PENGUIN BOOKS
FROM SOUTHEAST ASIA TO INDO-PACIFIC

Amitav Acharya is distinguished professor of international relations and the UNESCO Chair in Transnational Challenges and Governance at the School of International Service, American University, Washington DC. He won American University's highest honor, the Scholar-Teacher Award, for 2020.

Before taking up his current appointment in 2009, Acharya held professorships at University of Bristol, Nanyang Technological University, Singapore, and York University, Toronto, and was a Fellow at Harvard University's Asia Center and John F. Kennedy School of Government.

Acharya has received numerous fellowships and chairs around the world. He was the Nelson Mandela Visiting Professor in International Relations at Rhodes University, South Africa and the inaugural holder (2016–18) of the Boeing Company Chair in International Relations with the Schwarzman Scholars Program at Tsinghua University, Beijing.

He became the first non-Western scholar to be elected (2014–15) as the president of the International Studies Association (ISA), the most respected and influential global network of scholars in international relations. He has received three Distinguished Scholar Awards from ISA, for his contribution to non-Western scholarship in international relations and to the study of international cooperation.

ALSO BY AMITAV ACHARYA

Tragic Nation Burma: Why and How Democracy Failed (2022)

From Southeast Asia to Indo-Pacific

Culture, Identity, and the Return to Geopolitics

Amitav Acharya

PENGUIN BOOKS
An imprint of Penguin Random House

PENGUIN BOOKS

Penguin Books is an imprint of the Penguin Random House group of companies whose addresses can be found at global.penguinrandomhouse.com

Published by Penguin Random House SEA Pte Ltd
40 Penjuru Lane, #03-12, Block 2
Singapore 609216

First published in Penguin Books by Penguin Random House SEA 2025

Copyright © Amitav Acharya 2025

All rights reserved

10 9 8 7 6 5 4 3 2 1

The views and opinions expressed in this book are the author's own and the facts are as reported by him which have been verified to the extent possible, and the publishers are not in any way liable for the same.

Please note that no part of this book may be used or reproduced in any manner for the purpose of training artificial intelligence technologies or systems.

ISBN 9789815162080

Typeset in Garamond by MAP Systems, Bangalore, India

This book is sold subject to the condition that it shall not, by way of trade or otherwise, be lent, resold, hired out, or otherwise circulated without the publisher's prior consent in any form of binding or cover other than that in which it is published and without a similar condition including this condition being imposed on the subsequent purchaser.

www.penguin.sg

Contents

Introduction vii

PART I: CREATING IDENTITY

Chapter 1: History, Culture, and the Origins of Southeast Asia — 1

Chapter 2: Bandung 55 and the Rise of Southeast Asia — 23

Chapter 3: The ASEANists and the Emergence of Southeast Asian Identity — 45

PART II: CONTESTING FREEDOM

Chapter 4: Debating Human Rights — 65

Chapter 5: Is Democracy Good for Development and Stability? — 87

PART III: COPING WITH RIVALRY

Chapter 6: Will ASEAN Survive Great Power Rivalry? — 117

Chapter 7: A Region in Crisis — 143

Chapter 8: Demons and Angels: The Future of
      Southeast Asia   157

PART IV: STUDYING SOUTHEAST ASIA

Chapter 9: The Emergence and Evolution of
      Southeast Asian Studies   177

Chapter 10: The Indo-Pacific Idea: Myth and Reality   195

Notes   203

Introduction

Until the 20th century, there was no Southeast Asia in name, but there was always a sense of a separate, but connected universe of lands and waters. Indians called it *Suvarnabhumi* (golden earth) while the Chinese called it *Nanyang* (South Seas). Inside a vast geographic space east of India and south of China, there were different imperial centres, called *mandalas*, such as Srivijaya, Angkor, Bagan, Majapahit, Ayutthaya, Malacca, to name a few.

This chapter then discusses how Southeast Asia emerged through colonialism, war, revolution, and great power geopolitics. During World War II, Southeast Asia acquired its name in popular imagination through the Allied South East Asia Command under Lord Louis Mountbatten. In the 1950s and 60s, Southeast Asia was viewed by Western geopolitical experts as the 'Balkans of the Orient'[1] and a 'region of revolt'.[2] Its newly independent states were seen as 'dominos' that were about to fall in the tide of Soviet- and Chinese-backed communist movements.

By the 1980s, however, perceptions had changed. Southeast Asia had become part of East Asia's 'economic miracle'[3] and the 'Asian century'. The end of the Cold War in the early 1990s marked the high point of Southeast Asia's rise on the global stage. When the Berlin Wall fell, the dominos in Southeast Asia were rising! The world's attention focused on Southeast Asia's economic dynamism, relative political stability, and its ability to settle conflicts like Vietnam's occupation of Cambodia. The leaders of all the major powers of the world flocked to the region, meeting not only in traditional diplomatic hubs like Bangkok and Singapore, but in unlikely places like Yangon and Vientiane. President Obama's first state visit after re-election in 2012 was to Laos, not London. All the big players of the world, namely China, US, Japan, the European Union, India, and Russia, became 'dialogue partners' with the Association of Southeast Asian Nations (ASEAN) and gave a nod to its role as *the* leader of Asian cooperation.

But the tide is turning now. The past few years have been especially challenging for Southeast Asia. Great power rivalries have affected the region's stability, intra-regional cooperation and the efficacy of ASEAN. China has started flexing its growing military and economic muscles in the region, one of several reasons behind the US–China conflict. America and China have moved from being reluctant partners to outright rivals. This has drawn in other powers, namely Japan, India, Russia, and Australia, and has raised the prospects of a new Cold War in Southeast Asia. Southeast Asian states are under pressure to choose sides in this contest. At the same time, the COVID-19 pandemic, and the 'de-globalization' process set in motion by the 2008 global financial crisis, have darkened the region's economic and security prospects.

The previous era of great power rivalry, i.e., the Cold War from the 1950s to the 1990s, actually made the rise of Southeast Asia possible. In its fight against communism, the US extended a security umbrella over pro-Western nations and the vital Sea Lines of Communication (SLOCs) in the region. The Cold War also helped stimulate common purpose and unity among Southeast Asian nations, namely Indonesia, Malaysia, Singapore, Thailand, and Philippines, due to their fear of being entangled in great power politics. This led to the creation and consolidation of ASEAN. Moreover, investments from Japan, a US ally and Asia's fastest rising economy then, helped the industrialization of several countries in the region. The resulting rapid economic growth created greater domestic and regional stability.

Will the return of geopolitical rivalry have a similar impact? This is by no means assured. In fact, the opposite could happen. The new geopolitical realities are quite different from their Cold War counterpart. China is a much bigger economic and military power now than it was then. Not only has China replaced Japan as Asia's number one economy, it has also increased its military lead over all other Asian nations. Unlike Japan, which embraced its defeat in World War II and became a benign power, China still harbours grievances against Western and Asian powers, including Japan, owing to its mistreatment pre-dating World War II. Where Japan was a provider of investments to Southeast Asia, China has diverted them from it. While Japan has had no territorial disputes with Southeast Asian states, China has staked claimed to nearly all of South China Sea, including areas claimed by five Southeast Asian nations.

Moreover, Southeast Asia's capacity to offer a collective response to current geopolitical realities has come under challenge. ASEAN has expanded from the original five to ten nations. It has to reconcile a wider range of national positions. The nature of security threats facing the region has expanded, from territorial conflicts and domestic rebellions, to pandemics, climate crisis, and terrorism. These not only endanger Southeast Asian states, but also make it difficult for them to devise common and effective responses.

These developments affect Southeast Asia's reputation and threaten the region's appeal that was once built on successes from economic growth and political unity. They also affect the notion of Southeast Asia as a distinct sociopolitical entity separate and apart from the region becoming pawns in the hands of great powers yet again.

'Nations come and go, why not regions?'[4] The role of ASEAN has been crucial to keeping the idea of Southeast Asia alive. ASEAN's recent achievements have been impressive, but it faces critical challenges. These challenges include intra-ASEAN disputes, differences over how to deal with the China-US competition, and competing approaches to regional cooperation presented by the USA and China. A key challenge to ASEAN comes from the fact that now the US, Japan, India, and Australia, none of whom are Southeast Asian nations, are aggressively promoting the notion of the 'Indo-Pacific'—a trans-ASEAN understanding of shared futures that geographically stretches from Indian-Ocean-facing Africa to Pacific-facing North and Latin American nations. Will the Indo-Pacific idea sink ASEAN, drowning the very idea of Southeast Asia?

This book argues that there are three main forces that will decide whether Southeast Asia remains a viable, even vibrant idea, or sinks into oblivion, subsumed and supplanted by its rising neighbours, China and India, and the escalating rivalry between the US and China.

The first and foremost factor is building regional identity. This means recognizing some of its historical roots, whereby Southeast Asia simultaneously embraced outside influences that enhanced its autonomy, while rejecting those that made it an appendage to the civilizations of India and China. It also means building upon and strengthening the distinctive brand of regionalism, fostered through ASEAN, which engages all outside powers without being dominated by any of them. Chapter 1 discusses the historical and cultural origins of Southeast Asia, while the second chapter discusses the political rise of Southeast Asia and the birth of ASEAN. Chapter 3 further elaborates on the continuing relevance of ASEAN to the region.

A second factor critical to understanding the viability of Southeast Asia's regional identity deals with fostering freedom. This has not been Southeast Asia's strong point. ASEAN's embrace of human rights and democracy has been far too limited and conditional. The region is beset by enduring territorial disputes among nations with vastly different regime types, spanning democracy, civilian and military dictatorships, and monarchy. The occasional flowering of democracy has been repeatedly hindered by relapses into authoritarian rule. While authoritarian systems may have helped nurture economic progress for some states, such as Malaysia and Singapore, other states like Myanmar and East Timor have been repeatedly made vulnerable to domestic instability. Southeast Asian states are not likely to emulate Western-style liberal democracy. However, greater political openness might create longer-term conditions for regional stability. To understand how freedom has affected Southeast Asia, Chapter 4 wades into the debate on the universality of human rights and the concomitant rise of the Asian Values Debate. Chapter 5 focuses on regime type differences and the relationship between democracy and development.

A third factor affecting Southeast Asia's future is its ability to cope with the 'return of geopolitics', or the growing great power rivalry, especially between the US and China. This would require focus on neutrality, hedging, balancing, and preserving ASEAN centrality in regional cooperation. Chapters 6, 7, and 8 discuss the facets of the emerging rivalry and its ramifications for the future of Southeast Asia.

This book does not, and cannot, answer all the questions related to the future of Southeast Asia. But it offers clues by discussing the region's long history, its growing sense of identity, its strengths and weaknesses, and its achievements and failures. In so doing, it hopes to contribute to a better understanding of Southeast Asia's past, to invigorate an informed debate about the region's future. Southeast Asia is home to 8 per cent (and counting) of the world's population and is of immense strategic value.

As of 2016, nearly 21 per cent of all global trade, including 30 per cent of the world's crude oil needs, transits the Strait of Malacca, which connects the South China Sea, and by extension the Pacific Ocean with the Indian Ocean.[5] As such, understanding the region's prospects for peace and conflict is of critical importance to scholars and policymakers alike.

Let me end the introduction with two important caveats. First, this book is reflective rather than research intensive, so it is different from most of my other books on the region. This is in keeping with the mandate of the publisher, Penguin Random House Southeast Asia. Second, the book's main purpose is to identify some general and long-term trends about Southeast Asia. The focus is historical with limited updates after the COVID-19 pandemic. A common predicament for writers dealing with a fast-changing region and world is that things can get out of date by the time their books or journal articles are published, even in online versions. One cannot keep updating the narrative. Yet, highlighting long-term trends that defines a topic or an area of the world is useful as a benchmark for judging emerging developments as they unfold and shape the future.

PART I

CREATING IDENTITY

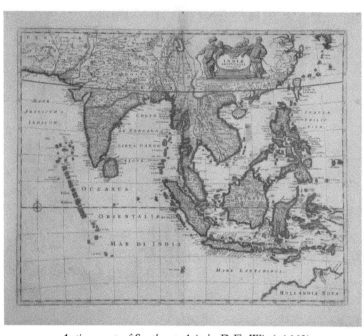

Antique map of Southeast Asia by D.E. Wit (c.1662)

Chapter 1

History, Culture, and the Origins of Southeast Asia

A Network of Mandalas

To a large extent, the conception of Southeast Asia as a region is a product of the historian's imagination. In the aftermath of World War II, some Western historians working on Southeast Asia began to 'imagine' its past as a distinctive region. They were rebelling against an excessively Indo-centric and Sino-centric view of Southeast Asia. What had been called 'Southeast Asian studies' had been traditionally dominated by Indologists and Sinologists, many of whom saw the region as a cultural appendage of India and China, two of the oldest civilizations in the neighbourhood, which had left a powerful influence on the assortment of mainland and maritime units that comprise today's Southeast Asia. In this sense, Southeast Asia was 'East by South': i.e. East of India and South of China, an expression which was as much a cultural statement as a geographic fact.

Moreover, as a result of the profound impact of the changes brought about by colonialism and Westernization, 'many Southeast Asian historians have interested themselves primarily in external stimuli, to the detriment of the study of indigenous institutions.'[6] Post-World War I views of Southeast Asia, shaped by indigenous nationalist thinking and Western scholarship, began to imagine Southeast Asia's cultural and ideational autonomy from India and China. Additionally, Southeast Asians were viewed, not as passive recipients of Indian and Chinese ideas, but active borrowers and modifiers. They were recast as makers, rather than victims, of history. The demand for an 'autonomous' history of Southeast Asia built upon the work of a Dutch economic historian, Jacob Van Leur, who had, in 1932 (translated into English in 1955) challenged the notion that Indian cultural and political ideas were imposed or imported onto Southeast Asia through commerce (by Indian merchants or *Vaisyas*) and conquest (by Indian warriors, or *Khastriyas*).[7] Van Leur argued that Southeast Asian rulers had 'called upon' the Indian civilization through the medium of the *Brahmans* (Hindu priests), because Hindu political concepts helped them enhance their legitimacy and organize their small territorial units into larger states. Hindu religious establishments were seen as commerce-friendly that helped entrust rulers with large funds that were then used to promote more trade and benefits to the local economy. Historians also pointed out that ancient Southeast Asians were actually quite selective in what they borrowed—ideas which they found useful and legitimizing (such as the *Code of Manu* or Kautilya's *Arthsastra*) were accepted, while those which did not fit into local traditions and beliefs (such as the Indian caste system) were rejected.

Van Leur's 'idea of the local initiative' was joined by similar constructs. The art historian, H.G. Quaritch Wales, spoke of 'local genius' that modified Hindu-Buddhist art and architecture by infusing it with local meaning and forms.[8] The historian O.W. Wolters coined the notions of 'localization' and 'relocalization' to describe how Southeast Asian borrowers adapted Indian, Chinese, and other foreign ideas to fit indigenous traditions in the field of religion, arts, law, poetry, and politics.[9]

Inspired by demands for an 'autonomous' history, Southeast Asia's geographic size—then accepted by area specialists and policy-makers—was reduced. No longer were India and China included in the region. More importantly, Southeast Asia was no longer considered part of South Asia or East Asia—a crucial factor to the development of regional identity and concept.[10]

Table 1.1: Selected Pre-Colonial States of Southeast Asia

Empire	Time Period	Geographical Scope
Funan	1st–6th century A.D.	Ancient Hindu state extending over the Mekong delta, the greater part of modern Cambodia, the lower Menam area and the coastal regions of the Malay Peninsula.
Champa	2nd–17th century A.D.	Ancient state in central and southern coastal regions of Vietnam.
Pagan	1044–1287 A.D.	Ancient empire of Myanmar in the Irrawaddy River region. The Pagan empire extended its influence over a region roughly the size of modern Myanmar.
Srivijaya	7th–13th century A.D.	Powerful maritime empire with hegemony over Bangka, Sumatra, and the Malay Peninsula.
Angkor	9th–15th century A.D.	Ancient Cambodian empire, which extended from the tip of the Indochinese peninsula northward to Yunnan and from Vietnam westward to the Bay of Bengal. The Angkor empire was one of the largest, most prosperous, and most sophisticated kingdoms in the history of Southeast Asia.

Majapahit	13th–16th century A.D.	Major maritime empire covering Java, Bali, Madura, Sumatra and the Malay Peninsula, Borneo and the Lesser Sunda Islands, the Celebes, and the Moluccas.
Sukhothai	1238–1350 A.D.	Ancient Thai kingdom in north central Thailand. The Sukhothai kingdom was the first independent Thai state in Thailand's central plain and its hegemony extended north into Laos, west to the Andaman Sea and south to the Malay Peninsula.
Ayutthaya	1350–1767 A.D.	Powerful state in continental Southeast Asia. Its influence extended over most of modern Thailand, the Menam basin, and a substantial part of the Malay Peninsula.

Historians also began to reconstruct Southeast Asia's past in ways that claimed to uncover distinctive patterns of spatial organization and governance that dotted its ancient political landscape. The most famous of these was Wolters' characterization of precolonial polities in Southeast Asia as mandalas. While mandalas lacked territorial specificity, they did represent an acute concentration of political management and moral authority which made it possible to speak of a distinctive political order in Southeast Asia. For Wolters, despite being 'demographically fragmented', politically 'multicentred', and socially 'characterized by stubborn small-scale sub-regional identities'[11], premodern Southeast Asia did develop a common pattern of intra-regional authority thanks to the 'patchwork of often overlapping *mandalas*, or "circles of kings" in each of which one king, identified with divine and universal authority and defined as the conqueror, claimed personal hegemony over the others, who in theory were bound to be his obedient allies and vassals.'[12] He identified several mandalas which existed between 7th and 14th centuries, the most prominent of which are Srivijaya, Angkor, Ayutthaya, and Majapahit.

> A glance at some of the famous mandalas which adorn the textbooks of earlier Southeast Asian history shows that each of them increased flow of communications between some of the many centres in different parts of the region. We may too often tend to strike contrasts between these earlier states and the modern states as though great men in the past made exciting impressions in their own day but left nothing behind them of consequence. But there were some enduring consequences which helped to reduce the multicentric character of earlier Southeast Asia.[13]

Others joined Wolters in describing common and overlapping political forms in classical Southeast Asia. Stanley Thambiah, for example, proposed the idea of 'galactic polities' to describe the Buddhist political world of mainland Southeast Asia.[14] While Wolters focused on court politics and the religious 'great traditions', Anthony Reid, another prominent historian of Southeast Asia, urged students of Southeast Asian history to focus instead on 'popular beliefs and social practices of ordinary Southeast Asians.'[15] To Reid, this is what defined the 'the common ground' among Southeast Asians, notwithstanding the region's 'bewildering variety of language, culture, and religion' and 'historic openness' to foreign trade. Reid identified a number of such social institutions and practices, particularly those which were absent in India and China, such as 'the concept of spirit or "soul stuff" animating living things, the prominence of women in descent, ritual matters, marketing and agriculture, and the importance of debt as a determinant of social obligations.'[16]

More importantly, Reid directed his attention to commercial interactions in building a pre-colonial region of Southeast Asia. In Reid's view, the period between the 15th and the 17th centuries constituted an age of commerce in Southeast Asia. During this period, Southeast Asian port cities, already sharing cultural and linguistic commonalities, were bound together in a structure of close economic interdependence. While the Indian Ocean trade network extended from eastern Africa and the Arabian Peninsula to Japan, within this structure the most intense commercial networking was developed among the port cities of Southeast Asia.

Reid also focused on the high degree of commercial intercourse connecting the great maritime cities of Southeast Asia, like Melaka, Pasai, Johor, Patani, Aceh, and Brunei. The growth of intra-regional trade reduced cultural barriers, which helped in the spread of Malay as the language of commerce. Despite the pan-Asian nature of the trade networks, Reid found evidence that until the arrival of the Dutch East India Company in the 17th century, the 'trading links within the region continued to be more influential than those beyond it.'[17]

> [M]aritime intercourse continued to link the peoples of Southeast Asia more tightly to one another than to outside influences down to the seventeenth century. The fact that Chinese and Indian influences came to most of the region by maritime trade, not by conquest or colonization, appeared to ensure that Southeast Asia retained its distinctiveness even while borrowing numerous elements from those larger centers. What did not happen (with the partial exception of Vietnam) was that any part of the region established closer relations with China and India than with its neighbours in Southeast Asia.[18]

This historical imagination of Southeast Asia has not gone unchallenged, however. Critics argue that no firm archaeological evidence exists that can decisively affirm Van Leur's idea of the 'local initiative.' Reid has been accused of unduly reifying intra-Southeast Asian commercial transactions, which could not realistically be isolated from the larger Indian Ocean network, and also of ignoring crucial mainland-maritime variations in classical (as well as contemporary) Southeast Asia's political and commercial landscape. Wolter's 'mandala concept' has been attacked as an Indocentric notion (after all, Wolter was an Indologist), whose very existence cannot be proven given the paucity of archaeological evidence. Yet, these criticisms do not detract from the important influence the project of historical imagination has had in drawing attention to the regional identity of Southeast Asia. Regions are imagined constructs, and no one does a better job of offering legitimacy to the act of imagining than the historian who can claim familiarity with an era long gone by.

'Indianization': Myth or Reality?

Select Hindu-Buddhist ('Indianized') states of ancient Southeast Asia

'Southeast Asia is the maritime crossroads of the Nirvana Route, the place where the civilizations of India and China meet.'[19] While China exercised a certain amount of geopolitical influence over the region, India's was mainly ideational. India and China were to Southeast Asia what Greece and Rome were to the Mediterranean, respectively. One was a cultural superpower and the other a geopolitical one.

While Indian influence in China was mostly through the spread of Buddhist philosophy, in Southeast Asia, it was more often a complex combination of Hindu-Buddhist ideas. Both religions were fused together to shape states and societies in early Southeast Asia.

There is a fair amount of charged debate among historians of the region as to how and why Indian ideas travelled to Southeast Asia. The debate pits three theories that argue over the prominence of three sets of actors: the Vaishya/Vaisya (merchants), the *Kshatriya* (warriors) and the Brahmana (priests). The first theory holds that Indian culture was brought by traders and merchants to support their economic interests. The second sees warriors and adventurers seeking glory and kingdoms as the principal actors, while the third focuses on proselytization by Indian priests. In reality, all three blended their influence and impact in the region.

Whoever the agent, they were, however, not colonizers. The thesis of Indian 'colonization' of Southeast Asia was put forth by historians like R.C. Majumdar, who claimed that Indian 'intercourse in the region first began by the way of trade, both by land and sea. But soon it developed into regular colonization, and Indians established political authority in various parts of the vast Asiatic continent that lay to the south of China and to the east and southeast of India.'[20]

Such assumptions stoked Indian nationalism, and were promoted by India's top leaders, including Jawaharlal Nehru and Rabindranath Tagore. The Greater India Society, founded in Calcutta in 1926 under the patronage of Tagore, reminded the British, and the Indian people at large, that India, too, was capable of colonization.

Despite the use of the rhetoric of colonization, in reality, there is no evidence of largescale Indian colonization (in the political sense) of Southeast Asia, except migration (to Myanmar for example)[21] and of trading settlements like the Kampong Keling (Kalinga Village) in Malacca.[22]

Indian culture was brought to Southeast Asia not through outright Indian colonization, but through a process that can only be called 'proselytization in reverse': Indians were 'called upon' by Southeast Asians to meet their political and religious needs. It was Southeast Asians, contends Australian historian of Southeast Asia, Milton Osborne, who sought out and then 'adapted these foreign ideas to suit their own needs and values.'[23] As a result, as Dilip Sardesai put it, Southeast Asia as a whole 'adopted the alien cultural traits without in the process losing its identity.'[24] As such, the influx of Indian ideas enhanced Southeast Asian identity.

Evidence that Southeast Asians did not merely copy Indian culture and architecture abound throughout the region. The largest Hindu and Buddhist temples anywhere in the world are both in Southeast Asia (Angkor Wat in Cambodia and Borobodur Temple in Indonesia respectively). But neither is very Indian in its appearance, and therein lies a story.[25]

Angkor Wat temple, Cambodia

When I set my first sights on Angkor Wat in 1990, as the country was still emerging from the genocidal rule of the Khmer Rouge, I had expected to see a traditional design for a Hindu temple, whether in the South Indian style or in the classical temple architecture of Odisha, whose capital city, Bhubaneswar, is widely regarded as India's temple city as it is dotted with dozens of temples dating back to 7th century A.D. But the Angkor Wat I saw was nothing like any temple architecture in India, although it was conceptually founded on the sacred Mount Meru.

Similarly, during a visit to Borobudur, the Buddhist temple resembled a pyramid of megalithic overtones more than an Indian stupa (although stupa-like structures adorn its top). This confirmed my impression that while Southeast Asia had absorbed Indian influences, it was never an outright Indian imitation or colony. Unlike the Greek colonizers of the Mediterranean, who founded Greek city-states (Polis), temples and marketplaces (*agoras*) that are exact replicas of those in the motherland, the Indian monuments in Southeast Asia looked different not only from those in India but also from each other. For example, the basic architecture of public buildings in the Greek colonies of Syracuse in Sicily are almost exactly the same as those in Miletus, and I have visited and studied both places closely. But the Ananda Temple in Bagan is dramatically different in design from the Temple of the Emerald Buddha (*Wat Phra Sri Rattana Satsadaram*) in Bangkok, a mere 1,000 kilometres away.

There is another difference. The Greek temples and polities in the Mediterranean were made by the Greeks and for the Greeks. Not so the Indian temples and polities in Southeast Asia. They were 'Indianized' but not Indian, as is often mistakenly believed by many Indians.

The Hindu epic of *Ramayana*, which remains very popular in Southeast Asia, is another example of this Indianization sans Indian, as it comes in different versions and variations in different parts of Southeast Asia.

But Indian ideas did have a political effect, as they did in China. Just as Tang emperor Wu Zetian in the late 7th century A.D. portrayed herself as a *Maitreya* or *Bodhisattva Vimalaprabha* ('The Radiance of Purity') to seize the imperial crown, in 7th Century Cambodia, King Jayavarman I claimed to be a 'portion' of *Shiva*, while another Khmer King Bhavavarman is claimed to have used Shiva's *Sakti* or divine to 'seize the kingship'.[26] In Bali, *Vishnu* gets presented as a 'rising prince', who emerges to infuse the community with renewed spiritual energy and status.

However, in helping to transform Southeast Asia's small polities into more stable, stronger states (as in Pegu, Champa, Srivijaya, Sukhothai, Ayutthaya), and even empires (Angkor, Pagan, and later Majapahit), India's influence was not always a peaceful force. Rather, it combined compassion with conquest. Competition over who was the Buddhist *chakravartin* (Buddha's secular counterpart) led to war between Burma and Thailand. While Indian traders and adventurers helped the political rise and economic prosperity of Southeast Asia, Chola imperialism—empire based in Southern India from 600 B.C. to 13th Century A.D.—destroyed Srivijaya, one of Southeast Asia's most prosperous maritime kingdoms.

An important turning point of Indian cultural influence is Malacca. In 1396 A.D., a Srivijayan prince from Palembang on the coast of Sumatra, fleeing an invasion by a Javanese army, landed on the island of Tumasik (the future Singapore of Sir Stamford Raffles). However, this prince, with the name of Parameswara ('supreme lord'), wanted to seize power for himself and killed his host. But Tumasik was protected by the kingdom of Ayutthaya (as the Thai kingdom was known then), and soon Thai forces were marching to punish the usurper. Parameswara fled north along the Malayan coast, and after about 130 miles, took rest on the banks of a river. Legend has it that there he saw an extraordinary sight: his hunting dog was being kicked by a mousedeer. He decided to establish a new kingdom there.

Thus, Malacca was founded. Over the next hundred years, it became Southeast Asia's premier port city. In the words of Portuguese writer Duarte Barbosa, 'Whoever is Lord in Malacca has his hand on the throat of Venice.'[27]

Malacca's rise and fall owed much to migrants from Kalinga, starting with the merchant Mani Purindan, whose descendants married into a Malaya family and became intimately involved in palace politics that weakened the port-state.[28] The fall of Malacca to the Portuguese in 1511 marked the end of classical globalization in Asia and ushered in the era of European imperialism.

Inventing History: The Mediterranean Analogy

The 'Mediterranean analogy' describes attempts by Southeast Asian historians to imagine an autonomous and internally coherent region of Southeast Asia, similar to the Mediterranean, that enjoys a great measure of internal connectivity, especially through commerce, and a connectivity created by the common exposure of its units to the sea and through the diffusion of ideas and political institutions. Sutherland points to several instances of this analogy.[29] For example, Georges Coedes, who directed France's prestigious Ecole Francaise d'Extreme-Orient (EFEO) from 1929–1947, referred to the Southeast Asian waters enclosed by the South China Sea, the Gulf of Siam, and the Java Sea, as a 'veritable Mediterranean', and a 'unifying factor' for the peoples in the region.[30] In another instance, during a Franco-German conference organized in 1997 by French scholar Denys Lombard, who served as Director of EFEO from 1993 to 1998, a German scholar, Roderich Ptak, from the University of Munich, considered the idea of an Asian Mediterranean.[31] Historians such as Reid and Lombard were 'inspired' and 'fascinated' by Braudel's classic study of the Mediterranean[32] not just because of its multidisciplinary approach and focus on the sea, but also because, as Sutherland put it, Braudel's work sought 'parallels between Southeast Asia and the civilizations of the Mediterranean [which] seemed to offer a solution to nagging doubts regarding Southeast Asian identity and agency.'[33]

But the Mediterranean analogy proved to be highly controversial. Sutherland's critique of the analogy rested on three main arguments. Firstly, Southeast Asia lacked the unity and cohesion that was found in the Mediterranean. Historians who used the analogy tended to exaggerate the geographic unity of Southeast Asia, which led to an inaccurate rendering of a coherent history for the region, creating the illusion of the region's autonomy from external influences. Critics also pointed to the 'dangers of Euro-centric model-making', and argued that 'the history of the Asian seas could be [and should be] rewritten from an entirely Asian perspective', and that Braudel himself tended to see the Mediterranean from a 'northern European' point of view.'[34] Thirdly, Braudel himself could not assume the unity of the Mediterranean, as he viewed it 'not so much a single entity as a "complex of seas".'[35] How could one then be so sure of 'the coherence and authenticity of Southeast Asia as a region?'[36]

While historians led the discourse on Southeast Asia's Mediterranean analogy, they did not actually perform any detailed comparisons. Historians such as Reid, Coedes, and Lombard who invoked the Mediterranean in considering Southeast Asia did not actually compare Mediterranean culture, society, and politics with that of Southeast Asia. Instead, they focused on the cultural, political, social, ethnic, and linguistic similarities among the units (states, societies, groups) within the region they studied, namely Southeast Asia, but scarcely ventured to study similar institutions and processes in the Mediterranean. Here, political scientists and scholars of international relations are better suited to provide tools for detailed comparisons.[37]

Perhaps the most useful way to look at the Mediterranean analogy is to view it from the prism of three approaches: 'autonomous history' (Reid)[38], 'comparative history'

(Lieberman)[39], and 'connected history' (Subrahmanyam)[40]. The idea of autonomous history derives from John Smail's famous call for freeing Southeast Asian history from its colonial baggage.[41] Autonomous history corrects a regional history that has been defined primarily by outsiders, using their own prisms and prejudices, while ignoring local dynamics. Autonomous historians are primarily concerned with establishing the identity and coherence of the region on its own terms. It is therefore different from what Lieberman calls 'externalist' history of the region, authored primarily by Indologists and Sinologists. Autonomous history is more about establishing the internal dynamics of the region under study, than about exploring similarities and differences between the studied region and other regions.

In contrast, such comparisons are central to comparative history. These scholars may be so labelled because they see Southeast Asian history in less distinctive terms and dismiss the idea of its limits being clearly defined. The main figure in this school in Southeast Asian studies is Victor Lieberman. Lieberman criticized the emphasis on Southeast Asia's internal coherence, especially targeting Anthony Reid's autonomous history approach in terms of its failure to distinguish 'mainland trajectories and those in the archipelago as well as between various patterns on the mainland.'[42] He also recognized 'the critical impact of global currents' by drawing 'strange parallels' between state formation in mainland Southeast Asia to Russia, Japan, France and the Islands.[43] Lieberman argued that 'in terms of linear-cum-cyclic trajectories, chronology, and dynamics, the mainland [Southeast Asia] resembled much of Europe and Japan, but diverged significantly from South Asia and island Southeast Asia.' As such, he found it problematic to consider Southeast Asia as a coherent region at least in terms of Reid's 'Age of Commerce' thesis.[44]

But Lieberman's comparative approach has been criticized for some of the same reasons as that of autonomous history. Critics contend that Lieberman is as prone to generalizations across regions as Reid's autonomous approach is within the region. Subrahmanyam critiques both autonomous history and Reid's approach for exaggerating the regional coherence of Southeast Asia (especially the extent of intra-regional similarities and interactions) as well as Lieberman's 'comparative history' approach for ignoring the links between mainland Southeast Asia and the Bay of Bengal littoral parts of modern-day India. Subrahmanyam's own solution to these problems is that of 'connected history':

> ... we not only compare from within our boxes, but spend some time and effort to transcend them, not by comparison alone, but by seeking out the at times fragile threads that connected the globe, even as the globe came to be defined as such. This is not to deny voice to those who were somehow 'fixed' by physical, social and cultural coordinates, who inhabited 'localities' in the early modern period and nothing else, and whom we might seek out with our intrepid analytical machetes. But if we ever get to 'them' by means other than archaeology, the chances are that it is because they are already plugged into some network, some process of circulation.'[45]

Despite his critique, Subrahmanyam nonetheless concedes that the Mediterranean analogy of Southeast Asia 'allows us to transcend or refashion national boundaries in the search for meaningful objects for historical analysis, a procedure that is absolutely essential as one moves back in time to an epoch when the nation-state was as yet a distant prospect.'[46] He also accepts that comparing the Mediterranean with 'other Mediterranean's' (Southeast Asia included) 'enables us to practice meaningful forms of what today has begun to emerge as "world history". Comparative history thus has helped to project Southeast Asian history on a world stage.'[47]

The debate over Southeast Asian historiography notwithstanding, it is clear that the three approaches are useful and that they are not mutually exclusive. There cannot be any meaningful regional analysis without autonomous history which does not approach a region from a purely externalist perspective. In the case of Southeast Asia, autonomous history would imply autonomy not just from colonial perspective, but also from Indo and Sinic vantage points. Hence, even though both Coedes and Reid invoked the Mediterranean analogy, they were different. The former did not see Southeast Asia as autonomous from Indic influences, although his work certainly helped to uncover a precolonial, indigenous cultural matrix. Similarly, comparative history helps correct some of the excesses, parochialisms, and reifications of autonomous history. It allows the development of theoretical tools, in historiography and political science alike, that makes it possible to generalize a region's distinctiveness and patterns of intra-regional interactions and extra-regional influences, which are empirically sustainable and analytically useful. Finally, connected history is absolutely vital when one thinks of relations between regions. It allows us to focus on interactions between regions, including the flow of ideas, goods, peoples, and institutions. No region is an island, and while the presence of inter-regional interactions does not negate the existence of regions, they should not be downgraded in favour of an exclusive or excessive focus on intra-regional similarities and interactions.

Southeast Asia in the Modern Nation-State System

The conception of Southeast Asia as a geostrategic and political region of modern nation-states draws from far more recent events in historical time. Its original referent point was Lord Mountbatten's Allied Command for Southeast Asia established during World War II. This command, which was ironically headquartered in Ceylon (modern day Sri Lanka), helped to make

Southeast Asia a 'fixed and practical term even in the United States' during World War II.[48] Another strand of Southeast Asia's geopolitical lineage came with accelerated decolonization and the outbreak of the Cold War. Southeast Asia now acquired a growing familiarity as a 'region of revolt', as 'the Balkans of the Orient', and as a hotbed of communism, making it a key flashpoint of the Cold War. The region's proneness to strife became a distinctive feature, prompting comments like one of the factors 'which makes Southeast Asia a "region" is the widespread incidence of conflict, along with some attempts at cooperation', and that 'instability is the one feature of Southeast Asia that gives the region much of its contemporary importance.'[49] According to this view, conflict was a form of contact and communication, since much of it involved the interference of Southeast Asia's leaders in the affairs of neighbours. 'The communications developed as a result are one factor which perhaps more than anything else compels us to accept the fact that, now, a sense of "region" does exist in Southeast Asia.'[50]

This negative strategic perception of Southeast Asia would not change until the 1970s, when the region finally shed its image as a conflict zone, especially in light of more intense and enduring conflicts in neighbouring South Asia, West Asia, and North Asia. Yet, where great power geopolitics let off, domestic politics took over in defining Southeast Asia's regional identity in primarily negative terms. The new pro-Western states of Southeast Asia made a collective descent into authoritarianism in the course of the late 1960s and 70s. While the European Community defined its regional identity as a grouping of liberal democracies, underpinned by the Kantian dictum that democracies avoid warring against each other, Southeast Asia developed its own version of illiberal peace, a regional system in which authoritarian states developed long-term habits of peaceful existence out of a common concern for regime survival, fiercely buoyed by a reluctance to intervene in each other's internal affairs.

Moreover, throughout the post-1975 period, Southeast Asia remained ideologically polarized. Vietnam, leading an Indo-China bloc that included Laos and the auto-genocidal Khmer Rouge regime in Cambodia (renamed by its captors as Kampuchea), challenged the regional conception developed by its rival grouping, ASEAN, which had organized itself since 1967. While the latter professed to represent the whole of Southeast Asia, Vietnam laid a firm and coercive claim to Indo-China as a distinctive and 'single strategic unit'.

Wang Gungwu's distinction between 'moderate' and 'revolutionary' types of nationalism elegantly explains the strategic polarization of Southeast Asia as a by-product of the region's competing conceptions of nationalism. The three countries swept by revolutionary nationalisms—Indonesia, Vietnam, and Burma—also proved to be the least amenable to regional identity and cooperation at the outset of the postcolonial era. While Burma drifted toward isolationism, Sukarno's Indonesia proved expansionist. Communist Vietnam showed open contempt for ASEAN's vision of regional cooperation. On the other hand, countries which experienced a more moderate nationalism, such as Malaysia and Thailand, played an instrumental role in regional cooperation. The ASEAN-Indochina ideological polarization between the mid-1970s and late 1980s, which is usually seen as a by-product of the Cold War, was thus not entirely unrelated to the political legacy of colonialism. The moderates and revolutionaries held radically different conceptions of Southeast Asia as a region. Where the revolutionaries rejected the idea of a region dominated by Western powers, the moderates had more to fear from a region dominated by China. While the revolutionaries hoped for a confederated region, the moderates would only accept regional cooperation based on the principles of equality and sovereignty. The moderates desired a region freely and multilaterally linked to the outside world, and the revolutionaries would accept this only if the communist powers were integral to this external linkage.[51]

It was not until the final Vietnamese withdrawal from Cambodia in 1989 and the subsequent Paris Peace Agreement securing Cambodia's future as an independent nation that the decades-long polarization of Southeast Asia finally ended. Regional elites were quick to point out that their forerunner's alleged dream of 'one Southeast Asia' was now close to fruition. ASEAN quickly expanded its membership to include the ten nations that regional elites insisted were always meant to be part of Southeast Asia (thereby conveniently ignoring the fact that Sri Lanka had been invited to join as a founder of ASEAN, an invitation it had declined, to its regret much later). But even after the realization of the One Southeast Asia concept, old divisions have persisted. Integration of the Indo-Chinese states, and more importantly, of Myanmar (Burma) into ASEAN, carried out with undue haste and with little advance planning (in marked contrast to the EU's project of membership expansion) has proven to be a daunting task, a burden that has undermined Southeast Asian regionalism to a much greater extent than the economic crisis of 1997.

If the impact of political and strategic forces in the making of Southeast Asia was ambiguous and indeterminate, the other key material determinant, intra-regional economic linkages, was even more problematic. Colonialism had terminally damaged the 'age of commerce' in Southeast Asia. Postcolonial Southeast Asian nations, like their counterparts in other parts of the developing world, maintained closer economic links with their former colonial masters than with each other. Their raw material producing economies were competitive vis-à-vis each other, rather than complementary.

Since economic interdependence was not a given, it had to be created. Yet, non-communist Southeast Asia was noticeably unsuccessful in organizing itself into an economic region, despite professing this objective for over three decades. It has taken ASEAN over fifty years since its founding to experience an intra-regional trade rate of 58 per cent of the region's total trade.[52] The organization's unruly membership expansion has accentuated the perils of economic diversity among member countries. The ASEAN Free Trade Area, the ultimate agreement that could deliver the idea of an economically integrated region, is mired in uncertainties and exclusions (of items from the tariff-reduction list), as well as attempts by Singapore to leapfrog the region and develop free trade links unilaterally with major economic powers outside. Sub-regional cooperation (the so-called 'growth triangles') proved more appealing and hopeful in the 1990s, but is rarely spoken of now, especially in the aftermath of the regional economic downturn caused by the Asian Financial Crisis, the Global Recession and the decelerated growth owing to the COVID-19 pandemic. In the meantime, Southeast Asia established and nurtured inter-regional linkages with Northeast Asia, to the neglect of intra-regional connections. The emergence of macro-regional entities, such as Asia-Pacific Economic Cooperation (APEC), the ASEAN Regional Forum (ARF) and the ASEAN Plus Three attest to this reality.

History and Culture Not Enough

Southeast Asia's physical, political, social, and cultural diversity is too immense to qualify it as a distinctive personality. Yet, what gives it coherence must count as one of the finest acts of collective self-imagination undertaken by a region's nationalist political elites in the wake of their liberation from European and American colonialism. My book, entitled, *The Quest for Identity: International Relations of Southeast Asia*, argued that, as with nationalism and nation-states, regions may be 'imagined', designed, constructed, and defended.[53]

My approach to the study of regions and regionalism shares many elements of Benedict Anderson's classic approach to the study of nationalism and the nation-state, as expounded in his book, *Imagined Communities: Reflections on the Origin and Spread of Nationalism*. There are many parallels between 'imagining the nation' and 'imagining the region'. Particularly, Anderson's focus on the collective 'imagining' of the nation by a nationalist elite is mirrored in my explanation of Southeast Asian region-building as a process of elite socialization. But drawing upon the work of Wolters, Reid, and others, I place more emphasis on the role of traditional political-cultural frameworks and pre-capitalist commerce (while Anderson focuses on print capitalism) in building modern social identities. I also believe that the term 'proximities' more accurately reflects the degree of socialisation and bonding evident in the case of Southeast Asia than the term 'communities' used by Anderson to describe nations. Although a certain sense of community can develop within the region, as has been the case in Southeast Asia, the continued salience of state sovereignty (despite claims about its alleged obsolescence and erosion) makes regional communities fundamentally different from nation-states. Southeast Asia is still a region inhabited by highly sovereignty-conscious actors.

> Southeast Asia is a region built on shared human and physical characteristics and endeavours, external geopolitical and economic currents, and collective social imagination. But its claim to be a region should be seen as being based as much on the construction of a regional identity as on the sum total of shared physical attributes and functional interactions among its units. The development of a regional identity may not necessarily conform to the 'facts' of geography, history, culture, or politics. The notion of Southeast Asia as a homogenous cultural or geographic entity can indeed be overstated. But its social and political identity, derived from the conscious

promotion of the regional concept by its states, societies, and peoples, is what makes it a distinct idea in the latter part of the twentieth century.[54]

To make the story of the emergence of Southeast Asia complete, we need to examine its regional identity as a political project, an act of political engineering by a group of like-minded elites, who have nurtured and employed a wide variety of tools, including myths and symbols (such as the 'ASEAN Way'), as well as notions of collective identity (such as 'One Southeast Asia'). How this happened with the creation of ASEAN is the subject of the next chapter.

Chapter 2

Bandung 55 and the Rise of Southeast Asia[55]

The Colombo Powers—The five Prime Ministers who sponsored the Bandung Conference

In his opening address to the Asian-African Conference at Bandung in 1955, Indonesia's president Sukarno described the gathering as 'the first intercontinental conference of coloured peoples in the history of mankind.'[56] Despite its path-breaking nature, a confluence of Western hostility, Eastern myth-making, and a paucity of primary sources on the Bandung Conference, have obscured or distorted its true significance for international order-building. To compound matters, mainstream international relations scholarship, with its limited and parochial conception of what the field should study and how to study it, has ignored the significance and legacies of this conference. Yet few events in the post-war era offer a more fertile ground for rethinking the established boundaries of international relations as an academic field than the Bandung Conference.

Sponsored by five Asian countries—India, Pakistan, Ceylon, Burma, and Indonesia (collectively known as the Conference of South-East Asian Prime Ministers or the Colombo Powers)—the Bandung Conference took place from 18–24 April 1955. It was attended by thirty countries: Afghanistan, Burma, Cambodia, Ceylon, China, Cyprus, Egypt, Ethiopia, Gold Coast, India, Indonesia, Iran, Iraq, Japan, Jordan, Laos, Lebanon, Liberia, Libya, Nepal, Pakistan, Philippines, Saudi Arabia, Syria, Sudan, Thailand, Turkey, Democratic Republic of Vietnam, State of Vietnam, and the Kingdom of Yemen. The African National Congress attended as an observer. The conference was not the first international conference of 'coloured' or non-Western countries, per se. There had been gatherings against racialism before, notably the 'Ligue contre l'impérialisme et l'oppression coloniale' (League Against Imperialism and Colonial Oppression) held in Brussels in 1927, and two Asian Relations Conferences in New Delhi in 1947 and 1949 (the latter was also called the Conference on Indonesia). However, as Sukarno mentioned in his opening address at the Bandung Conference, it was at the Brussels meeting in 1927 where 'many distinguished delegates who are present here today met each other and found new strength in their fight for independence'. The Bandung Conference was distinctive and noteworthy because:

> [The Brussels meeting] was a meeting place thousands of miles away, amidst foreign people, in a foreign country, in a foreign continent. It was not assembled there by choice, but

by necessity. Today the contrast is great. Our nations and countries are colonies no more. Now we are free, sovereign and independent. We are again masters in our own house. We do not need to go to other continents to confer.[57]

The first New Delhi Conference in 1947 was technically unofficial as it was hosted by a think-tank, the Indian Council on World Affairs. Participants included Tibet, as well as yet-to-be independent governments. Even the host country India was still under British colonial rule and would continue to be for a few more months after the conference. Moreover, both the New Delhi conferences were not exclusively a gathering of coloured peoples. Australia, the US, and the UK attended the 1947 gathering as observers, and Australia was included in the 1949 conference as a full participant. However, Australia was not invited to the Bandung conference and neither did it wish to be invited.[58] According to a declassified British document, Prime Minister Menzies 'shares our [British] views of [the] mischievous nature of proposed Afro-Asian Conference and expressed annoyance at suggestions in Australia (from the Australian Labor Party) that Australia should have been invited . . . He takes dark view of activities which, under guise of peaceful co-existence, in fact are stirring up colour prejudices.'[59] Another British document points out that the Australian government 'neither wanted an invitation nor the opportunity to refuse one.'[60]

Why is the Bandung Conference a critical event in international order-building? Using a body of primary sources on the conference, including archival sources previously unavailable or underutilized, I will discuss some of the key legacies of the conference that challenge the conventional perceptions of the conference and attest to the 'agency' of the newly independent states in the making of the post-war international order.[61] A summary of the conference's legacies are as follows:

- By having successfully involved the participation of thirty countries, the Bandung Conference frustrated Western (UK and US) efforts to 'sabotage' it.
- It influenced the positions of the newly independent 'Third World' states in the Cold War by delegitimizing US-sponsored collective defence pacts, while simultaneously laying the foundation for the global Non-Aligned Movement (NAM).
- The conference strengthened the emerging global normative framework by not only advancing decolonization, but also by affirming universal human rights, support for universalism, and the UN.
- It affirmed the 'comity of civilizations' over the racialized 'clash of civilizations' thesis.
- The Bandung Conference also enabled the rise of Southeast Asia as a site of regionalism, especially by diminishing the relative influences of both India and China and by paving the way for the emergence of a regionalism led by the weaker states of Southeast Asia, as a precursor to ASEAN.

Frustrating Western Hostility

The first legacy of the Bandung Conference is really, to put it bluntly, a thrilling story of Western paranoia, conspiracy, sabotage, and ultimate frustration at their failed attempts. With the declassification of diplomatic sources in recent years, it now seems unquestionable that Western powers, especially the UK and the US, felt a great deal of apprehension, even threat, from the Bandung Conference. The UK was fearful the conference would further stoke anti-colonial sentiments in its remaining possessions in Asia, Africa, and elsewhere (that were yet to gain their independence), which, although diminishing, were still substantial.

The US, for its part, was deeply anxious that the conference could dent the isolation of communist China and give it and the Soviet Union a major platform to increase communist influence in Asia and Africa. The British initially wanted to persuade pro-Western countries to boycott the conference, but later realized that this would be difficult and counterproductive. As such, the British Cabinet 'decided not to encourage foreign governments to attend, to discourage Gold Coast and Central African Federation from accepting their invitations for full participation, and generally to play down [the] importance of [the] conference.'[62]

Eventually, the British succeeded in preventing the leaders of Singapore (David Marshall) and Ghana (Kwame Nkrumah), both under dominion status, from attending the conference. Moreover, the British, in coordination with the US and France, sought to manipulate the conference through friendly governments in attendance, like Turkey, Pakistan, Philippines, Iran, Iraq, and Thailand.[63]

The British had three goals for sabotaging the conference: (1) to prevent the emergence of an Afro-Asian bloc, (2) to prevent any resolution deemed 'advantageous to the communists or inimical to British interests', and (3) to 'cause the maximum embarrassment to the communists.' These objectives were developed at two meetings that were held on 2 and 3 March 1955 at the UK Foreign Office.[64] British 'guidance' documents dealing with Britain's approach to a variety of issues involving its Asian colonies were sent to their diplomatic missions in thirty-seven countries, including some countries not attending the Conference. These dealt with the existence of 'communist colonialism,'[65] the need for a ban on strategic goods exports to communist China, communist violation of the Geneva Agreements on Indo-China, the dangers of the Five Principles of Peaceful Co-existence (promoted by India and China), the lack of religious freedom in the communist world, and the implications of the hydrogen bomb (the goal being to discourage any resolution against the bomb due to the risk of massive radiation). Through these documents, the British missions were asked to urge friendly nations to 'resist proposals that the Conference should endorse controversial claims for extensions of sovereignty,' and to offer advice to 'our more trustworthy friends [who] should be warned to beware of projects for any kind of Afro-Asian bloc designed to disrupt existing regional organizations (Colombo Plan, specialized agencies of UN on SEATO, etc.).'[66]

Yet, as will be seen later, at Bandung, sovereignty was extended to cover non-participation in Cold War Pacts, and SEATO was delegitimized. At the same time, no guidance was issued on the issue of racialism, even though some British officials were anxious to portray Bandung as a racialist gathering—due to the exclusion of countries like Rhodesia and the apartheid regime in South Africa—as the issue made the West vulnerable.

In the US, the Eisenhower administration also advised the American missions 'to avoid an open show of interest' in the conference. While Secretary of State Dulles publicly told the media that the 'US had always taken a sympathetic attitude', that Bandung would 'serve a useful purpose', and that the US attitude towards the conference would be one of 'benevolent indifference',[67] the country was deeply worried that the conference would 'offer communist China an excellent propaganda opportunity,' and 'enhance communist prestige in the area and weaken that of the West.'[68] The US further worried that the conference might 'lull the anxieties of friendly and non-committed countries and place the blame for present world tensions on the policies of the United States.'[69]

To counter this, the US urged collaboration among its friends to counter the neutrals and China. The Americans followed the UK's lead in offering friendly governments—such as Japan, Turkey, South Vietnam, Lebanon, Philippines and Thailand—

advice and guidance on how to behave and what to say. The US not only had an advance copy of the Philippines lead representative Carlos Romulo's opening speech at Bandung, but also gave him (less than two weeks before the conference) a draft resolution on Taiwan, which he promised to use (and did use) at Bandung.[70]

These Western efforts at manipulation initially had the effect of fuelling controversy and bickering, which at one point threatened to derail the whole conference. For example, the British had provided an aide-memoire to Ceylonese Prime Minister John Kotelawala, one of the sponsors of the conference, urging that 'full attention should be directed to communist colonialism', referring to Eastern Europe under Soviet dominance. Kotelawala was supposedly in the so-called *neutralist* camp, but actually sympathized with pro-Western positions, albeit within limits imposed by his fear of Indian disapproval. After he launched into an attack on communist colonialism at Bandung, a British official mused: 'Sir John Kotelawala made good use of his brief.'[71] But his attack not only angered Chinese Premier Zhou Enlai, causing him to lose his cool for the only time during the entire conference, it also enraged Indian Prime Minister Jawaharlal Nehru, who rejected the parallel between Western colonialism and the situation in the Soviet bloc countries in Eastern Europe and confronted Kotelawala angrily. Kotelawala subsequently toned down his position on communism considerably.

Despite such incidents, the conference was able to reach a consensus on almost all major issues and produce a Final Communique. To a large extent, Western efforts at manipulation were borne out of exaggerated fear of the intentions of the Bandung countries, especially the neutralist camp led by India and Indonesia. The latter were not really pursuing any anti-Western (certainly not a pro-Soviet) agenda, but in some cases, the collective interests of the newly independent countries, like advancing decolonization or developing an independent common voice in international affairs, seemed anti-Western to the leading Western powers. There was no downplaying of the opposition to Western colonialism (relative to communist colonialism) at Bandung, and the Anglo-American effort to cause 'maximum embarrassment' to China was an outstanding failure. So was their effort to prevent the emergence of an independent collective voice and movement of the postcolonial states, although this might not have been apparent in the immediate aftermath of Bandung. Despite differences and divisions among the participants, the Bandung Conference provided the first major instance of the postcolonial countries' collective resistance to Western dominance in international relations.

Influencing Cold War Dynamics

A second legacy of the Bandung Conference, and closely related to the thwarting of Western efforts as mentioned above, lies in shaping the attitudes of newly independent countries towards the Cold War by laying the foundation of the Non-Aligned Movement (NAM). Contrary to a popular myth, neither Tito of Yugoslavia nor Nkrumah of Ghana came to Bandung. NAM was established through the efforts of Nehru and Indonesia as Bandung's host country. Bandung also owes its success to another engaged and popular participant—Egypt's new leader Gamal Abdel Nasser, who was instrumental in negotiating compromises without which the Final Communique would not have been possible.

Before Bandung, Nasser had been described in secret American assessments as pro-Western. If that were the case, Nasser certainly left the conference a changed man. He heard Nehru's arguments against the dangers posed by the Cold War pacts being promoted by US Secretary of State Dulles, which reinforced Nasser's own misgivings about the Baghdad Pact and its offshoot, the Central Treaty Organization (CENTO). At Bandung, Nehru gave full vent to his bitter opposition to such pacts, especially the Southeast Asia Treaty Organization (SEATO). Speaking of the decision of some countries represented at Bandung, namely Turkey, Pakistan, Thailand, and Philippines, Nehru lamented: 'It is an intolerable thought to me that the great countries of Asia and Africa should come out of bondage into freedom only to degrade themselves or humiliate themselves in this way.' As he saw it, membership in such pacts rendered a country a 'camp follower' and deprived it of its 'freedom and dignity'.[72]

Nehru came under criticism for using such harsh words, and the conference compromised by listing among the Ten Principles (*Dasa Sila*) of its Final Communique, 'Respect for the right of each nation to defend itself singly or collectively, in conformity with the Charter of the United Nations' (Principle 6), as well as the principle of 'abstention from the use of arrangements of collective defence to serve the particular interests of any of the big powers.'[73] The abstention principle became one of the founding declaratory principles of NAM. Moreover, while the conference affirmed the right of collective self-defence, it had the effect of discouraging any further new members for SEATO as had been hoped for by its supporters. In fact, SEATO was doomed. As a UK Foreign Office Assessment of Bandung later acknowledged, '. . . any hope that might have existed that additional states could be attracted to SEATO has now vanished, and a growing tendency towards a neutralist attitude in line with India's position is to be expected.'[74]

As noted above, Nasser's experience at the conference seemed to transform his policy, although no direct link could be established from available primary sources. Within four months after returning from Bandung, Nasser signed a historic arms deal with Czechoslovakia, and less than a year thereafter, in July 1956, he nationalized the Suez Canal Company, prompting the trilateral invasion by the UK, France, and Israel that would change the history of the Middle East and the course of the Cold War. Whether he actually solicited Soviet weapons during his meetings with Zhou Enlai in Bandung, weapons the Soviet Union eventually provided him through Czechoslovakia, is a matter of conjecture, but some analysts believe it did happen.[75] According to an Egyptian political writer, during their meeting in Bandung, 'Chou-en-Lai promised Abdel-Nasser that he would speak to the Soviets to see if *they* could furnish weapons to Egypt. His mediation on Egypt's behalf led to the Czech arms deal.'[76] Nasser went on to join Nehru and Tito as a leader of the Non-Aligned Movement that emerged in the 1960s.

Another Cold War dynamic that was affected by the Bandung Conference was the slowly increasing rift between the Soviet Union and China. It was a rare multilateral conference in which communist China attended without the Soviet Union being present. There is little evidence that China consulted the Soviet Union to discuss and develop a common stand. Bandung allowed the PRC to show its independent face in international affairs, rather than as the representative of a monolithic communist bloc. As Homer Jack noted in a study of the conference: '. . . Bandung saw the emergence of China as a great Asian power and not merely as an isolated partner of Russia.'[77]

In the end, the conference might have contributed to Chinese diplomatic independence from the Soviet Union. In fact, some Asian leaders, including Nehru, overcame initial opposition from some countries (Ceylon in particular) to invite China to the conference precisely on the ground that it might help draw it away from the communist bloc. China could develop its identity as an Asian nation seeking peaceful relations with its neighbours, rather than as a communist nation promoting subversion and instability in the region. George McTurnan Kahin noted in his study of Bandung that the conference gave a chance for Chinese leaders to get more acquainted with the 'realities of China's international environment', and for its neighbours to create 'moral restraint against possible Chinese tendencies of aggression'.[78]

Challenging and Broadening Global Norms

Notwithstanding its challenge to Western dominance, the Bandung Conference also contributed to and strengthened the emerging post-war global normative framework to better reflect the positions and concerns of the newly independent and decolonizing nations. The conference contributed to the extension and deepening of the idea and norms of universal sovereignty.[79] The meaning of non-intervention was extended to include non-participation in unequal military alliances conceived in the Cold War context. The dominant Western perspective today might view this contribution in a negative light, given its tendency to view sovereignty and non-intervention as a threat to both collective action and collective morality, especially for the protection of human rights. But in the immediate postwar context, sovereignty was a deeply emancipatory idea for countries that had lost it to predatory and profoundly immoral Western powers for a few centuries.

The conference's normative contribution also included its staunch support for universal human rights—something often overlooked by Western governments as well as human rights scholars and transnational activists. There is a persistent myth that the Bandung countries were, if not anti-human rights, at least cultural relativists. But there was no hint of cultural relativism in the discussions about human rights at Bandung. The very first of the Ten Principles called for the 'respect for fundamental human rights and for the purposes and principles of the Charter of the United Nations'.[80] And this was not because of Western pressure. Nehru, no stooge of the West himself, took the lead by urging a dose of self-criticism at the outset of the debate over human rights. As he put it, 'We have no right to criticize others for violating human rights if we ourselves do not observe them.'[81] The Bandung Declaration 'takes note of the Universal Declaration of Human Rights as a common standard of achievement for all peoples and all nations'. But it broadened its support for human rights by also recognizing 'the fundamental principles of human rights as set forth in the Charter of the United Nations'.[82] In that sense, the conference advanced the earlier efforts of the Latin American countries in promoting universal human rights and presaged the subsequent efforts of the developing countries in advancing the global human rights agenda at the UN.[83]

The conference also strengthened support for the UN. Western nations had feared that the conference might undermine the UN and the principle of universalism by creating an alternative Afro-Asian bloc. Nine of the thirty participants at Bandung were not yet UN members. But the Bandung Declaration stated that 'membership in the United Nations should be universal' and demanded that the UN Security Council admit those Bandung participants that were not yet members of the UN. In short, the conference defended universalism and sought its expansion, rather than suggesting an alternative to it.

A Comity of Civilizations

Finally, the Bandung Conference offered one of the most vivid and powerful displays of the comity of civilizations—investigating which is a key concern of the burgeoning field of Global International Relations. Hosted by the world's largest Muslim country, whose motto is 'unity in diversity', the conference brought together leaders of diverse faiths, ethnicities, languages, and cultural heritage. The leaders of the largest Hindu, Muslim, Buddhist, and Confucian nations were there. Even among the Islamic nations, there were significant cultural differences— for example between Saudi Arabia and Turkey. Yet, aside from adjusting the dates of the conference to avoid the Muslim fasting month, and despite Western-backed efforts to highlight the lack of religious diversity of communist societies, religion was a non-issue in shaping positions, alignments, and interactions during the conference. One of the most powerful alliances was between Muslim Pakistan, secular-minded Turkey, Catholic Philippines, and Buddhist Thailand. Religious tolerance was the dominant ethos and the interactions among leaders at the conference were remarkably multi-cultural and interpersonal (including sharing of food and common eating spaces for leaders). The identity that mattered and shaped Bandung was the constructed political identity of the newly independent and marginalized forces of world politics, rather than the parochial identities of cultural or civilizational blocs. There was not even the faintest hint of Huntington's 'clash of civilizations' at Bandung.

Negative Legacies

Some contemporary assessments tend to gloss over the negative legacies of the Bandung Conference. But these did exist and must be recognized. A key negative legacy was the polarization of Asia between pro-Western, communist, and non-aligned countries. While these divisions had already become evident, having been influenced by the Cold War, Bandung helped to accentuate them considerably. Another negative legacy was that the conference may have contributed to increasing authoritarianism in Asia and Africa. Pro-Western nations such as the Philippines, Thailand, and Pakistan, who claimed victory at Bandung for the *free world*, were blinded to their domestic failings, which resulted in military takeovers of their political systems. It is not unreasonable to assume that the euphoria generated by the success of the conference might have accentuated Sukarno's authoritarian impulses. At the very least, it may have provided a diversion from his increasing domestic troubles. Yet another negative legacy was to encourage regional adventurism and interventionism by some of the larger participating nations. Egypt's Nasser returned from Bandung emboldened not only to take on the West, but also to assertively seek an Egyptian sphere of influence over his neighbours in the interest of pan-Arabism, including by carrying out military interventions in the region. Sukarno's nationalistic foreign policy towards his neighbours—which led to a militant opposition (*Konfrontasi*) to the creation of Malaysia in 1963—may well have received a boost from the conference.

A Bandung Balance Sheet

Among its most conspicuous failures, it has been suggested that the conference did not develop any permanent organization of Asian-African nations, as had been feared by the West, and desired by some participants, especially China. But this had less to do with Western manipulation as with Indian misgivings, because Nehru, learning from his earlier attempt at an Asian relations organization, had by now realized the practical difficulties of creating a permanent organization. Perhaps he was already looking to the future when a larger and more global movement of postcolonial nations could be established (this came to fruition in the creation of the NAM in 1961).

Some Western analysts noted that the condemnation of colonialism and the expression of anti-Western sentiments at the conference was muted. While this may be seen as a victory for Western governments, especially the UK, the fact was that the leading participants like India and China had no intention of turning the conference into an anti-Western talk fest. The Bandung Conference advanced decolonization and the right of former and current colonies to exist as sovereign entities, alongside their former colonizers. Aside from laying the foundation of the NAM, it directly inspired Nasser's pan-Arabism and Nkrumah's pan-

African movements, the latter having a pronounced anticolonial function, since Africa had fallen behind Asia on that score. As George McTurnan Kahin noted, the conference proved to be a 'substantial denominator of anti-colonialism'.[84]

Indeed, one way to assess these overall implications of the conference would be to take a look at the confidential assessments of those very Western nations who had both feared its results and disparaged its significance in mobilizing an Afro-Asian consensus. These may be more credible, given that assessments by the conference's main supporters—such as China, Indonesia, and India—are likely to be perceived as biased in highlighting its successes.

Despite their initial hostility and misgivings about the purpose and likely outcome of the conference, Western powers had to accept, however grudgingly, its significance. In a patronizing tone, a British assessment noted that:

> The East is no longer age-old, inscrutable, unchanging. It is young, eager, drunk with new nationalism and freedom, but also desperately anxious to behave with maturity and make a good showing before its elders if not betters. It loses its angularity only when treated as a grown-up and an equal, and like all adolescents is easily offended, and as easily influenced for good.[85]

In a less comical tone, an intelligence assessment by the US State Department, noted:

> In fact, the nations assembled at Bandung, with little prior experience in running large international conferences and with only decades or less of independent participation in world politics, managed to organize a meeting which rejected the discipline of any of the Conference's five sponsoring powers,

yet found its way to common ground with efficiency and dispatch. The Conference succeeded in demonstrating that there is an Asian-African consensus.[86]

Some British documents also conceded that the conference 'strengthened the self-confidence' of the participating nations and 'gave them a greater sense of their importance in world affairs' and encouraged them to 'evolve policies of their own'. The documents further noted that an Afro-Asian 'common purpose' had been 'strengthened', leading to a corresponding 'weakening of Western leadership.'[87] While indicating a Western bias towards viewing strength as zero-sum, this assessment did not elaborate on how strengthening among Afro-Asian nations spelt weakening of Western leadership.

Although questions such as who won and who lost and whether the Bandung Conference was a success or failure may never be settled, at the very least, it produced 'the evident feeling of the delegations that the meeting represented a fresh stage in international relations,' as the British Ambassador to Indonesia put it.[88] The conference underscored the real and substantial *agency* of the non-Western nations in the construction of the post-War international order in areas such as anti-colonialism, universalism, and human rights. It marked the rise of the *regionalism of the weak in world politics*. It also had an 'educational function': 'a fuller and more realistic understanding of one another's point of view.'[89] Legacies of the Bandung Conference can be better understood not in terms of categories such as positive and negative, but in terms of how it shaped and reshaped international order in Asia and the world, the analysis of which has been dominated by the centrality of great power geopolitics to the neglect of the perspectives and agency of non-Western, non-great power actors.

Conclusion

The Bandung Conference offers a unique and important point of reference for advancing the study of Global IR. The conference was not an event of deep antiquity. It is still of immense significance in the *longue durée* conception of international relations, as Sukarno's reference to it being the first intercontinental gathering of coloured peoples in his opening address clearly reminded. What Sukarno said next is no less important: 'It is a new departure in the history of the world that leaders of Asian and African peoples can meet together in their own countries to discuss and deliberate upon matters of common concern.'[90]

Bandung was the first time when nations in different continents were holding a multilateral intergovernmental meeting on their home turf, instead of in the imperial capitals of London, Paris, Brussels, or Berlin. Their purpose was not just to advance decolonization, which was already well under way (except in Africa), but also, as the Secretary General of the Bandung Conference, Roselan Abdulghani, later wrote, 'The formulation and establishment of certain norms for the conduct of present-day international relations and the instruments for the practical application of these norms.'[91] The fact that they accomplished the objective, at least in the normative sense, with the articulation of the Ten Principles, and despite the gaps between the principles and how they were applied, does not detract from the conference's contribution. While the international system they were born into was European in its origin, it would be misleading to simply call it—in the manner of the early English School theorists—as the European states-system writ large.[92] The new actors had to adapt those European rules to fit local postcolonial realities. At Bandung, they did so by broadening the meanings of non-intervention, control over natural resources, and the delegitimization of regional cooperation under the orbit of great powers akin to the Concert of Europe. Later through the NAM, which was born at Bandung, and other fora where developing countries networked with one another, they would advance these and other principles, including human rights.

The Bandung Conference aspired to contribute to an international order that recognized indigenous non-Western forms of interaction.[93] It decided against adopting any elaborate or formal rules of procedure, preferring to keep things informal, and rejected voting so that decisions could be reached through deliberations and consensus. Abdulghani, the Indonesian Secretary-General of the conference, characterized these rules as 'deep-rooted and unquestioned practice' of Indonesian, and other Asian and African societies. 'The object is to reach an acceptable consensus of opinion, and one which not only hurts the feeling or the position of no one, but which actually tends to reinforce the community feeling.'[94]

The Bandung Conference's extension of universal sovereignty and its realization of a substantial Afro-Asian consensus—as acknowledged by its Western detractors—on issues such as decolonization and human rights (as well as other issues such as development, disarmament, and self-determination not discussed here owing to lack of space) constitute a powerful act of agency by the non-Western countries. Agency here means something quite different from how it is employed by Europeans under their 'standard of civilization' formula, which referred to a state's capacity and right to play the game of power politics. The agency at display at Bandung was a normative agency, i.e., an ability to interpret, localize, formulate, and strengthen the rules of international relations to advance freedom, peace, and order. While some of these rules were not always upheld in practice and gaps developed between these normative aspirations and subsequent realities in Asia and Africa, this does not detract from the fact that they remain integral to the contemporary global normative order supported by a majority of both developed and developing countries.

The Bandung Conference also shed light on the nature and implications of the current global power shift. Many emerging powers of today have a strong connection to Bandung. Six of the G-20 members, the premier global forum that brings together both emerging and established powers, attended Bandung: China, India, Indonesia, Japan, Turkey, and Saudi Arabia. (South Africa, which along with India and China belongs to the BRICS forum—Brazil, Russia, India, China, and South Africa—also attended as an observer state representing the African National Congress). While there were differences at Bandung, there was also a substantial measure of consensus among many about the need for reforming the existing global order to make it more just and democratic. The same demand underpins the policies of contemporary emerging powers, and, as such, should be counted as a legacy of the Bandung Conference. Indeed, the gap between then pro-Western Turkey on the one hand and India and China on the other has narrowed. While the West hopes that these powers may somehow be co-opted into the existing international order without it having to make significant concessions, these hopes are likely to prove illusory. The normative aspirations of the emerging powers are more consistent with the Bandung Declaration, with its quest for greater justice and equality among nations, than with past great power initiatives, be it the Congress of Vienna that marginalized weaker states by creating the Concert of Europe, or the Berlin Conference that carved out Africa.

Reshaping Intra-Asian Relations and Regionalism

A final and perhaps the most enduring legacy of the Bandung conference was the rise of Southeast Asian regionalism, minus India and China. Before and at Bandung, there was no separation between Southeast Asia and South Asia as the five sponsors—the Conference of Southeast Asian Prime Ministers—included Pakistan, Ceylon, and India, which are now part of South Asia. Similarly, there was no conception of the 'Middle East'—an imperial British concoction. The very fact that the conference was called the Asian-African Conference signifies that the Arab countries, Iran, and Turkey were simply regarded as part of Asia, with Egypt straddling its space between Asia and Africa.

The rise of Southeast Asia as a distinctive region apart from South Asia was the result of the diminished influence of Asia's two major powers—India and China—that Bandung brought about. This assertion may seem surprising to those who accept the conventional wisdom that the conference was a contest for influence between the Indian Prime Minister Nehru and his Chinese counterpart Zhou Enlai, which the latter won decisively. But the assertions of any India–China competition at the time of the conference are quite exaggerated, as the Chinese genuinely respected Nehru and depended on his counsel in the lead up to and at the conference.[95] A British diplomatic dispatch about the conference noted that 'Chou had at one stage said that any English phrase which was acceptable to Nehru would be acceptable to him.'[96] Chinese documents collected and translated by this author show that while the Chinese did recognize differences between their and India's aims and objectives, especially over the creation of a permanent organization out of Bandung, which China wanted but India rejected, there was more convergence than competition in the interests and approaches of the two leaders.

If this were a contest, the consensus among observers is that Chinese Premier Zhou Enlai won. Nehru was seen to have been at least sidelined by Zhou. He was criticized for his arrogant manner while observers praised Zhou's impressive demeanour. He appeared calm, mature, restrained, and conciliatory. Yet, the reality may well be that neither won. While Bandung might have undercut Nehru's prestige and influence, it did not end suspicions of China, especially after China continued and stepped up its support for communist insurgencies in its neighbourhood. The Australian Ambassador to Indonesia, W.R. Crocker, who closely monitored the conference and its outcome, offers a more balanced assessment of the Nehru–Zhou rivalry than most media reports of the time:

> It is commonly said at Djakarta today that Chou's rise in prestige was proportionate to, and indeed the cause of, Nehru's decline in prestige. Some at least of this argument originates from identifiable sources, some of it is wishful, and some is exaggerated. It was, after all, Nehru who insisted on Chou's being invited, who indoctrinated him carefully before the Conference, and who sponsored him in the difficult opening days at Bandung. Mr. Nehru did not strike me as feeling that he had been supplanted by Chou. He might of course have been concealing his feelings but during the time I spent with him after the conference he spoke highly of Chou's performance and he seemed to be pleased with it.[97]

Yet, one might argue with the benefit of hindsight that the real winner at Bandung was neither China nor India, but the future ASEAN. Suspicion of both India and China, generated at Bandung, paved the way in Asia for a regionalism of smaller nations to emerge, led by none of the big powers. ASEAN's establishment in 1967 was the realization of that goal. What is more, the Bandung Conference gave Japan an opportunity to emerge from its isolation and passivity following its defeat in World War II. At Bandung, Japan focused almost exclusively on economic issues, and might have gotten some ideas and a taste of regionalism without the kind of hegemonic framework that had underpinned its Greater East Asia Co-Prosperity Sphere concept. By paving the way for regionalism of the smaller nations, which Japan, later, came to back strongly, by providing crucial economic support to ASEAN, the Bandung Conference might have decisively shaped the trajectory of Asian regionalism, which continues, to this day, to be ASEAN-centric. What is more, the informal, interpersonal, and consensus-driven nature of interactions among the top leaders at Bandung might have presaged the 'ASEAN Way'—the non-coercive and non-legalistic mode of interactions that marked the formative years of ASEAN.

To understand this enduring and most important legacy of the Bandung Conference, the next chapter elaborates on the circumstances that led to the creation of ASEAN and the organization's role in shaping Southeast Asian regional identity.

Chapter 3

The ASEANists and the Emergence of Southeast Asian Identity[98]

In Chapter 1, I discussed the role of Western historians and colonial geopolitical dynamic that underscored the understanding of the emergence of Southeast Asia as a distinctive region. However, the story is still incomplete. Southeast Asia was also the product of the ideas and policies of what might be called 'ASEANists'—the generation of leaders who founded ASEAN.

Unlike in Europe, regionalism in Southeast Asia has been constructed to serve the interest of nationalism. 'The search for national solidarity and unity,' wrote Alejandro Melchor, a Filippino Cabinet member, 'is replicated, albeit on a broader scale and less urgent, but equally persistent, in the relations among nations of Southeast Asia.'[99] 'The isolation of centuries,' he added, 'had to be breached; lost ties had to be restored.'[100]

The founders of ASEAN, the first generation of ASEANists, saw their region and the organization as a quest for unity in diversity. The nations of Southeast Asia—Brunei, Cambodia, Indonesia, Laos, Malaysia, Myanmar, Philippines, Singapore, Thailand, Timor Leste, and Vietnam—are too diverse in terms of their political, social, and cultural make up to be regarded as part of a natural region. Not only is Southeast Asia a 'chaos of races and languages',[101] its nation-states differ significantly from each other in terms of religion, political system, colonial past, and level of economic development.

Consider this. Buddhism is the religion of the majority in Cambodia, Myanmar, and Thailand, Islam in Malaysia, Brunei, and Indonesia, and Christianity in the Philippines. Confucian values are latent in the societies of Singapore and Vietnam. Hinduism thrives in Bali and remains an underlying cultural force in many Southeast Asian societies. One can find both inter-state as well as intra-state religious and ethnic diversity.

Colonialism of all hues and colours have shaped Southeast Asia's recent history. All major colonial powers were here—the British in Myanmar, Malaysia, and Singapore, the Dutch in Indonesia, the French in Indochina (Cambodia, Laos, and Vietnam), the Spaniards and the Americans in the Philippines. The Portuguese ushered in the era of Western colonialism by conquering the Sultanate of Malacca in 1511 and stayed in East Timor until 1975. Japan occupied much of the region during World War II.

Despite these multi-faceted diversities, the term 'Southeast Asia' has stuck, at least since World War II. Why so? This is mainly because ASEAN's founders set about a deliberate process of collective identity-building while recognizing the cultural diversity of their members and fully respecting their sovereignty as nation-states. Unlike the European Union, this was not a sovereignty-defying project. Supranationalism was incompatible with their long and hard-fought struggles against colonialism. But socialization, especially elite socialization, was undertaken as a way of reducing the tyranny of structural diversity and pre-empting postcolonial divisions from erupting into violent conflict. As a result, the original members of ASEAN have not fought a war against each other since 1967. Conflicts have been 'swept under the carpet', admittedly to reappear now and then, but as yet to a degree that could justify resorting to war. Nationalism has not waned, but has rather gotten subsumed under a socially constructed framework of regionalism.

The Prelude to ASEAN Identity

ASEAN's identity is not a cultural given. Rather, it has been constructed out of self-conscious social interaction. The Declaration of ASEAN Concord, an important document of Southeast Asian regionalism signed by ASEAN's five original members in 1976, clearly stated that 'member states shall vigorously develop an awareness of regional identity and exert all efforts to create a strong ASEAN community.'

ASEAN's forerunner was the establishment of the Association of Southeast Asia (ASA) in 1961 with the membership of Malaya, Thailand, and the Philippines. This organization was the result of an unlikely development. The idea of ASA was initially proposed by Tunku Abdul Rahman, Malaya's first Prime Minister, soon after it became independent in 1957. He envisaged a regional grouping to fight communist subversion by targeting what he deduced to be its major cause: poverty. At a meeting with Philippine President Garcia in January 1959, the two had agreed on a Southeast Asian Friendship and Economic Treaty as the core of a regional association. The objectives of the proposed group, as revealed in portions of Tunku's message to Sukarno, dated October 28, 1959, were:

> to encourage closer relations among the countries of Southeast Asia by discussion, conferences, or consultation, and to achieve agreement freely. It is hoped by this method that countries will be able to understand each other more deeply. It is also the objective of this association to study ways and means of helping one another—particularly in economic, social, and cultural and scientific fields . . . You will understand that because of

> historical circumstances, the economic growth of most of the countries in Southeast Asia in this century has been influenced by relations with countries outside the region. Because of this, the feeling of 'one region' has been stunted, ... and because of these historical circumstances, we have looked for help and examples from the outside and seldom look to ourselves ... [102]

Tunku's idea received support from the then Thai Foreign Minister Thanat Khoman, who wanted a broad, inclusive grouping, except for North Vietnam. The Thais also prepared a 'Preliminary Working Paper on Cooperation in Southeast Asia',[103] which emphasized the need for an organization with minimal administrative machinery. Although Tunku attempted to convince other regional leaders of his idea, Indonesia remained suspicious of the organization, viewing it as a front for SEATO. While the idea of a broader grouping failed, ASA was set up by three members in 1961.

ASA's stated objectives included social and cultural cooperation, and the 'promotion of Southeast Asian studies'.[104] Tunku described ASA as 'an alliance of three friendly countries formed to build a happy region in South-East Asia.'[105] The purpose of ASA was to 'show the world that peoples of Asia can think and plan for themselves.'[106] Tunku also stressed ASA's role in fostering a regional identity:

> In the past—and this is one of the faults of our history—the countries of South-East Asia have been very individualist, very prone to go different ways and very disinclined to co-operate with each other. In fact, those with more rather tended to look down on others with less, there was no desire to try and help one another.[107]

The Philippines's Vice-President and Secretary of Foreign Affairs, Emmanuel Pelaez, saw ASA as helping its members towards 'meeting the increasing challenge of economic blocs from other parts of the world.' For this reason, he called for ASA to 'fully explore and exploit the possibilities and potentialities of greater intra-regional trade.'[108]

For Thanat Khoman, ASA was rooted in 'Asian culture and traditions'. In his view, ASA reflected a faith 'in our capability to shape and direct for ourselves the future destiny of our nations.'[109]

Another precursor to ASEAN was Maphilindo, conceived by Philippine President Diosdado Macapagal as a loose confederation of the three independent states of the Malay stock (Malaysia, Philippines, and Indonesia). Seen as a response to Sukarno's opposition to the Malaysian Federation and the resulting policy of Konfrontasi, the Macapagal Plan aimed to 'restore and strengthen the historic unity and common heritage among the Malay peoples, and draw them to closer political, economic, and cultural relations.'[110] Despite its failure, Maphilindo was important for the Philippines' own regional identification. It signalled Manila's realization that the Philippines could not live alone in the region, and that the US defence umbrella was an important but insufficient basis for security. Regional identification was deemed necessary.

The ASEANists' Political Imperative

Like their counterparts in other parts of the developing world, Southeast Asian elites saw colonialism imposing artificial boundaries on nations as well as regions. As such, postcolonial Asian elites could see in the end of colonialism both an imperative and an opportunity for reconstituting lost regional linkages and identities.

The creation of ASEAN was not simply a reflection of global trends like the Cold War. It was largely the product of local circumstances. The immediate motivating factors behind ASEAN had to do, firstly, with a common desire for collective diplomatic clout against external powers. ASEAN was expected to enhance the bargaining power of its small and weak members in their dealings with the great powers. ASEAN might not enable its member states to prevent the great powers from interfering in the affairs of the region, but it could, as Prime Minister Lee Kuan Yew of Singapore pointed out, help them to 'have their interests taken into consideration when the great powers make their compromises.'[111] Adam Malik, the Indonesian Foreign Minister made the same point:

> Southeast Asia is one region in which the presence and interests of most major powers converge, politically as well as physically. The frequency and intensity of policy interactions among them, as well as their dominant influence on the countries in the region, cannot but have a direct bearing on political realities. In the face of this, the smaller nations of the region have no hope of ever making any impact on this pattern of dominant influence of the big powers, unless they act collectively and until they develop the capacity to forge among themselves an area of internal cohesion, stability and common purpose.[112]

As ASEAN members were beginning to pursue similar development strategies, there emerged a certain ideological commonality among them, which provided an important political foundation for the organization. With the war in Indochina having prompted its members to lay urgent emphasis on economic growth within the free-market model, Ghazali Shafie of Malaysia proclaimed that:

> The concept of free enterprise as they apply [sic] in the ASEAN region is the philosophical basis of ASEAN. The appreciation of this is vital in the understanding of ASEAN and its sense of direction. The countries of the ASEAN region

had come together to protect the system of free enterprise as a counterpoise against communism on the one hand and monopolistic capitalism on the other . . . When the leaders of Malaysia, Indonesia, Philippines, Singapore and Thailand got together in Bangkok in 1967 to officiate at the establishment of the Association of Southeast Asian Nations, they were in fact making a commitment to jointly strengthen and promote the system of free enterprise in their countries in the belief that together they could harness the strength of the system to bring about the kind of national and regional resilience that would serve as a bulwark against communism.[113]

Adam Malik, the Foreign Minister of Indonesia, explained this norm most forcefully in 1974:

Regional problems, i.e., those having a direct bearing upon the region concerned, should be accepted as being of primary concern to that region itself. Mutual consultations and cooperation among the countries of the region in facing these problems may . . . lead to the point where the views of the region are accorded the primacy they deserve in the search for solution.[114]

Singapore's Foreign Minister, S. Rajaratnam, urged that Southeast Asia should stay out of great power rivalry:

The British decision to withdraw from the region in the seventies brings . . . to an end nearly two centuries of dominant European influence in the region. The seventies will also see the withdrawal of direct American influence in Southeast Asian affairs. For the first time in centuries, Southeast Asia will be on its own. It must fill what some people call the power vacuum itself or resign itself to the dismal prospect of the vacuum being filled from the outside ... We can and should fill it ourselves, not necessarily militarily, but by strengthening our social, economic and political foundations through cooperation and collective effort.[115]

ASEAN's focus on socio-cultural identity also made it reject any proposal to turn it into a military alliance. At the Bali summit of 1976, the Prime Minister of Malaysia, Hussein Onn, stated:

It is obvious that the ASEAN members do not wish to change the character of ASEAN from a socio-economic organization into a security alliance as this would only create misunderstanding in the region and undermine the positive achievements of ASEAN in promoting peace and stability through co-operation in the socio-economic and related fields.[116]

Creating the ASEAN Way

Signing of the Bangkok Declaration to establish ASEAN, 8 August 1967 (AESC)

The founding ASEANists provided the articulation of the ASEAN Way. General Ali Moertopo of Indonesia argued that the success of ASEAN was due to 'the system of consultations that has marked much of its work, what I may call the ASEAN

Way of dealing with a variety of problems confronting its member nations.'[117] He ascribed the ASEAN Way to 'the fact that most of the leaders representing the ASEAN member countries for the past seven years or more of its existence have mostly been old friends who know one another so well.'[118]

Malaysia's Ghazali Shafie argued that 'our common cultural heritage', especially the *kampung* (village) spirit of 'togetherness', not only was a key factor behind secret Malaysia–Indonesia negotiations to end *Konfrontasi*, but also formed the basis of the establishment of ASEAN.[119] For him, the very fact that the Bangkok Declaration was called a declaration and not a treaty (unlike the Treaty of Rome) was significant, because 'treaty presupposes lack of trust'. Moreover, the word 'association' was meant to differentiate ASEAN from an 'organization' and thereby convey a sense of looseness and informality.[120] ASEAN's founders believed that such informality was necessary in light of the diversity of views and positions held by the ASEAN members. Estrella Solidum, a Filipino scholar, believes that the ASEAN Way 'consists of cultural elements which are found to be congruent with some values of each of the member states.'[121]

Carlos Romulo, the Foreign Secretary of the Philippines, said: 'I can pick up the telephone now and talk directly to Adam Malik [Indonesia's Foreign Minister] or Rajaratnam [Singapore's Foreign Minister]. We often find that private talks over breakfast prove more important than formal meetings.'[122] Explaining the rationale behind the informal setting of ASEAN, Malaysia's Prime Minister, Hussein Onn, observed at the 1976 Bali summit: 'ASEAN has been able to absorb national differences because it is a relatively informal organization without rigid rules of procedure and without elaborate structural machinery.'[123] Agerico Lacanlale, a Filipino scholar, has pointed out that ASEAN's organizational set-up was:

> flexible enough to accommodate a diversity of interests without causing the collapse of the organization . . . it is the reluctance to

commit themselves to rigid rules of conduct that seems to have strengthened ASEAN. The less the member states feel bound by certain rules, the more willing they are to consult with one another and adopt a common position on common concerns. The fact that the coercive element in their collective conduct is minimized means that joint decisions are arrived at out of free choice and in the spirit of consensus and cooperation.[124]

Later, speaking at the height of a regional economic crisis that took place three decades after the formation of ASEAN, Singapore's Foreign Minister, S. Jayakumar, offered a rare account of the principles considered to be integral to the ASEAN Way. In his words, 'The ASEAN Way stresses informality, organizational minimalism, inclusiveness, intensive consultations leading to consensus and peaceful resolution of disputes.'[125]

A related aspect of the ASEAN Way is the role of the Track-Two dialogues and consultative mechanisms in formulating ideas and contributing to policy debates. Although the idea of Track-Two is by no means unique to Southeast Asia (a Western example would be the Ditchley Park conferences in Britain), it has been quite significant to the evolution of ASEAN's security role in the 1980s and 1990s. Track-Two processes are meetings (both bilateral as well as multilateral) sponsored by NGOs (usually think-tanks) that bear explicitly and directly on policy-relevant issues. Such mechanisms have two main characteristics. First, the think-tanks involved are, in most cases, closely linked to their respective national governments, and rely on government funding for their academic and policy-relevant activities. As Stuart Harris puts it, Track-Two diplomacy is dependent 'upon the consent, endorsement and commitment, often including financial commitment, of governments.'[126] Second, these meetings feature participation by government officials alongside academics and other non-official actors, although officials usually participate *in their private capacity*. Although the participating officials seldom venture beyond the position of their respective governments, the principle of private capacity enables governments to test new ideas without making binding commitments and, if necessary, back-track on positions.[127]

Expansion of Southeast Asia

After the founding of ASEAN, the 1970s and 1980s saw an expansion of Southeast Asia in terms of its geography, politics, economies, and cultures.

The expansion of ASEAN to assimilate Vietnam, Cambodia, Laos, and Myanmar after the end of the Cold War represented a new phase in the process of regional construction. Sukhumbhand Paribatra argued that having all ten countries of Southeast Asia under the banner of a single regional grouping would 'enhance the region's security and well-being' and represent 'the fulfilment of a dream to create a region-wide organization, which had begun some three decades before'.[128] Documents such as *Shared Destiny: Southeast Asia in the 21st Century*, issued in 1993, and *Southeast Asia Beyond the Year 2000: A Statement of Vision*, issued in 1994, attest to the fact, as Carolina Hernandez writes, that 'one Southeast Asia . . . is a goal increasingly captivating the imagination and support of the region's political and other opinion leaders from academe, the media, the private sector, and other professionals.'[129]

Despite the enthusiasm and effort meted out to the endeavour, there remain several gaps in the social construction of Southeast Asia as a region, gaps which I have extensively discussed in my 2000 book, *The Quest for Identity*. Failure to extend the socialization process from the elite level to the people at large is especially debilitating to the future of Southeast Asia. Regional coherence is undermined by the avoidable squabbling between Singapore and Malaysia, the group's founding member-states.

Furthermore, the social construction of Southeast Asia is also challenged by the forces of globalization. The Asian economic crisis in the late 1990s underscored the vulnerability of Southeast Asian economies to the forces of global capitalism. Similarly, the threat of transnational terrorism, SARS (2003), the COVID-19 pandemic, and the growing rivalry between the US and China, leading to what has been called the 'return of geopolitics' further Southeast Asia's vulnerability and challenge the very notion of Southeast Asia as a region.

To overcome these challenges and maintain their distinctive identity into the 21st century, Southeast Asian states must return to the building blocks and develop their political will to preserve their hard-earned regional identity. Increased regionalism, at the level of governments and civic organizations, is the only hope for the region to remain a region in the face of dark clouds that have gathered on the horizon since the outbreak of the Asian economic crisis in 1997. But Southeast Asia will remain a politically important, if analytically fuzzier, notion as long as local governments and elites find it useful to advance their common economic, political, and geo-strategic interests and objectives. Regionalism and regional identity-building will continue to be a key determinant of the idea of region.

Constructing ASEAN-Ten

It was not until the Vietnamese withdrawal from Cambodia in 1989 and the subsequent Paris Peace Agreement of 1991 that secured Cambodia's future as an independent nation that the Cold War polarization of Southeast Asia finally ended. ASEAN quickly expanded its membership to include Vietnam, Laos, Myanmar, and Cambodia, thereby completing the ASEAN-10, and claiming the realization of its 'One Southeast Asia' concept.

The One Southeast Asia concept challenges one of the more enduring tendencies among Southeast Asian specialists, which is to view Southeast Asia in terms of its constituent nation-states, rather than in a holistic, regional sense. While diversity among Southeast Asian states and the nation-state system are not disappearing, it does make sense to view the region as more than the sum of its individual states because of growing economic interdependence, the unmistakable differences between the region and its larger neighbours, India and China, and the shared vulnerabilities of Southeast Asian countries to transnational challenges.

Yet, the ideal of One Southeast Asia should not obscure some persisting political fault lines. Regional coherence is undermined by a lingering mistrust and squabbling among neighbouring states, most recently between Thailand and Cambodia over the ownership of land near the Hindu temple of Preah Vihear. The integration of the states that made up Indochina, and more importantly, of Myanmar into ASEAN, has proven to be challenging. ASEAN is a group of 'haves' and 'have-nots', and it will take some time and considerable effort to bridge this development divide. Politically, democracy has advanced, especially in Indonesia and now in Myanmar, but authoritarianism remains a feature of the region's political culture, and Southeast Asia as a region continues to evoke serious human rights concerns. People, even in democratizing nations, continue to bear the legacy of an authoritarian past, in their education, livelihood, and dignity.

As can be seen from the preceding analysis, Southeast Asia's claim to be a region cannot be entirely justified on the basis of strategic, political, and economic factors alone. To complete the picture, we need to look at the idea of Southeast Asia from historical and cultural perspectives, and as a social construction, which is carved out of diversity through an act of political engineering by a group of like-minded elites through metaphors such as One Southeast Asia. Southeast Asian nationalists forged a disparate region carved up by colonialists, divided by geography, history, politics, and culture, into a coherent existence through dialogue and repeat interactions. In their effort to both adopt a regional identity and shore up their individual national identities that was hard won, leaders embedded a conciliatory decision-making approach. While this has affected ASEAN's effectiveness, the organization has also managed to weather successive storms in the form of coups, foreign intervention, economic crises, natural disasters, and pandemics.

ASEAN and Southeast Asian Studies

The emergence of Southeast Asian studies contributed much to the global recognition of Southeast Asia as a distinctive region. This was the result of two related and closely interacting forces in the post-war period.[130] The first was the slow but steady recognition of an emerging idea of Southeast Asia as a region in its own right. This, in itself, was a late, contrived, and contested process. It involved rejecting Southeast Asia as a cultural appendage of China or India.[131] Partly responsible for this rejection is what Reid has called the 'turning away' tendency in states that are in close proximity to larger powers, that is, Burma and Vietnam (as well as the Philippines in relation to the US).[132] A related development was the quest for an 'autonomous history' of the region.[133] Political and strategic developments, including the Southeast Asian Command (SEAC) established by the Allied Forces fighting Japan during World War II made Southeast Asia a more familiar geopolitical concept. But as late as 1955, the sponsors of the Asia-Africa Conference in Bandung—a group comprising India, Pakistan, Ceylon (later Sri Lanka), Burma (later Myanmar) and Indonesia—were still calling themselves officially the 'Conference of the South-East Asian Prime Ministers'. The existence of this group, also known as the Colombo Powers, suggests that the concept of Southeast Asia excluding Pakistan, India, and Sri Lanka (which would be later classified as belonging to South Asia) had not yet fully arrived, at least in the political and diplomatic arena.

The second important factor was the institutional development of Southeast Asian studies. Initially, European scholars were key to the debate over Southeast Asia's cultural matrix and autonomy.[134] Subsequently, 'the centre of this new field [Southeast Asia] was undoubtedly the United States,'[135] a 'coincidence between Southeast Asia's birth as a concept and the triumph of world power.'[136] In the US, the First and Second Indochinese wars had a major influence in advancing the concept of Southeast Asia and Southeast Asian studies as an academic discipline.[137] The increasing prominence of the United States in the field of Southeast Asian studies was reflected in the establishment of fourteen Southeast Asian Studies departments between 1947 and 1972 and a tenfold increase in specialists on the region from 1940 to 1984.[138]

ASEAN Creates a Community

ASEAN's quest for identity was forcefully reaffirmed in the aftermath of the Asian financial crisis in 1997 and the adoption of the ASEAN Community framework in 2003. The 10th general principle of the Bali Concord II, adopted in 2003, proclaimed that 'ASEAN shall continue to foster a community of caring societies and promote a common regional identity.' Among the goals listed by the ASEAN Charter that was adopted in 2008, there was special emphasis paid to the promotion of identity through a greater awareness of the diverse culture and heritage of the region.

ASEAN has since consistently stressed the slogan of 'One Vision, One Identity, One Community' in many of its official statements and documents.[139]

Yet, Southeast Asia's identity is not permanent. In the absence of an active and continuing process of imagination and construction, the regional personality of Southeast Asia runs a considerable risk of unravelling. Today, Southeast Asia's regional identity is shaped and challenged by a variety of forces. An important challenge is the impact of globalization. Globalization has had both positive and negative consequences on the region's economic and political stability. On the positive side, it has fostered economic development and interdependence among Southeast Asian states, through increased flow of trade, investment, and travel. Regional airlines such as Bangkok Airways, Silk Air, Air Asia, and Tiger Airways now connect small urban and cultural centres of Southeast Asia, such as Siam Reap, Yogyakarta, Solo, Lombok, Bandung, and Bagan, with the larger metropolises and more established cultural centres of the region. This is helping bring people of the region together.

The negative impacts include the vulnerability of the region to transnational dangers, such as the regional financial meltdown of 1997, the SARS pandemic of 2003, the terrorist attacks in Bali (2002, 2003) and later in Jakarta engineered by a transnational extremist network, and the problems of drug trafficking and people-smuggling, all of which brought Southeast Asia into international disrepute. Other challenges include the growing economic disparities not only between the nation-states of Southeast Asia, but also within them, i.e., between central urban centres and their peripheral areas. Of particular importance is the damage and destruction of Southeast Asia's environment, including rain forests, lakes, rivers, and mangroves, to various forms of threats, including commercial plantations, land reclamation, and urbanization. Globalization and industrialization have affected the Southeast Asian peoples' traditional way of living, leading to a loss of traditional values, including the community spirit that is characteristic of Southeast Asian cultures.

Not Yet a People's Region

Another challenge to building Southeast Asia's regional identity is the lack of attachment and empathy among the people of Southeast Asia to the regional idea. There is a growing sense of an ASEAN identity among the region's elites, in keeping with ASEAN's progress in developing associated regional communities like the ARF, Asia-Pacific Economic Cooperation (APEC), and the Regional Comprehensive Economic Partnership (RCEP). A survey published in 2017 by the Jakarta-based Economic Research Institute for ASEAN and East Asia (ERIA) found that 'awareness of ASEAN increased significantly after 2014'. More importantly, the survey revealed that 'more than three-fourths of all respondents felt 'moderately' to 'very much' as ASEAN citizens.' Combined with those who indicated feeling 'somewhat' as ASEAN citizens, a sense of belonging to ASEAN was shared by virtually all the respondents. But much of this identity is due to the publicity surrounding the ASEAN Economic Community (which came into force in 2015), as well as the natural effect of geographic proximity. It's significant that for a regional organization, which unlike the European Union has no program for a common citizenship, 'only 3 per cent of the respondents said they did not feel like they were ASEAN citizens.'[140]

But the idea of Southeast Asia in general and ASEAN in particular, has been and remains the handiwork of Southeast Asia's political elites. It is yet to trickle down to the societal level and engage the people's consciousness. Although there is a slogan of creating a 'people's ASEAN', this remains a far cry from reality. The notion of Southeast Asia is also in many ways an urban construct. How many people living in the peripheries of Southeast Asia consider themselves as ASEANs or Southeast Asians? The modern territorial nation-states of Southeast Asia are themselves artificial constructs of Western colonialism, harbouring an elite-centred nationalism. One consequence of the colonial rule over Southeast Asia was the separation of singular ethnic communities across the territorial boundaries of modern nation-states. The idea of citizenship in the modern nation-state context stands in the way of restoring the historic cultural and ethnic links forged during the classical *Mandala* era of Southeast Asian history. Hence, while the official inter-governmental regionalism of Southeast Asia has made much progress, it is yet to reintegrate the communities divided by colonialism and the construct of the nation-state. This regionalism remains a top-down, rather than a bottom-up phenomenon. Igniting the people's imagination towards the idea of Southeast Asia is one of the most pressing needs in building a genuine regional community.

PART II

CONTESTING FREEDOM

Chapter 4

Debating Human Rights[141]

Human Rights Discourses in Southeast Asia

As the Cold War was coming to an end, the issue of human rights began to emerge as a significant and highly controversial element in the foreign policy and regionalism agendas of Southeast Asian countries. Several developments contributed to this emerging preoccupation. One factor had to do with the professed commitment of leading Western countries to the spread of democratic governance and to the use of aid conditionalities to promote human rights around the globe. These policies were reinforced by the sense of triumphalism and self-vindication that marked the West's 'victory' in the Cold War and Fukuyama's 'end of history' hypothesis that saw the cessation of further historical challenges to the realities of liberal democracy and market capitalism. Western governments with political, economic, and security interests in the region had to pay greater attention to the issue, as human rights questions increasingly crept into their development assistance and regional security agendas (both bilateral and multilateral).

These developments were seen by key Southeast Asian elites as both a threat to their sovereignty and as a divisive and a somewhat alarming aspect of the emerging post-Cold War international order. This led to periodic clashes between Southeast Asian governments and their otherwise 'like-minded' Western partners (especially ASEAN's 'dialogue partners'—the US, Canada, Australia, and the EU) and prompted the latter to articulate a common response to human rights issues in international fora.

Another reason for the increasing preoccupation with human rights was that Southeast Asia's economically successful but politically authoritarian regimes were facing increasing pressure from their own populations, especially from an expanding middle class and increasingly active domestic and regional human rights groups. The rise of more politically conscious citizens put pressure on governments to be more sensitive to human rights issues. Owing to these factors, human rights and democracy had become a major determinant of conflict and cooperation between Southeast Asia and the West, as well as between Southeast Asian governments themselves, with significant implications for regional economic and security affairs.

The promotion of human rights in Southeast Asia was complicated by several policy dilemmas and choices. For Southeast Asian regimes, one of the main dilemmas lay in reconciling the demand (both domestic and external) for greater respect for human rights with the need to maintain authoritarian political control, which they believe was needed for continued economic growth and, therefore, regime legitimacy. Another was the challenge of maintaining friendly and mutually beneficial relations with the West while rejecting the latter's attempts to exert pressure on them on human rights questions. For Western countries, the problem lay in how to take advantage of the region's rapid economic growth, and the market and investment opportunities created by it, while maintaining a strong commitment to human rights that are consistent with their national political objectives. While adversarial relations with individual Southeast Asian countries over human rights issues could undermine lucrative economic and trade relationships with the rest of the region, ignoring human rights abuses by regional governments would also be politically difficult to attempt and explain to their domestic human rights pressure groups and constituents.

The need to resolve these dilemmas and the growing awareness among Southeast Asian elites that they cannot gain international status and respectability commensurate with their demonstrated economic success without a positive record on human rights, contributed to the issue of human rights emerging in the forefront of the foreign policy agendas of Southeast Asian countries. This chapter examines several related aspects of Southeast Asia's foreign policy dilemmas concerning human rights. It begins with an analysis of the government or elite perspectives on the place of human rights in the emerging post-Cold War international order, including those responses which form the basis of an alternative and culturally specific understanding of human rights. This is followed by a brief look at the emergence and role of non-governmental human rights groups and its implications for the human rights debate (this section is supplemented in the appendix with an interview of a prominent Indonesian human rights activist). The next section examines attempts by Southeast Asian governments to develop a regional approach to human rights issues, including ASEAN's policy of 'constructive engagement' originally developed in the context of Myanmar and which has the potential to become a more general framework for managing inter-state relations on human rights questions. Finally, the chapter assesses the role and effectiveness of policy instruments employed by external powers, including donor countries, in the promotion of human rights in Southeast Asia.

Debating Human Rights During the Cold War

There had never been a singularity of voices within Southeast Asia on the issue of human rights, although until recently it had become fashionable to project an 'Asian view on human rights' that derived almost exclusively from a relatively narrow set of official and elite opinions. A closer examination of the issue shows that not only the views of governments and elites clash with those of non-governmental organizations and individuals, but there are also important differences among the individual governments themselves. Indeed, differences in perspective on the human rights issue are greater between governments within the region than among the non-governmental organizations and individuals, who have quite self-consciously cultivated the habit of speaking in one voice at major international events.

The fact that Southeast Asian governments did not necessarily speak in one voice over the human rights issue was evident in a report on how US officials viewed the position of various countries towards the 1993 Vienna World Conference on Human Rights, organized under the auspices of the UN. The report suggested both intra-ASEAN and intra-Asian divisions on human rights. Thus, US ranked China, Pakistan, Indonesia, and sometimes Singapore as among the 'worst' group of 'vocal' human rights 'violators' and 'particularizers', while Malaysia, Myanmar, and India were regarded as 'unhelpful.' The positions taken by the Philippines, Japan, and South Korea were viewed as 'correct' and constructive, although these states were seen as being unwilling to take on their Asian colleagues.[142]

The noted scholar and policy analyst Carolina Hernandez argued that differences among the ASEAN states on human rights questions arose because their governments:

> follow different paths (1) in the way they interpret human rights and democracy, (2) in their assumption of international legal obligations as indicated by their acceptance of international human rights norms embodied in various international human rights documents, (3) in the manner in which they have organized their domestic constitutional, legal and judicial

systems as they relate to human rights concerns, and (4) in the degree of political openness of their societies . . . .[143]

Other analysts, such as Matthew Davis of Australian National University, argue that Southeast Asian countries can be divided into three groups based on their track record of human rights: 'progressive' countries like Indonesia and Philippines, as both have put significant efforts in adhering to human rights law and have embraced democracy; 'cautious' countries like Singapore, Malaysia, and Thailand as these states have refused to accept global standards in civil and political rights; and 'recalcitrant' countries like Cambodia, Laos, Myanmar, Brunei, and Vietnam as they have made very slow progress in human rights law compliance.[144]

Despite their varying human rights records, it is possible to discern two broad areas of relative agreement in Southeast Asian governments' perspectives on human rights. The first can be termed as a relativist argument, the other, a developmentalist argument. A third argument, concerning national security was also prominent, especially in the immediate post-colonial period, although it came to be subsumed under the relativist position.

The relativist argument, as stated by a former Thai Prime Minister, implied that implementation of human rights should 'vary because of differences in socio-economic and cultural backgrounds.'[145] At a regional preparatory meeting of Asian countries before the Vienna World Conference on Human Rights, ASEAN worked with other like-minded Asian countries (including China) to draft a declaration which stated that human rights 'must be considered in the context of a dynamic and evolving process of international norm-setting, bearing in mind the significance of national and regional particularities and various historical, cultural and religious backgrounds.'[146] To reinforce this point, Singapore's Foreign Minister, Wong Kan Seng, drew attention not only to differences between the West and the Third World, but among Western countries as well. Differing standards of human rights could result from different stages of development. In his view, the definition of human rights had changed over time and was influenced by centuries of history and culture. UK, France, and the US had taken over 200 years to evolve into full democracies. 'Can we therefore expect the citizens of many newly-independent countries of this century to acquire the same rights as those enjoyed by the developed nations when they lack the economic, educational and social pre-conditions to exercise such rights fully?'[147]

The relativist viewpoint was also forcefully argued by Malaysia's Prime Minister, Mahathir Mohamad, who claimed to speak for the entire ASEAN membership:

> The West tells us that democratic freedom and human rights are fundamental for the achievement of economic and social development. We in ASEAN never disputed that democracy for the people and opportunity for the individual to develop his or her own greatest potentials are indeed important principles. We disagree, however, that political systems qualify as democratic only when they measure up to certain particular yardsticks. Similarly, the norms and precepts for the observance of human rights vary from society to society and from one period to another within the same society. Nobody can claim to have the monopoly of wisdom to determine what is right and proper for all countries and peoples. It would be condescending, to say the least, and suspect for the West to preach human rights to us in the East.[148]

An important aspect of this cultural relativist position was a communitarian view of governance prevalent among the ruling elites of Southeast Asia. Indonesian Foreign Minister Ali Alatas, then working under President Suharto, told the Vienna Conference that Indonesia and the developing world have to maintain a balance between an 'individualistic approach' to human rights and the interests of their societies as a whole. 'Without such a balance, the rights of the community as a whole can be denied, which can lead to instability and even anarchy.'[149] Singapore went further by invoking the Confucian principle of 'community over self',[150] while ASEAN Foreign Ministers collectively supported Alatas' idea of 'balance' which was necessary not only to ensure 'freedom, progress, and national stability' within the region, but also to create a political framework 'through which many individual rights are realized.'[151]

Accordingly, contended Mahathir, ASEAN states had been correct in placing 'a high premium on political stability by managing a balance between the rights of the individual and the needs of society as a whole.'[152] The multi-ethnic composition of states in Southeast Asia and the sensitive relationship between the dominant and minority ethnic groups added to the need for Southeast Asian governments to emphasize social stability and national security by exercising strict control over freedom of speech and the media. Singapore and Malaysia openly asserted the need for such control, citing examples from the past when inflammatory racial speeches had sparked ethnic riots (especially the 1969 racial riots in Malaysia).

The developmentalist argument on human rights, a common aspect of Third World platforms, had found a particularly powerful echo in Southeast Asia because of the region's relative success in ensuring rapid economic growth. This position focused on the principle of 'non-selectivity', or the notion that political freedom and justiciable rights should not be stressed over the economic and the social welfare of citizens. At the Vienna Conference, Malaysia called for a universal conception of human rights to go beyond political rights and to establish 'particularly its linkage with development'.[153] ASEAN Foreign Ministers, meeting in Singapore in July 1993, issued a statement contending that:

> ... human rights are interrelated and indivisible comprising civil, political, economic, social and cultural rights. These rights are of equal importance. They should be addressed in a balanced and integrated manner and protected and promoted with due regard for specific cultural, social, economic and political circumstances ... the promotion and protection of human rights should not be politicized.[154]

In championing 'non-selectivity', ASEAN states sought to detract attention from the emphasis placed by the West on the restrictions on political rights within ASEAN. A report issued by the ASEAN Institutes of Strategic and International Studies (ASEAN-ISIS) argued thus, 'The emphasis placed by ASEAN countries on development and basic needs is a testament to the underpinnings of human rights in the region, particularly the right to development and the necessities of life in such areas as food, health, shelter education and employment.'[155]

The argument was that without fulfilling the basic economic needs of their societies, developing countries could not ensure the necessary conditions under which the political rights of citizens could be upheld. 'Only those who have forgotten the pangs of hunger will think of consoling the hungry by telling them that they should be free before they can eat ... Economic growth is the necessary foundation of any system that claims to advance human dignity and that order and stability are essential for development.'[156] To stress both the communitarian and developmental context of human rights, Singapore's leaders put forward the notion of 'good government'. The key element of this notion consisted of 'wise and honest' leadership. A 'good' government must be efficient and able to deliver on the economic front, but it need not provide for political openness. On the contrary, Lee Kuan Yew contended that the two goals were negatively correlated. Singapore's leaders, however, when pressed by their Western colleagues, did concede that the notion of good government might include a core group of human rights, such as absence of torture, slavery, arbitrary killings, disappearances, or 'shooting down of innocent demonstrators'.[157] But this concession did not extend to political and civil liberties.

In considering the merits of the cultural and communitarian view of human rights, two points are especially pertinent. First, governments who argued that the scope of human rights must be delimited by culture would highlight only those elements of traditional cultural norms that justify authoritarian political control and serve the regime's political and economic agenda. It is interesting that in Asia, governments which had once rejected traditional culture when it conflicted with their modernization goals (e.g. China's earlier rejection of Confucianism as a factor behind its economic backwardness) were now invoking it to deflect criticism of their human rights record.

But more importantly, the definition of what constituted cultural norms was not uniform between or within Southeast Asian countries and societies. Singapore's invoking of Confucian values could not have been shared by Islamic Malaysia or Catholic Philippines or Buddhist Thailand. Nor would values converge within individual ASEAN states. In multi-ethnic ASEAN states, any attempt by the ruling elite to articulate a 'national' position on human rights would, like the notion of 'national security', become an 'ambiguous symbol'. In the words of one critic, 'Attempts to define the community as coterminous with the state may have less to do with culture than with political self-interest [of the ruling elite].'[158] Thus, one cannot talk about a national or regional collective cultural/communitarian position on human rights when individual countries were unable to overcome inter-ethnic competition within their own territories. Against this backdrop, Yash Ghai's critique is particularly apt:

> The communitarian argument is, however, Janus-faced. It opposes the claim of universal human rights by distinguishing

between the allegedly Western, individual-oriented approach and the community-centred values of the East. But at the same time, it is used to deny the claims and assertions of communities in the name of national unity and stability.[159]

Critics of cultural relativism also argued that such a position masked cultural arrogance. Moreover, cultural particularities need not preclude a set of values common to all cultures that would provide the basis for universal standards of behaviour with respect to human rights.[160]

Civil Society Perspectives

As noted, the growing prominence of human rights in the foreign policy agenda of Southeast Asian states at this time was not just a function of external pressure. At the domestic level, Southeast Asian governments faced increasing demands for respect for human rights from domestic circles, including human rights NGOs (especially in Thailand, Malaysia, Indonesia, and the Philippines).[161] Despite scant resources and government suppression, these groups felt encouraged by the favourable international climate to their cause. Their perspectives contrasted sharply with those of the Southeast Asian elites and provided an alternative channel for the development of human rights norms.

Non-governmental organizations in Southeast Asia concerned with human rights issues vary in their strength and performance. In the early 1990s, the NGO community was especially well-developed in the Philippines and Thailand, while in Malaysia and Indonesia, such groups faced far greater government control. Singapore, Brunei, Vietnam, and Burma had no human rights NGOs. While the development of human rights NGOs in Southeast Asia owed partly to financial support from Western donor countries, the groups that existed did have strong domestic roots.[162] Some of the larger human rights NGOs in the region developed as responses to political crackdowns by their own governments without being prompted by the West. This was the case in the Philippines after the declaration of martial law in 1972, the establishment of the Legal Aid Institute (later called the Indonesian Legal Aid Foundation) in Indonesia in 1971, and the emergence of Thai human rights groups after the coup of 1973.

Apart from action within the domestic sphere, there had been some concerted international action by Southeast Asian human rights NGOs. In March 1993, a group of regional and international NGOs issued a declaration on human rights that was a clear rejection of the 'Asian Concept of Human Rights' promoted by ASEAN governments. The meeting revealed strong coordination among Southeast Asian NGOs (especially Thai, Malaysian, Filipino, and Indonesian), as well as between South Asian and Southeast Asian NGOs. Subsequently, representatives from Southeast Asian human rights groups tried unsuccessfully to submit a set of recommendations to the ASEAN foreign ministers during the inaugural meeting of the ASEAN Regional Forum (ARF) in July 1994. The meeting accused the ASEAN foreign ministers of adopting 'double standards by only showing concern for problems outside the region such as Bosnia and Rwanda while not demonstrating similar concern for problems that exist within the region, especially in Burma and East Timor.' The Bangkok NGO forum declaration also pointed out that while the ASEAN foreign ministers were rejecting Western policies linking workers' rights, labour standards and environmental issues with trade as a new type of protectionism, 'the ASEAN governments should primarily be held responsible for continued violations of workers' rights, the undermining of labour standards and degradation of the environment in their respective countries.' The forum also viewed existing national institutions as having failed to promote and protect human rights and as lacking both independence and effectiveness.[163]

The wider transboundary focus of human rights NGOs became more pronounced in the case of Thai groups, who went regional and organized joint meetings with Indonesian human rights groups. This development prompted one observer to note that 'official solidarity [among the ASEAN members] is mirrored by a greater sense of regionalism among non-governmental activists' even at the risk of undermining the Thai government's tolerance of local NGOs.[164]

While the development of human rights NGOs in Southeast Asia remained limited, the emergence of an NGO perspective on human rights already had important policy implications. Among other things, it ensured that the demand for human rights extended to and became more vocal in every Southeast Asian country. It refuted the government view that the issue of human rights was an externally imposed subject supported by the liberal segments of the West. It contributed to a more receptive audience for Western human rights policies in Southeast Asia. Finally, the pressure from NGOs was part of the reason for forcing some Southeast Asian governments to show greater sensitivity toward human rights, such as Indonesia's creation of a national human rights commission in June 1993. For the donor countries, providing support to human rights NGOs such as the Indonesian Legal Aid Foundation became a more productive and less controversial alternative to sanctions and aid conditionality in promoting human rights in Southeast Asia.

Towards a Regional Approach

Attempts to develop a regional approach to human rights in Southeast Asia began in the immediate post-Cold War period. Indeed, many Southeast Asian governments considered the rising prominence of human rights in recent years as a direct result of the end of the Cold War. The anti-communist thrust of Western policy, which tolerated blatant human rights abuses by pro-Western Asian governments in the past, was no more. Instead, the promotion of human rights was seen to constitute the core element of the 'New World Order'. As Lee Kuan Yew would put it:

> Unfortunately, with the end of the Cold War, U.S. policies toward China, Japan and the countries of East Asia have not been guided by strategic and economic considerations as they used to be. Issues of human rights and democracy have become an obsession with the U.S. media, Congress, and the administration.[165]

In general, Southeast Asian governments were facing increasing pressure from the West over their human rights record, one which came under intense international scrutiny. Apart from regular and periodic reports issued by Western human rights organizations (such as Amnesty International and Asia Watch) and media sources, some events brought human rights issues in Southeast Asia to international limelight. The most infamous of these was the shooting by Indonesian security forces of anti-state demonstrators in the East Timorese capital of Dili in November 1991. Amid an outcry in international media over the incident, two Western donor countries, namely the Netherlands and Canada, suspended their aid to Indonesia. Indonesia retaliated by organizing a new aid consortium that excluded the Netherlands. However, Jakarta's international image had suffered a major blow. While the US did not cut off aid, it prevented a sale by Jordan of US-made fighter aircrafts to Indonesia, citing the country's East Timor policy.

Other Southeast Asian countries, especially Malaysia and Singapore, had been criticized by human rights watchdogs for their internal security detention laws and lack of press freedom.

Faced with a loss of jobs to foreign competition (especially East Asian), trade unions and human rights groups in the US appealed for linking trade privileges with countries like Malaysia with their allowance of workers' rights. Additionally, violent military suppression of minority groups in Thailand, the Philippines, and Indonesia attracted a great deal of publicity for their human rights implications.

In responding to the human rights campaign from the West, Southeast Asian leaders often accused Western states of double standards. While Western states justified their promotion of human rights in the name of their universality, some ASEAN policy makers saw this as a highly selective exercise. Foreign Minister Wong Kan Seng of Singapore argued that 'concern for human rights [in the West] has always been balanced against other national interests.'[166] Attesting to 'hypocrisy' in the West's application of its human rights standards, Kishore Mahbubani, then a senior Singaporean Foreign Ministry official contended:

> . . . while human rights campaigns are often portrayed as an absolute moral good to be implemented without qualification, in practice Western governments are prudent and selective. For example, given their powerful vested interest in secure and stable oil supplies from Saudi Arabia, Western governments have not tried to export their standards of human rights or democracy to that country, for they know that any alternative to the stable rule of the Saudi government would very likely be bad for the West.[167]

To underscore this point further, Mahbubani contrasted the case of Saudi Arabia with Algeria, where Western governments had acquiesced to a military coup, which overthrew an elected government with a strongly Islamic orientation.[168] In this context, the enforcement of human rights standards by the West was not only selective, but also intensely political. Indonesia's Ali Alatas wondered whether there were any 'disguised political purposes' behind the West's human rights campaign that were designed to 'serve as a pretext to wage a political campaign against another country.'[169]

Furthermore, Southeast Asian elites found the Western campaign for human rights as being reflective of the power disparities in the international system. Malaysian Foreign Minister Abdullah Ahmad Badawi suggested that 'attempts to impose the standard of one side on the other . . . tread upon the sovereignty of nations.'[170] As the incumbent Chair of the Non-Aligned Movement (NAM), Indonesia warned that 'in a world where domination of the strong over the weak and interference between states are still a painful reality, no country or group of countries should arrogate unto itself the role of judge, jury and executioner over other countries on this critical and sensitive issue.'[171]

ASEAN Warms to Human Rights?

Southeast Asia has seriously lagged in the arena of human rights protection. ASEAN's initiative on human rights, the ASEAN Inter-Governmental Commission on Human Rights (AICHR), was inaugurated in 2009. This was followed a year later, by another body—the ASEAN Commission on the Promotion and the Protection of the Rights of Women and Children (ACWC). Yet, more than a decade later, not much progress has been made in moving ASEAN human rights mechanisms towards becoming credible and effective for the protection of human rights in Southeast Asia. For example, the AICHR took no action when civil rights groups from Malaysia, Indonesia, and the Philippines 'reported' the Malaysian government to the AICHR for its suppression of demonstrations by the group 'Bersih.'

The functions of ASEAN human rights commissions remain limited to information-sharing, rather than advocacy, not to mention enforcement. Their activities consist mainly of organizing seminars, workshops, and preparing audio-visual material to raise peoples' awareness of rights in a broad range of areas such as the rights of people with disabilities, campaigns against trafficking in persons, and corporate social responsibility. Such efforts are not without merit, however. Indonesian scholar Abubakar Eby Hara, citing the views of some human rights activists such as Rafendy Djamin, points out, 'People may not know their rights in regard to their states, since they are more often told by their governments about their obligations than their rights as citizens.'[172] Hence a campaign to promote 'awareness of rights ... is part of the protection, because people and officials will know what kind of human rights protection they have.'[173] This is of additional value to those ASEAN members, such as Cambodia, Laos, Myanmar, and Vietnam (CMLV) that 'had experienced gross human rights violation and have not enjoyed the benefit of human rights' who are in special need of these activities.[174] Moreover, ASEAN human rights commissions have helped to increase awareness of international developments concerning human rights and maintain contacts with international human rights NGOs.

It may be tempting to explain ASEAN's limited progress in providing human rights protection as reflecting a relativist view of human rights, i.e., the view that human rights should conform to the particular socio-economic and cultural context of the countries concerned. It may also reflect a position that economic rights or the right to development should take precedence over civil and political liberties. Such views, which are found throughout the developing world, are by no means uniform among ASEAN members and they are no longer expressed as vigorously today as was the case in the 1980s and 1990s. Certainly, this strong attitude of cultural relativism does not reflect the official positions of countries such as Indonesia. In the past, ASEAN states bemoaned the human rights double-standards of Western countries as a defensive mechanism to justify their own lack of enthusiasm for human rights. But this has become less of an issue now, not least because Western championing of human rights has itself slackened. But the more important reasons have to do with domestic considerations, especially the limited democratization of ASEAN states and their continuing faith in the non-interference doctrine. Democratic transitions have produced a shift towards a more liberal attitude towards human rights, as has been the case after the fall of the Suharto regime in Indonesia and under the short-lived second Mahathir government in Malaysia. However, the non-interference principle has discouraged criticism of human rights violations in fellow ASEAN members. Assessing the performance of AICHR, a statement from Southeast Asian NGOs noted:

> From 2010 to 2018, AICHR spent over six million USD conducting 121 activities . . . Unfortunately, these activities have not resulted in any significant improvement in the human rights situation on the ground, or for the peoples of ASEAN who need its protection. The human rights commission chooses to hide behind the non-interference principle of ASEAN and to sideline the rule of law, democracy, and respect for fundamental freedoms. This has resulted in the grave neglect of fulfilment of human rights on the ground and continually resulted in the irrelevance of AICHR and ASEAN as a whole to address people's struggles.[175]

Even noteworthy improvements like the adoption of the ASEAN Human Rights Declaration in 2012 fell short of international human rights standards. The continued emphasis on noninterference and national sovereignty have stalled the creation of a regional human rights body that can work not just on human rights promotion, but on rights protection.[176] National particularities, regional peculiarities, and cultural specificities still dominate the human rights discourse.

In an environment of constant criticism from Southeast Asian civil society organizations as well as foreign pressure about ASEAN's lukewarm human rights work, the body has taken steps towards redressing its lack of emphasis on human rights. Since 2015, the EU and ASEAN established an EU-ASEAN Policy Dialogue on Human Rights (PDHR), which functions as 'a high-level platform to discuss shared concerns on human rights, identify key challenges, and articulate a strategic framework for EU–ASEAN collaboration. The biennial dialogue is alternately hosted by EU and ASEAN.'[177] The most recent PDHR took place in Brussels in October 2023, where thirty ASEAN delegates representing four organizations and various divisions of the ASEAN Secretariat participated. The dialogue covered various thematic areas, including civil and political rights, business and human rights, environmental rights and climate change, gender equality and inclusion, rights of the child and persons with disabilities, migrant workers' rights and trafficking in persons, freedom of expression and assembly, digital and human rights, and respecting human rights while countering violent extremism. The last issue was of special concern as it brought to light ASEAN's stern reactions to Myanmar's role in exacerbating the Rohingya crisis.

Smarting under intense international scrutiny and criticism, ASEAN felt compelled to react in the Rohingya crisis in Myanmar, the most significant human rights crisis in Southeast Asia since the formation of AICHR. The simmering Rohingya crisis has posed a particularly daunting challenge to ASEAN's reputation. In its February 2017 report, a UN mission to Bangladesh investigating the conditions of Rohingya refugees described the 'level of violence' as 'unprecedented', including 'the killing of babies, toddlers, children, women and elderly, opening fire at people fleeing, burning of entire villages, massive detention, massive and systematic rape and sexual violence, deliberate destruction of food and sources of food.'[178] The crisis led to a massive refugee exodus, estimated at a million people in Bangladesh,[179] as well as about 25,000[180] internally displaced people in Myanmar.

Among ASEAN members, the most vocal criticism of Myanmar came from Malaysia's Najib government, which went to the extent of accusing the Burmese authorities of 'genocide' and calling for a review of Myanmar's membership in ASEAN.[181] Even at the time, the Prime Minister's reaction was intended (and was seen as such) to respond to domestic pressures in the Muslim-majority country and to burnish the Malaysian government's Islamic credentials and divert attention from his domestic troubles. Moreover, Malaysian security forces, between January and March 2020 pushed boats filled with Rohingya refugees back into the sea to prevent them from coming to Malaysian shores. Overall, ASEAN's response to the crisis was restrained, focusing on diplomacy and humanitarian support, rather than human rights abuses committed by an ASEAN member-state.

Amid the international furore against Myanmar, ASEAN members encouraged the Burmese government to create an independent commission of inquiry into the allegations of human rights abuse by the Tatmadaw (Burmese military) against the Rohingyas and to allow and facilitate the voluntary repatriation of Rohingyas. Some ASEAN members made contributions to Myanmar, Bangladesh, and to international relief agencies to help Rohingya refugees on a bilateral basis, while ASEAN provided some relief aid for internally displaced persons in Rakhine State. But this led 'human rights observers . . . to accuse ASEAN of prioritizing diplomacy over human rights concerns.'[182]

ASEAN has continued to recognize and support the Myanmar government's official position on the issue. A statement by the ASEAN Chair at the 34th ASEAN Summit that was held from 20–23 June, 2019 indicates the organization's tacit support to Myanmar. The statement, while not using the term 'Rohingya' in deference to Myanmar's wish, 'stressed the importance of and expressed [ASEAN's] continued support for Myanmar's commitment to ensure safety and security for all communities in Rakhine State as effectively as possible and facilitate the voluntary return of displaced persons in a safe, secure and dignified manner.'[183] ASEAN also drafted a 'preliminary needs assessment' for the repatriation of Rohingya refugees in Bangladesh, but since this was done without consulting the refugees themselves, it raised concerns whether the repatriation would be voluntary. According to Human Rights Watch, 'ASEAN governments' focus on repatriation over safety and accountability reveals a callous disregard for Rohingya lives . . . ASEAN member states should drop their harmful 'non-interference' mantra and express their readiness to respond to Myanmar's abuses and lack of cooperation with international agencies.'[184]

ASEAN's soft approach to the Rohingya crisis has had mixed outcomes. On the one hand, it made it politically easier for Myanmar to accept bilateral humanitarian aid from fellow ASEAN members and may have eased their resistance to the repatriation of Rohingya refugees to Myanmar. On the other hand, it may have also increased Myanmar's defiance of the wider international community, including the kind visible in Aung San Suu Kyi's appearance before the International Court of Justice in December 2019 (which failed to win international support for her country).[185]

Burma's deteriorating internal crisis was further aggravated by its February 2021 coup. The country's already precarious human rights situation became even more catastrophic in the wake of the coup that led to massive protests, increase in violence against protestors, as they were met with a disproportionate use of force, creating an even more appalling human rights situation. For their part, ASEAN urged the junta to refrain from violence and release political detainees, all the while tempering their demands while being sensitive to their sovereignty and non-interference principles. But individual ASEAN countries have used stronger language and called for more intrusive action. On the whole, though, ASEAN as a group has been more impatient with the military regime in Myanmar than with the military regime that came into power in Thailand as a result of the 2014 coup carried out by General Prayut Chan-o-cha. Unlike its response to the Thai coup, ASEAN's response to the 2021 coup in Burma had some concrete initiatives, like the 'Five Point Consensus'. However, the coup unravelled the organization's decades-long efforts to create political stability in the country. Beyond timid responses condemning the violence, ASEAN could not achieve much. [186]

The toothless approach towards protecting human rights in both Thailand and Myanmar, beyond showcasing ASEAN's reluctance to get drawn deeper into their domestic affairs, was also aggravated by the states' preference for national responses to COVID-19 rather than a regional-institutional response. Not only did the pandemic pose a significant threat to the continued relevancy of ASEAN, it also afforded *regimes with authoritarian tendencies the opportunity to further suppress political dissent, and consolidate their power.*[187] In typical authoritarian fashion, Southeast Asian leaders used the pandemic as cover to silence political opponents, reduce space for civil society to operate, and attack media freedom. However, in a sign of resiliency and the slow growth of democracy in the region, civil society organizations defied efforts to shut down protests, while some found creative ways around censorship and control, indicating the staying power of democratic norms and practices in a region habituated to autocratic expressions of control. [188]

Chapter 5

Is Democracy Good for Development and Stability?

After the fall of the Berlin Wall, the international community gave considerable attention to the spread of democracy around the globe. What Huntington and some others labelled as democracy's 'Third Wave'[189] was seen, in the aftermath of the Cold War, as being an even wider, more irresistible, and long-term phenomenon. Thus, Rustow referred to democracy as a 'global revolution',[190] while Karl and Schmitter highlighted the phenomenon of 'democratization around the globe'.[191] Thomas Frank went a step further by claiming that 'the emerging right to democratic governance' has laid the foundation for 'an international democratic order'.[192] Larry Diamond spoke of the 'globalization of democracy' and anticipated a '"democratic moment" when the idea of democracy and the democratic countries of the world lack serious rivals on either the geopolitical or ideological planes.'[193] Francis Fukuyama affirmed Diamond's claim in what he believed was the 'end of history', when no serious challenges could emerge to market capitalism and liberal democracy.[194]

Yet, looking at political trends in Southeast Asia in the early 1990s, it seems that the region remained firmly under the grip of authoritarian and semi-authoritarian rule. Southeast Asian states have had an on-again, off-again relationship with democracy. It was not entirely absent in the region. Singapore, Malaysia, Thailand, and the Philippines all claimed to have democratic political systems. Indonesia had its period of 'Guided Democracy', while the Suharto regime spoke glowingly of 'the maturing' of *Pancsila* Democracy. But these countries, with the exception of the Philippines after Marcos, remained under some form of authoritarian rule ('soft authoritarianism' has been the catchphrase of scholars in describing many of Southeast Asia's political systems). Chan Heng Chee's observation that many Southeast Asian countries 'emerged from the colonial era experimenting with Western liberal democracy, but each abandoned the original model for variations of authoritarian forms which accommodate degrees of democracy'[195] still held true for Singapore, Malaysia, and Indonesia. Although the democratic experiments in Thailand and the Philippines seemed to be quite robust, it was too early to rule out a return to authoritarian rule, especially in the form of military control over the political process. For Cambodia, the issue was not of democratic transition, but of consolidation, as its fledgling democracy, created by the largest peace-building operation undertaken by the international community, continued to unravel, if not completely, then at least partially. Vietnam and Laos, which continued to be ruled by communist regimes while undertaking economic liberalization, provided a test case for theoretical arguments concerning the linkage between capitalist economic development and democracy made by modernization theorists and scholars within the liberal tradition. Brunei and Burma remained under absolute monarchy and military dictatorship respectively. For them, the process of democratization had to begin with transitions from authoritarian rule.

Thus, the term 'democratization' or 'democratic transition' in a Southeast Asian context could only be applied in its broadest or most varied sense—covering several related processes such as transition from authoritarian rule, political liberalization, democratic consolidation and further institutionalization, and greater political openness. The question about Southeast Asia's democratic future, then, was not just about whether more Southeast Asian countries will become democratic or not, but also whether some Southeast Asian countries will become more or less democratic?

Why did Southeast Asia fail to catch this supposedly global trend of democratization? This is especially puzzling since as an influential argument by Samuel Huntington put it, 'Democratization occurs most frequently and also most easily in countries that have reached the upper-middle income levels of economic development.'[196] Other approaches, including the Marxist-inspired perspectives on democratization in Southeast Asia,[197] while not going this far, also broadly agreed on the importance of rapid economic growth as a catalyst for democratization. Indeed, a common thrust of all the major approaches to the study of democratization in Southeast Asia in the 1990s was that economic growth held the key to prospects for political change.

But the situation in Southeast Asia in the decades of rapid economic growth it underwent had resisted these theoretical expectations. On the contrary, Southeast Asia remains a mostly authoritarian region. For the most part, Southeast Asian leaders have viewed democracy as a threat to economic growth and political stability. Let me discuss these in the following sections.

Democracy versus Development

The leading voice of those who saw political democracy as a threat to economic development was Singapore's late Prime Minister Lee Kuan Yew. He put it most starkly: 'The exuberance of democracy leads to undisciplined and disorderly conditions which are inimical to development.'[198] Lee also deplored the 'obsession with the U.S. media, Congress, and the administration' with 'issues of human rights and democracy'. In his view, this represents an 'unfortunate' neglect of important 'strategic and economic considerations', which, in the past, 'used to be' the guiding framework of US policy.[199] Western policies of humanitarian intervention, 'democratic peace' (the belief that democracies do not fight each other), and aid conditionality came to be viewed by Southeast Asian ruling elites as instruments for Western domination of the developing countries. Malaysia's then Prime Minister, Mahathir Mohamad, attacked what he saw as a Western effort to impose a particular standard of democracy on ASEAN countries. The West, in his view, could not 'claim to have the monopoly of wisdom to determine what is right and proper for all countries and peoples.'[200] In the wake of the economic crisis, Mahathir continued his attack on Western human rights policies, claiming that the calls for linking human rights to trade 'are ideas which originate in the rich' and 'whose advantages seem to accrue only to the rich.'[201]

Dr Surin Pitsuwan, the late former Foreign Minister of Thailand and former Secretary General of ASEAN, once bemoaned that the focus on economic growth stymied democracy in the region. As he put it, 'socio-economic development reinforced an unhelpful tendency by many of the countries in the region to rate economic development higher than democratization.' In his view, 'Development and prosperity . . . became the 'state ethos', with 'less importance . . . given to democracy, participation, accountability, and transparency.'[202]

But these views were not unchallenged. What Southeast Asia needed was 'democracy that delivers', a sentiment echoed by President Ramos of the Philippines, who had succeeded Cory Aquino, and who reminded Mr Lee that the authoritarianism of the Marcos era contributed in no small way to his country's economic ruin and political stagnation. Anwar Ibrahim, the then deputy Prime Minister of Malaysia between 1993 to 1998, also refuted Lee Kuan Yew in the following terms:

> . . . today, we see Asian, especially Confucian, values now being invoked in support of the proposition that democracy is inimical

to political stability and economic growth. But this notion has been effectively debunked by the experience of both Thailand and Malaysia. Political liberality is *not* incompatible with strong economic performance; these countries have sustained growth for more than three decades while practising open and vibrant forms of democracy. As for Asian values, they have produced great civilisations in the past. If these values are to contribute towards an Asian renaissance, however, they must serve as a source of liberation. Asian cultural renewal must mean the cultivation of all that is true, just and caring from our heritage, not by perpetuating the narrow and oppressive order of the feudal past.[203]

But those who critiqued democracy not only continued to dismiss the suitability of Western-style democracy for the region, they also argued that external pressures, including economic sanctions, would not be effective in bringing about democratic change. They further warned that the West's democratic zeal risks undermining the foundations of regional stability based on the inviolability of state sovereignty. The very notion of democratic assistance militates against one of the most vaunted ASEAN norms: the doctrine of non-interference in the internal affairs of member-states. ASEAN did not see Vietnam's communist political system as a barrier to its membership in the organization. ASEAN was also instrumental in resisting Western calls for sanctions against the military regime and in pushing for a policy of 'constructive engagement.'[204] Buoyed by ASEAN's backing, neither Vietnam nor Burma saw democratization as a way of ending their international isolation, in the manner of the South Korean elites in the 1980s. The admission of Burma into ASEAN despite a chorus of international protest and condemnation confirmed ASEAN's policy that a country's political system was not a criterion of membership into the regional organization.

The Asian financial crisis of 1997 challenged Lee Kuan Yew's 'democracy is bad for development' argument. Unlike Indonesia, South Korea and Thailand were able to find political alternatives to their existing regimes with relative ease, with leaders distancing themselves from the mistakes of their predecessors and adopting measures to rectify the situation. When one compares the nepotism and cronyism that surrounded Suharto's regime in Indonesia with Kim Dae Jong's novel approach to Korea's economic woes, it is noteworthy that a democratic form of government can help a country cope with rapid economic change.[205] Madeleine Albright, the US Secretary of State, stressed the same point. In her view, democratic governments in South Korea, the Philippines and Thailand, had made progress in overcoming the economic crisis 'in part because their people were able to elect new governments, which started work in a climate of openness and trust, and with the moral legitimacy to call for shared sacrifice.'[206] Indonesia, in her view, now had a chance to follow their footsteps. Her views are supported by others within the Southeast Asian region. Outgoing President Ramos of the Philippines was even more blunt in his statement on the democracy-development nexus. Blaming the 'agony' of the Asian economies on a lack of 'transparency and democratic controls,' Ramos stated that 'the present economic crisis proves that in choosing democracy over authoritarianism, we Filipinos were on the side of history, rather than outside of it, as earlier believed.'[207]

Ramos' comment was an allusion to his earlier debate with Lee Kuan Yew which did not escape a riposte from the Singaporean statesman. 'Indonesia did better than the Philippines in the last 30 years, and may well do so again in the next 30 years,' said Lee, adding that '[i]t is better not to be black-and-white in categorising countries as democratic and therefore successful or authoritarian and prone to failure.'[208] Despite his earlier criticism of nepotism, Lee rejected the notion that Asian values contributed to the economic crisis in the region. As he put it, 'Having Asian values did not necessarily translate into having a general lack of transparency.' The fact that Singapore had Asian values and transparency did not spare it from the crisis, because of the regional contagion.[209] According to Lee, what the demonstrators in Indonesia were demanding was not democracy, but an end to corruption, cronyism, nepotism, and the rule of Suharto. The solution to Asia's economic problems did not lie in greater democracy, but in better government, or 'good governance,' including 'sound banking laws, rigorous supervision in the financial sector and proper corporate governance.'[210]

In July 2011, after Singapore's parliamentary elections when the ruling People's Action Party (PAP) had its poorest showing since Singapore became an independent nation in 1965, Lee restated his belief that democracy is not good for development. Democracy, he said, 'may satisfy the curious, but . . . what is required is good governance, eradication of corruption, economic development.'[211]

Democracy and Disorder

A second argument against democratization, oft quoted by Southeast Asian elites, is that it is bad for political stability. But this has little basis in fact. It is hard to associate democratization with political violence.

For example, comparing the violence accompanying the transition to democracy and the descent into authoritarian rule is instructive here. Pending detailed empirical studies, it seems reasonable to conclude from the experiences of Burma under Ne Win and the State Law and Order Restoration Council (SLORC), as well as the State Peace and Development Council (SPDC), Cambodia under Pol Pot, Indonesia under Suharto, South Korea under Chun Doo Hwan, Taiwan under Kuomingtang in the early period of its rule, and Thailand under Thanom and Suchinda, that authoritarian rule has produced more mass violence in Asia than has democracy. In fact, the very first observation about democracy and violence in Asia is that authoritarian regimes have presided over, and in many cases, themselves perpetrated, more violence and loss of lives than regimes engaged in democratic transitions.

Two cases of violence during authoritarian rule and democratic or semi-democratic transitions deserve notice. Between 1975 and 1978, the Khmer Rouge killed between 1.5 to 2 million Cambodians, whereas fewer than 1,000 Cambodians have died under semi-democratic governments, including the infamous Hun Sen regime, following UN-organized elections in 1993, according to the Uppsala Conflict Data Program. The bloody riots in Indonesia following the downfall of Suharto have done much to reinforce the myth of democratic violence among Asian apologists for authoritarian rule. But consider the following statistics: during 1965-66, between half a million to a million people died in the violence that accompanied Suharto's seizure of power, whereas the death toll in anti-Chinese riots in May 1998 has been put at 1190, excluding the violence in East Timor and Aceh. Even if we include the latter, which straddle both Suharto and the post-Suharto regimes, the toll does not exceed the killings during Suharto's rule. In fact, the East Timorese killings under Suharto were higher than those that followed the withdrawal of the Indonesian military in August 1999. Only in the Philippines did the violence contributing to civilian deaths, extra-judicial killings, and killings of journalists, in the democratic era of the Arroyo regime, seemed to match the levels of violence during Marcos's rule, although this claim needs to be more thoroughly verified.

The Limits of 'Democratic Assistance'

Another reason why democracy failed to take root in Southeast Asia has to do with external factors. Barring a few exceptions, Western governments have generally viewed economic liberalization and political stability in Southeast Asia as being more important than democracy. The US attitude towards the fall of Suharto—Southeast Asia's longest serving dictator—in 1998 is a case in point. A declassified memorandum of conversation from 1970 between President Nixon and President Suharto indicates the close relationship and cooperation between the US and Indonesia.[212] The Clinton administration continued backing the Suharto regime until its very final moments. While US officials did call for 'restoration of order without violence and a genuine opening of a dialogue on political reform,'[213] it was not a demand for linking IMF loans to political reform. Rather, Washington was demanding Suharto's compliance with the IMF's economic and financial prescriptions. As Indonesia's large maritime neighbour, Australia explicitly rejected any linkage between economic and political reform in Indonesia. Peter Costello, the Australian Treasurer, argued that 'at the end of the day, it's economic reform which is going to improve opportunities for people in Indonesia', while Prime Minister John Howard praised Suharto's last-ditch plan for handing over power as 'statesman-like'.[214]

Democracy and ASEAN

Finally, ASEAN's role has also been important in maintaining authoritarianism in Southeast Asia. ASEAN emerged as a club of authoritarian rulers. The association's strict non-interference policy prevented the group from acting against military coups or supporting pro-democracy forces.

To be sure, ASEAN's norm of non-interference has come under attack. In the aftermath of the Asian financial crisis, the then Thai Foreign Minister, Surin Pitsuwan argued: 'It is time that ASEAN's cherished principle of non-intervention is modified to allow it to play a constructive role in preventing or resolving domestic issues with regional implications.'[215] Pitsuwan urged that 'when a matter of domestic concern poses a threat to regional stability, a dose of peer pressure or friendly advice at the right time can be helpful.'[216] Despite gross human rights violations perpetrated by the Khmer Rouge or Suharto's regime in Indonesia, in general, ASEAN governments refrained from any expression of support for regime change in either country. Singapore's then Prime Minister Goh Chok Tong maintained that political unrest in Indonesia was its 'internal affairs', which was up to the government of the country to handle.[217]

Hopes that the departure of Suharto may lead to a softening of ASEAN's support for authoritarian regimes among the member states proved too optimistic, however. Even Thailand's Foreign Minister and future ASEAN Secretary-General Surin Pitsuwan, who had called for using human rights and democracy as the 'primary determinants of foreign policy', admitted that 'if our policy of promoting human rights and democracy hurts the interests of our traders along the border, the policy will encounter domestic political resistance and be ultimately unsustainable.'[218]

This does not mean that ASEAN's attitude towards democracy and authoritarianism have not changed at all. There have been occasional hints of opposition to military coups. One such hint came in 1997, when Cambodia's Prime Minister, Prince Norodom Ranariddh, was forcibly ousted by his government's coalition partner, Hun Sen. Addressing the ouster, Singapore's then Foreign Minister, S. Jayakumar, stated: 'Any unconstitutional change of government is cause for concern. Where force is used for an unconstitutional purpose, it is behaviour that ASEAN cannot ignore or condone.'[219]

In 2004, ASEAN's Socio-Political Community Plan of Action laid down the principle that 'ASEAN Member Countries shall not condone unconstitutional and undemocratic changes of government'.[220] Moreover, in the ASEAN Charter, which came into force on 15 December 2008, democracy and human rights get mentioned three and seven times respectively. The charter's section entitled 'Purposes' includes a call 'to strengthen democracy, enhance good governance and the rule of law, and to promote and protect human rights and fundamental freedoms, with due regard to the rights and responsibilities of the Member States of ASEAN.' Further, principles (h) and (i) call for 'adherence to the rule of law, good governance, the principles of democracy and constitutional government' and 'respect for fundamental freedoms, the promotion and protection of human rights, and the promotion of social justice,' respectively.[221]

Despite the charter's provisions, it did not lead to much change. The anti-coup norm got tested by the Thai military coup in 2006, and subsequently by Myanmar's coups when ASEAN could do little but condone the military takeover and send envoys.

The Case of Post-Suharto Indonesia: Democracy, Development and Stability

Indonesia challenged the view that newly democratic states are likely to suffer from lower economic growth, greater internal strife, or turn rabidly nationalistic and seek war with their neighbours.[222]

Indonesia is the fourth most populous nation in the world after China, India, and the US. It is also the world's largest Muslim majority country and the third largest democracy. Its economy is currently the 16th largest and according to McKinsey predictions, it will become the 7th largest by 2030. Under Suharto, Indonesia had achieved stability and economic growth, but suffered from persistent internal conflicts, particularly the insurgency in the northwestern region of Aceh. The Asian financial crisis demolished the idea that only an authoritarian regime can sustain economic growth and prosperity. Not only did Suharto fail to offer an effective response to the crisis, he was also toppled due to his inability to do so.

Suharto had been president for thirty-three years at the time of his downfall. Widespread riots accompanied the weeks before and after Suharto's downfall. Recalling the dark days after Suharto's downfall, Fauzi Ichsan, an Indonesian economist, said, 'The betting was not whether Indonesia would fall apart—breaking into half a dozen island states—but how soon.'[223]

But after a rocky start, Indonesia would show that democracy, development, and stability are not mutually exclusive, but mutually reinforcing. This is Indonesia's trifecta. As the then US Secretary of State Hillary Clinton put it, 'If you want to know whether Islam, democracy, modernity and women's rights can co-exist, go to Indonesia.'[224] Indonesia's former President Susilo Bambang Yudhoyono claimed that 'while outsiders focus on economic progress, the real achievement [of Indonesia] is democracy, and harmonizing democracy, development, Islam and human rights.'[225] In the decade immediately following Suharto's fall, i.e., between 2000–2010, Indonesia averaged a growth rate of 5.1 per cent, according to the World Bank, surpassing all the emerging economies except China and India, and was ahead of the other BRICS nations, namely Russia, Brazil, and South Africa.[226] In clocking a high growth rate and being projected to be among the top ten economies in the world, Indonesia demolished the view that countries transitioning from authoritarianism to democracy will be mired in political violence and not experience high levels of economic growth.

Owing to its impressive growth, Indonesia managed to silence critics of democratization, who blamed it for its internal violence, in the form of insurgencies, secessionist movements, terrorist organizations, and foreign adventurism like in East Timor. A democratizing Indonesia resolved to end its long-standing conflicts in East Timor and Aceh. Subsequent measures of decentralization and federal distribution of powers helped to foster greater national stability.[227] In terms of national security,

Indonesia has done a far better job than anyone had expected in managing the threats posed by radicalism and terrorism in the wake of the 9/11 attacks on the US and on Indonesia itself. Ironically, but importantly, Indonesia in 1965, when Suharto's dictatorship was established, and subsequently with Myanmar's coup in 2021, we can see that transitions to authoritarianism seem to be accompanied by greater levels of violence than are transitions to democratic rule.

However, successive general elections post-Suharto, like in 1999, 2004, 2009, 2014, and 2019, have not been free of electoral violence. For example, in the last presidential election, six people were killed and over 350 were injured during mass rallies against the re-election of President Joko Widodo.[228] Thus, Indonesia, like most postcolonial countries in the region, totter between the poles of democracy and its associated political stability, and political instability augmented by the reactionary forces of nativism.[229]

The Future of Democracy in Southeast Asia

Following the massive structural reforms that Indonesia undertook in 1998 to democratize, it is generally considered a beacon of democracy in the Southeast Asian region.[230] The democracy report card for the entire region would largely comprise of enduring authoritarian states, monarchies, anocratic mixed regimes and states that frequently oscillate between violent military takeovers or military dictatorships, like Thailand, Cambodia, and of course Myanmar.

The dramatic events in Myanmar since 2011, like the third time release of opposition leader, Aung San Suu Kyi, the holding of democratic by-elections which Suu Kyi won, and the limited release of political prisoners along with a restoration of press freedom, rekindled hopes for the further evolution of human rights and democracy in Southeast Asia. The Tatmadaw is one of the most politically strong militaries, and for them to hold elections and release Suu Kyi around an election time signalled Myanmar's slow march towards more openness and transparency.

Myanmar's political situation, although hardly exceptional in Southeast Asia, had been a potent symbol of the region's tryst with authoritarianism after decolonization. Myanmar was at the epicentre of debates over the 'cultural relativism' stance that ASEAN governments adopted around the Vienna World Conference on Human Rights in 1993. Myanmar was also a reminder of how Southeast Asian governments, as members of ASEAN, neglected the importance of promoting human rights and democracy as part of their agenda for regional cooperation. ASEAN's policy of 'constructive engagement' towards Myanmar, pursued in the aftermath of the 1988 military crackdown on pro-democracy forces as part of the 8888 Uprising, was widely criticized by the international community as shielding human rights abuses by the junta. The policy not only affected ASEAN's relations with Western nations, but also created an unfavourable international image for an otherwise respected grouping. The policy was also a reminder of the paradoxical impact of ASEAN's time-honoured non-interference doctrine, which has been credited with maintaining intra-mural peace, while aggravating the neglect of human rights and democracy in the region.

But democratization in ASEAN remained uneven and fragile. Even in Indonesia, despite successful direct presidential elections, one cannot take the democratization process as irreversible. The recent Thai experience warrants caution, even a bit of scepticism, that democratization in Southeast Asia is a linear process. Cambodia became increasingly intolerant of civil society activism.[231] Vietnam, a large and influential ASEAN member, is hostile towards its citizens promoting human rights.[232] Singapore's 2020 elections signalled a limited opening up of the polity to civil society autonomy, although the setback delivered to the ruling party there may be more due to the people's desire for greater humility and accountability from their government, rather than for democracy and human rights.[233]

Democracy's fragility in the region is also owing to the kind of civil society the countries have. In most Southeast Asian countries, civil society, even in the countries where it enjoys reasonable political space, remains nationally focused. When it seeks external economic and political support, it is usually from the West, rather than from neighbouring countries. In other words, the regional layer of civil society, one that operates between national and global levels, is rather thin, and the incentives and resources to develop a more robust regional civil society are lacking in the region. Neither is there sufficient political will for the cultivation of a pan-region civil society.[234]

Moreover, some of the new institutions created by ASEAN may have ironically constrained the growth of democracy and human rights in the region. It has been argued that the ASEAN Charter has recommitted the members, this time in a fundamental, constitutional way, to the principle of respect for sovereignty. The ASEAN Secretariat has little mandate and capacity for engaging civil society organizations. The efforts by the former Secretary General Surin Pitsuwan to develop a networked secretariat that would have involved greater civil society participation, was met with resistance from official representatives of member states to ASEAN. ASEAN's Committee on Permanent Representatives (CPR), the body comprising of official envoys from the member states, is opposed to an autonomous role for the secretariat and the secretary general, thereby hindering efforts to promote cooperation and collaboration between and across governments and civil society.

Lastly, the rise of China and its growing influence in the region is another constraining factor behind participatory regionalism and the seeding of democracy. A country whose own domestic civil society is heavily muzzled by its regime, China is increasingly an influential dialogue partner of ASEAN and a leader of wider East Asian regionalism through its membership in the East Asia Summit and the Shanghai Cooperation Organization. It is therefore unlikely to tolerate or support the growth of a regional civil society in East Asia which might encourage democratization in the region and thus pose a threat to its own regime's survival.

Past as Prologue

Southeast Asia remains an odd mixture of authoritarian, semi-authoritarian/monarchical and democratic regimes. Democratization in Southeast Asia has an uneven record. While elections are not uncommon, they have often produced conflicting trends towards political openness. For example, in Malaysia, the defeat of the ruling UMNO (United Malay National Organization) in the May 2018 elections, which has been in power since the country's independence, was a victory of pro-democracy forces against the corruption and repression by the preceding government. But the return of aging Mahathir Mohamad as the new Prime Minister, followed by his downfall in 2020, paved the way for UMNO's return, underscoring the limits and fragility of political change in the region.

Similarly, Thailand's 2011 general election took place in the backdrop of protest movements and a violent crackdown on protestors in 2010. That Thailand could conduct a peaceful election with a large turnout in the aftermath of these events suggested that the country's democratic development was moving forward, albeit slowly and cautiously. The 2011 results were also accepted by Thai military leaders, which implied that the military was attempting to become a more professional armed force.[235] However, the 2014 coup reversed these trends.

But the March 2019 elections in Thailand helped create a modicum of stability. However, thanks to the country's military-drafted 2017 constitution, the continuation of military dominance in Thai politics remains a certainty for the foreseeable future. While the constitution and the election outcome ostensibly advantage the military-backed parties led by incumbent Prime Minister Prayuth Chan-ocha to remain in power, they also gave the anti-military parties enough seats in the lower house to remain an effective and potentially disruptive political force. This bifurcation is still a cause for concern, as it could cause future political violence and instability. Thailand continues to face severe challenges to its political stability and democracy owing to growing and unprecedented student-led protests against the monarchy. Its long-term stability depends on preserving the legitimacy of the monarchy, or ensuring a smooth transition to a republican government, and in creating a political system that might bridge the political divide between the rich elites in Bangkok and the marginalized population residing in the northeast and southern parts of the country.

In the Philippines, despite an authoritarian turn under President Rodrigo Duterte, he failed to change the constitution to ensure another term in office, as his critics had originally feared. His brash governance style and violent anti-drug law enforcement measures did result in at least 1,800 extra-judicial murders within his first few months in office.[236] Duterte's reliance on the police and the military has undermined efforts at establishing adequate democratic controls over national coercive apparatuses. Moreover, his administration has also systematically and aggressively targeted political opponents, the judiciary, and media, and actively furthered disinformation campaigns, indicating the country's backsliding democracy.[237]

Myanmar's highly promising experiment with democracy was threatened by ethnic strife, distrust and tensions between the still powerful military and the National League for Democracy (NLD) led by Nobel Peace Prize-winning activist, Aung San Suu Kyi. However, her accommodationist stance towards the military led her to sacrifice human rights principles over the Rohingyas issue and cost her a great deal of international support. One could not rule out a dramatic reversal of the already fragile democratization process in Myanmar, resulting in the military's return to absolute control in the country. Cut to 1 February 2021, and the Tatmadaw had its tanks and other military vehicles patrol the streets of Yangon, having shut down telecommunications and having detained Suu Kyi and other NLD leaders. The coup came after a decade of political and economic opening, which signalled the country's desire to not remain a global pariah. This reversal was met with fierce resistance by the public in the form of labour strikes, civil disobedience movements, and campaigns to boycott the military. In retribution, as of March 2023, according to the Assistance Association for Political Prisoners, the military has arrested 19,982 people and killed over 3,000.[238]

Indonesia's President Susilo Bambang Yudhoyono won a second term in the 2009 elections, winning an impressive popular mandate, however Indonesia was mired in political stagnation.[239] Given its relative size, population, and regional weight, domestic politics in Indonesia is a key element of the regional order of Southeast Asia. The 2014 elections heralded a massive electoral victory to Joko Widodo (Jokowi), a non-establishment candidate from humble origins. In 2019, he returned to power with 85 million votes, receiving the highest vote count for any candidate in Indonesia's democratic electoral history.[240] But the aftermath of the election was marred by violence carried out by supporters of defeated candidate Prabowo Subianto. Although the violence subsided, and Prabowo has been co-opted into Jokowi's cabinet, the episode was ample warning that the rise of radical Islam will be a major factor in Indonesia's instability. On the positive side, Indonesia does not suffer a major insurgency similar to the ones in southern Philippines and southern Thailand. It has no minority persecution or refugee crisis like in Myanmar. While Islamic radicalism remains a risk, it has not translated into large-scale and wide-spread attacks. Some attacks are possible, but they are unlikely to destabilize the country or its legitimate government.

Overall, the domestic political situation in Southeast Asia varies widely from country to country. There is no region-wide trend towards either authoritarianism or democratization. There is a trend towards openness in Indonesia and Malaysia, while Cambodia and Thailand have the potential for deeper and long-term entrenchment in authoritarianism. In the past, Southeast Asia has been able to develop a common identity and achieve relative stability through significant regional cooperation despite widely different political systems and leadership styles. That is unlikely to change.

Against this backdrop, how is Southeast Asia responding to the current wave of populism seen around the world? While the West bemoans the rise of populism as a threat to world order, much of that threat is coming from within the West, with notable non-Western variations found in large countries such as India, Brazil, and Turkey. What is interesting is that Southeast Asian countries seem relatively less affected by the current wave of populism. Why so?

While populism and authoritarianism are conflated, they are not the same. Populism can afflict democratic states, and authoritarian regimes may not resort to populism. In some cases, populism is more of a danger to democracies, including non-Western democracies like India, where leaders, constrained by domestic institutions and rule of law, may resort to propaganda, policy manipulation, religious nationalism, anti-immigrant/anti-minority rhetoric and the use of real or imagined threats, to bolster their electoral prospects, and hold onto power. While Southeast Asia is not immune to this, its long-standing pattern of 'strongman rule' and authoritarian-leaning politics means there is a lesser need to resort to Western-style populism. Paradoxically,

Southeast Asia's experience with authoritarianism acts as a bulwark to the onset and growth of populism.

George Yeo, Singapore's former Foreign Minister, argues that Asian states are less likely to follow the same populist pattern of the West, because of the Asian system of 'rule by law', as opposed to 'rule of law', and cultural differences, especially in Confucian societies of Asia, that already allow them to control dissent and rebellion without resorting to overt populism.[241] While I agree that culture and 'rule by law' in Southeast Asia matter, my argument focuses more on the region's political dynamic, including the preexisting tradition of patrimonial authoritarianism, that makes populism less necessary as a tool for governments. Another relevant factor concerns the economic preconditions that make populism palatable. While contemporary Western populism is a reaction to the perceived harmful effects of globalization, Southeast Asia's general attitude towards globalization remains positive.

Other extra-regional developments that have not had a major political impact on the region include COVID-19 and the regional responses to mitigate the disaster. Learning from the prior epidemic experiences, namely Avian Influenza and SARS, Southeast Asian states leveraged on regional cooperation and preexisting health mechanisms to attenuate COVID's repercussions.

However, COVID's ravages do make political instability more likely in the region. Growing protests in Thailand against the military-dominated government and more notably the monarchy are an ominous sign. Governments have authorized a tightening of political control, increased surveillance, and used emergency powers as part of their COVID reduction efforts, thereby creating pockets of growing public resentment and disenchantment. There are reports of the government arresting dissidents and suppressing dissent for spreading disinformation (in Vietnam)[242] and for raising awareness related to COVID-19 (in Cambodia).[243]

In Thailand, the hand of the military has been strengthened. The government led by former General Prayut declared an Emergency Law and took attendant measures, which have been seen as clamping down on freedom of speech in the name of curbing the spread of false information about COVID-19. Some 21,426 people were persecuted for violating the emergency law and the Prime Minister bypassed parliamentary oversight and issued three royal decrees to borrow 1.9 trillion baht in April to deal with COVID-19 and for economic rehabilitation and restoration.[244]

While the line between pandemic dis/misinformation and political freedom of speech may be blurry, it is quite possible that the rules and regulations put in place to deal with the pandemic will discourage pro-democracy forces.[245] Overall, COVID-19 could discourage the further opening up of political space in Southeast Asia, which was already showing a trend towards authoritarianism.

Another impact on the political systems of Southeast Asia is the stress to leaders on how best to avoid political downturns as their population goes through economic hardship.[246] Economic pressure from COVID-19 has led to cabinet reshuffles in Southeast Asian countries. For instance, Indonesian President Joko Widodo criticized his cabinet publicly and threatened to reshuffle.[247] In Thailand, the resignation of a critical team of economic technocrats as well as the country's new finance minister made its economic recovery plan more uncertain.[248] Prime Minister Prayuth Chan-ocha also faces growing demonstrations critical of the monarchy, which has long been the 'third rail' of Thai politics.[249]

John Sifton, Advocacy Director for Human Rights Watch Asia, notes that 'democracy has been deteriorating in a few ASEAN states like Thailand, Malaysia, Indonesia, Singapore and the Philippines, while Vietnam, Laos, Brunei and Cambodia are not democratic at all.'[250] While the region is yet to overcome the perception that there is a trade-off between democracy and development[251], democracy's lag is mostly owing to national-level political instability. Coups in Thailand and Myanmar, and the centralization of power under the guise of curbing COVID-19, have decelerated the slow march of democracy. Myanmar's 2021 coup led to the country's military leaders becoming disinvited from ASEAN meetings and from the first-ever ASEAN Summit held in Washington DC in May 2022. The summit was meant to demonstrate America's commitment to the region, but senior Congress leaders also reiterated that issues like the need to protect human rights and reversing the region's democratic decline would be raised.

The region's democratic regression is also owing to historical divisions caused by ethnic and religious tensions. 'Religious, political, and ethnic identities are frequently exploited in Southeast Asia to promote conflict, spread discrimination and hate speech, and ultra-nationalist, ethno-nationalist and extreme religious agendas.'[252] Cambodia staged a sham election in August 2023 in which the main opposition, the Candlelight Party, was banned, and the ruling party of longtime Prime Minister Hun Sen took nearly every seat. Prior to the July 2023 elections, Hun Sen announced that he would hand the position over to his oldest son, Hun Manet, currently the army chief.[253] In Thailand, where the progressive Move Forward party won a plurality of seats in elections held in May 2023, military-aligned parties and royalist forces blocked the party's leader, Pita Limjaroenrat, from being named prime minister.

Meanwhile, Myanmar's junta keeps promising and postponing their own sure-to-be-sham elections, all the while conducting a civil war, where the Tatmadaw has intensified its horrific human rights abuses.[254] However, in a change of fortune, Myanmar's Ethnic Armed Organizations (EAOs) and the People's Defence Forces (PDF)—the armed wing of the civilian National

Unity Government—are on the offensive throughout the country (with the exception of Rakhine State), forcing the Tatmadaw into a defensive posture. 'In August, the military deployed massive numbers of troops in Kachin, Shan and Kayah states in an attempt to regain territory lost to EAOs and resistance forces. At the same time, it had to repel escalating attacks in Chin and Mon states.'[255] Labelling the resistance fights as Operation 1027, the EAOs and PDFs caused the junta to lose hundreds of outposts as rebel forces captured towns and several key border crossings in November and December 2023. In these areas, resistance forces also set up interim administrative bodies like a provisional legislature and judiciary and to provide public services in education, healthcare, and humanitarian assistance.[256]

Democracies and Poverty Reduction

Democracy's recent backsliding has not significantly dented the region's economic prospects, at least in the short run. Countries that were growing at a steady clip, like Vietnam, despite increasing their authoritarian hold, continued to maintain their economic growth. As China remains the biggest trading partner with Southeast Asian states and does not care about their domestic politics—China is also satisfied with the region's democratic regression[257]—the region has not suffered a reversal in its economic prospects. However, this may not hold in the long run.

A final question about democracy and development needs discussing: Are democracies better at reducing poverty than autocracies? In an address to the 14th Bali Democracy Forum on 9 December 2021, I made the following three main points:

First, poverty is a broad and relative notion: it cannot be measured by an economic benchmark alone, like the World Bank's official $2.15 per person per day criterion for the 'extreme poverty' line.[258] There is now the *idea of 'multidimensional poverty'*, developed by the Oxford Poverty and Human Development Initiative (OPHI) and released by the United Nations Development Program. 'Multidimensional Poverty is an index that captures the percentage of households in a country deprived along three dimensions of well-being—monetary poverty, education, and basic infrastructure services.'[259] This comprehensive understanding of poverty attempts to go beyond economic measures alone, by examining welfare service provision and regime type. This makes poverty a broader concept that considers indicators such as malnutrition, lack of healthcare, as well as limited access to clean water, electricity, education, and employment opportunities. These additional measures are part of a holistic understanding of welfare known as human security. As such, what matters in poverty reduction is not reducing the number of people below a certain income level but increasing human security for all people. Even if a country achieves growth and reduces poverty by counting income, it does not mean it has really reduced poverty or increased prosperity for its people.

Second, there is no question that democracies are not necessarily better in poverty reduction. In Asia, both China and India have done well in poverty alleviation, despite very different political systems. According to Pew Research Center, between 2001 to 2011, the poverty rate in 'India fell from 35 per cent in 2001 to 20 per cent in 2011. That meant that 133 million Indians exited poverty in that decade, the second-largest drop globally after China.' In China, about 356 million people were lifted out of poverty.[260] By this count, China did and continues to do better than India. But India, according to Oxford's Department of International Development, led the world in lifting as many as 270 million people out of multidimensional poverty between 2005–06 and 2015–16.[261] India also provides robust evidence that democracies do well in addressing famine. Independent and democratic India has been able to avoid famines that recurred throughout the British colonial period, the last of which killed 3 million people in Bengal in 1943.[262] As India's Nobel Prize winner in Economics, Amartya Sen, argues, democracies are less likely to suffer devastating famines.[263]

Some electoral democracies have not done as well, such as in Africa, although this has much to do with their weak institutional capacity, rather than democracy per se. At the same time, many authoritarian countries have done poorly in poverty reduction. North Korea is a striking example. And let us not forget, poverty levels increase when a country slides into authoritarianism. Thus, Myanmar after the 1962 military coup went from being the rice bowl of Asia to being one of the world's poorest nations.[264]

Here, one is again reminded of the famous controversy about the link between democracy and development in the 1990s. There was an argument that the 'East Asian economic miracle' happened because of authoritarian rule in key countries and territories: namely South Korea, Taiwan, Indonesia (under Suharto), Singapore, etc. China would soon join this group. Prime Minister Lee Kuan Yew held the view that democracy can be detrimental to development, while the President of Philippines, Fidel Ramos, countered his view and pointed out that Philippines was under a dictatorship for decades, yet achieved little growth. Under Ramos, Philippines improved in economic growth.

So did Indonesia under the authoritarian regime of Suharto. But it would also continue to do well after its democratic transition. Democratic Indonesia continues to provide evidence that democracy, development, and stability are complementary, or are in a virtuous cycle. I have discussed this 'trifecta' in my 2014 book *Indonesia Matters*, and also discussed it in a recent Jakarta Post article titled 'Will Indonesia's Trifecta Survive COVID-19?'.[265]

The cases of Indonesia or India beg the question: is it preferrable to live under a system that combines democracy, development and stability, as opposed to a system that provides only stability and development (perhaps at a little faster rate) but one that is not democratic? Authoritarian regimes with good institutions and governance may reduce poverty faster (again, depending on what one means by poverty), but the reduction also comes at a cost of civil liberties restriction, and limited mobility of people across different states and urban centres.

My third point is that democracy is certainly not sufficient for development and poverty reduction. Aside from institutional capacity, good governance also matters. On this score, Singapore and China have done well in poverty reduction. But good governance ultimately requires democracy. As noted democracy expert Larry Diamond says:

> Good governance involves the capacity and commitment to act in pursuit of the public good, transparency, accountability, citizen participation and the rule of law. Bad governance prevents the accumulation of the financial, physical, social, and political capital necessary for development. Democracy should provide a corrective to bad governance by holding corrupt, unresponsive, or ineffectual leaders to account and enabling citizens to participate in making policy.[266]

Owing to these reasons, I believe there is no excuse to justify authoritarian rule in the name of poverty alleviation. Elites who perpetuate their tight control may do so fearing instability that could affect their political survival. But poverty reduction and stability are better euphemisms for power and political survival.

Finally, there is a new danger now. A vicious cycle has emerged between the COVID-19 pandemic, poverty, and loss of democracy. COVID-19 has increased the level of poverty worldwide while reducing democratic space. This is worrisome. In October 2020, the World Bank predicted that owing to the pandemic, global extreme poverty would rise in 2020 for the first time in over twenty years, increasing the number of people in extreme poverty by 88 million to 150 million by 2021.[267] This means that extreme poverty will remain between 9.1 per cent and 9.4 per cent of the world's population in 2020, instead of dropping to 7.9 per cent had there been no pandemic. It also noted that the new poor will, disproportionately, be in countries with already high poverty rates.

This reinforces the already severe effect of the pandemic on poor people and minorities. A study of the impact of COVID-19 in five of the largest democracies: US, India, Brazil, Philippines, and Indonesia, by Joshua Kurlantzick of the Council on Foreign Relations, concludes that the pandemic has killed more poor people and minorities per capita than middle class or rich people in these countries.[268] This, along with ineffective government response, has reduced the number of wage-earners for affected families, making their future recovery even more challenging.

While poverty rates rise, democratic space is being reduced. According to an Asia Society Policy Institute study, people in Southeast Asian states are accepting, and even demanding stronger state intervention, which they believe will better address the pandemic.[269] Giving more authority to governments even for handling the pandemic always carries the risk of abuse and overall restriction of freedom, especially in a region known for its 'strong' and authoritarian regimes. This is particularly alarming in view of the worldwide reversal of democratization that started well before the pandemic.

PART III

COPING WITH RIVALRY

Chapter 6

Will ASEAN Survive Great Power Rivalry?

Pundits and policymakers increasingly see the changing great power politics in Asia (or the Asia-Pacific or Indo-Pacific, terms I use interchangeably) as an existential challenge to ASEAN. Of particular concern here is the growing military assertiveness of China in ASEAN's backyard, the South China Sea, and the US 'rebalancing' or 'pivot' strategy. Added to this picture are Japan's moves to amend its constitution to allow more room for forward military operations and India's growing military presence in the Indian Ocean extending to East Asian waters and its assertive diplomacy under Prime Minister Narendra Modi. Critics argue that ASEAN is both toothless and clueless in responding to these changes. Its main reaction has been to persist with regional institutions such as the ASEAN Regional Forum (ARF) and the East Asian Summit (EAS), disparagingly seen as 'talk shops'. While such an approach might have served a useful purpose when great power relations were less volatile in the immediate aftermath of the Cold War, it has now outlived its usefulness. Critics not only write off the idea of 'ASEAN centrality' in Asia's regional security architecture, but also the very survival of ASEAN as a regional community.

While ASEAN faces significant challenges, these have less to do with its external environment, such as great power policies and interactions. Much more important are strains to ASEAN's internal cohesion and capacity, especially owing to its expanded membership and agenda. ASEAN is not without precedent and advantages in dealing with great power politics. Its external environment is, in fact, more helpful to its security role than is commonly portrayed by the pessimists. If ASEAN's unity holds and it makes necessary changes to its ambitions and agenda, it should not only survive great power competition, but continue to play a meaningful role in managing that competition, at least in Southeast Asia.

What Great Power Competition?

In his book, *The Tragedy of Great Power Politics,* American political scientist John Mearsheimer argued that rising powers must expand to survive, which often leads them to seek at least a regional hegemony. He predicted that if the growth of Chinese power continues, it will seek regional hegemony, which in turn will provoke conflict possibly leading to war with the United States. He cited the examples of Nazi Germany, imperial Japan, and the United States before the 20th century to illustrate his thesis.[270]

A second perspective on great power politics, derived almost entirely from Europe before World War II, holds that international stability is a function of the number of great powers and the distribution of capabilities among them. A multipolar system, where the main actors are the great powers (the 'poles'), is usually more prone to instability and conflict than a bipolar system, such as what existed during the Cold War. Another distribution of power is unipolarity, and while not all realists agree that unipolarity is unstable, most concur that it is rare and that multipolarity is the least stable of power configurations. A multipolar system has more dyads, hence more opportunities for competition, which, in turn, renders interactions among the great powers less predictable.

Both scenarios point to a bleak future for ASEAN. Chinese regional hegemony, whether of the coercive Monroe Doctrine type or even a relatively benign one,[271] which provides Chinese aid, investment, and market access in return for loyalty to China in a manner akin to the old tributary system, is bad news for ASEAN. If it materializes, it will certainly cover at least parts of Southeast Asia, including the states involved in the South China Sea dispute. A multipolar system dominated by the great powers gives little space to smaller and weaker states, which would be made victims of great power politics. As Aaron Friedberg hypothesized, the end of the Cold War ushered in a multipolar system in Asia, like in Europe before World War II.[272] China, like Germany then, is a revisionist rising power, and wants to challenge the status quo of an American dominated liberal international order. Hence, Asia is 'ripe for rivalry', and can expect intensified great power competition leading to catastrophic breakdowns as happened in Europe in the early 20th century. Both these perspectives have been reinforced by Chinese moves in the South China Sea and East China Sea areas, which, along with Russian moves in Ukraine and Eastern Europe, many analysts see as signs of Chinese and Russian expansionism, a 'return of geopolitics' in the world, and the arrival of 19th century European geopolitics in Asia.

There are, of course, more optimistic and positive views about great power politics. Hedley Bull stressed the special responsibility of the great powers in the management of international order.[273] Karl Deutsch and David Singer rejected the idea that multipolarity invariably leads to great power competition and conflict. On the contrary, they argued that it may make war less likely by making a potential aggressor less sure about a state's alignments whereby the state can enlarge its size and power through coalitions.[274] Additionally, multipolarity increases interaction opportunities among the major players, creating cross-cutting pressures on their strategic designs. On occasion, multipolar interactions may also promote pluralistic common interests. This may sometimes lead to significant cooperation, as happened with the early 19th century European Concert system.

Even these relatively optimistic perspectives still assume great power primacy in maintaining stability. The concert of powers or its bilateral variant, a two-power condominium, (such as a G-2 between the United States and China), leaves ASEAN marginalized. None of the above perspectives recognizes the possibility of smaller and weaker players influencing great power politics. They are seen as objects and passive recipients of great power influence.

Yet, if the traditional perspectives are correct, ASEAN would have been doomed from its birth in 1967, as many Western and some Asian analysts had indeed predicted then and keep predicting. ASEAN is an anomaly in the universe of great power politics. Not only has it survived, but it has contributed significantly to conflict reduction and management in Southeast Asia and has served as the main anchor of regional cooperation involving all the major powers of Asia and indeed the world. As a result, Southeast Asia is the only region in known history where the strong live in the world of the weak, and the weak lead the strong. ASEAN's record has been a mixed one, but its existence, survival. and purpose turns traditional realism on its head.

Great power politics may be a constant through world history, but it does not reappear in the same way and for the same reasons. It is unfortunate that pundits keep using 19th century (mainly European) lenses to describe 21st century realities in Asia and the world. The term great power rivalry and competition is a bit misleading because of the significant and far-reaching cooperation that exists among the same great powers both at regional and global levels. This cooperation is underpinned by a type of interdependence that simply did not exist a century ago, when competition was de rigueur.

The term multipolarity, a Eurocentric notion, is also quite out of date now. It described a world of great powers and referred mainly to the number of actors and the distribution of power among them. It said much less about the substance and quality of their interactions. If one takes the latter into account, the dominant feature of today's world and Asia is not multipolarity, but multiplexity. Multiplexity, or the idea of a Multiplex World, differs from a multipolar system in significant ways.[275] Whereas the traditional conception of multipolarity assumed the primacy of the great powers, actors (or agents) in a multiplex world are not just great powers or only states (Western and non-Western). Multiplexity recognizes the importance of international institutions, non-governmental organizations, multinational corporations, and transnational networks (good and bad). A multiplex order is marked by complex global and regional linkages including not just trade but also finance and transnational production networks, which were scarce in pre-World War European economic interdependence. Moreover, interdependence today is not only economic in nature but also covers many other issue areas, such as the environment, disease, human rights, and social media. A multiplex order has multiple layers of governance, including global, inter-regional, regional, domestic, and sub-state. Regionalism is a key part of this, but regionalism today is open and overlapping, a far cry from 19th century imperial blocs that fuelled great power competition and war, and which are unlikely to reappear. A multiplex world is a decentred world. While power hierarchies remain, the overall architecture of a multiplex world is non-hegemonic. The world is unlikely to see global hegemons like Britain and the United States again. China is not going to be one, as I argue below. At the same time, a multiplex world is not a 'G-Zero' world,[276] but one that encourages pluralistic and shared leadership at both global and regional levels. ASEAN's prospects should be judged not in terms of old-fashioned, outdated notions of multipolarity, but in light of these unfolding changes towards a multiplex world, which also affect the Asia-Pacific region.

A Chinese Monroe Doctrine?

The key feature of the Asian strategic landscape is, of course, the rise of China, both as an economic and military power. Rising powers do not necessarily worry their neighbours simply with their rise. What matters more are changes to the balance of threat rather than the balance of power. ASEAN has serious reasons to worry about recent Chinese behaviour, especially in the South China Sea. While China's claims are not new, some of its tactics are, such as land reclamation work to create new 'islands'. These claims are backed by increasing Chinese military capability and financial clout, which is then used to buy support, for example, from Myanmar and Cambodia.[277] But the Chinese threat is only to the disputed offshore territories and waters of ASEAN members rather than to their metropolitan territory. China is not alone in the reclamation effort and talks to conclude a South China Sea code of conduct are proceeding, despite the delays and obstacles.

Some experts believe that China could follow America's route to great power status. Before it became a global superpower, the US not only expanded within the North American continent, but also imposed a sphere of influence in central America and the Caribbean. The US Monroe Doctrine denied these areas to European great powers and limited the independence of America's neighbours. Can China do likewise in Southeast Asia and Central Asia? Fears are growing of Chinese dominance in the South China Sea. America is concerned about freedom of critical sea lanes. Yet, the conditions that allowed the US to expand and become hegemonic are not found in Asia today. Back then, no European power—Britain and France included—was able to challenge US expansionism. Today, a Chinese Monroe Doctrine for Asia would be vigorously resisted not only by the US, but also by other powers, notably Japan, India, and Vietnam.

A somewhat different scenario of China's future is that it could revive its own past. That past harks back to the old tributary system that lasted for over a thousand years before the European colonial powers humiliated China in the 18th and 19th centuries. Under the tributary order, a powerful and prosperous China was the magnet for its neighbouring countries' trade and hence a key source of their prosperity. China also offered strategic protection to select neighbours and in the first half of the 15th century, even policed the sea lanes. Moreover, China's self-perception was not just as the leading state of Asia, but also of the world, a perception captured in the term, 'Chinese World Order'. Since China is once again powerful and prosperous, might Asia return to living under benign Chinese suzerainty? This scenario, which is believed by many inside China and a few outside, is unlikely. The revival of the old tributary system is undercut by the influence of US, Japan, India, and Russia. A regional order based on Confucian notions of hierarchy and deference may appeal to some inside China, but it is incompatible with Southeast Asia's emphasis on sovereignty and equality.

That leaves the third, and in some respects most dangerous scenario for Asia under rising Chinese power. Is China today the Germany of the late 19th and early 20th centuries? As Europe then, Asia is now moving towards multipolarity. Will the powerful combination of economic growth, military modernization, nationalism, and totalitarianism that took Germany on the road to expansion be replicated by 21st century China? This view conveniently ignores the fact that Germany's rise happened in an era marked by an 'orgy of imperialism' among the great powers. This is not the case today. Moreover, economic bonds in Asia and the world today are deeper and more far-reaching than those in Europe before World War I. Today, trade, financial flows, and cross-border production networks are defying the rules of sovereignty, rendering the German parallel for China implausible.

The view that South China Sea and Southeast Asia are a natural theatre for a Chinese version of the Monroe Doctrine, which can coerce, if not directly threaten, ASEAN, is based on both flawed logic and a false ghost from history. They focus on ASEAN's weaknesses in dealing with China, while ignoring China's difficulties and dilemmas in the South China Sea issue. The Monroe Doctrine was possible when the United States had no countervailing power in its neighbourhood. Spain had withered away as a great power. Britain and France, the European powers that could have challenged the US in its backyard, were too busy fighting each other in Europe and elsewhere, and later fighting a unified Germany together.

China faces a very different situation today. Any temptation it might harbour for creating a zone of exclusion in the South China Sea or a sphere of influence over Southeast Asia would be met with stiff resistance by the presence of not only the US, but also of India and Japan, along with America's allies, Singapore and Australia. Some ASEAN members, like Vietnam, are at least capable of raising the costs of Chinese military aggression. Moreover, in committing aggression or sea denial in the South China Sea, China has to consider the consequences for its own shipping through chokepoints where ASEAN navies have powers of reconnaissance, detection, and even interdiction, and the Indian Ocean, where the US and Indian navies are more active and superior. Unlike the Caribbean's role for America, geography is not on China's side in its maritime environment.

Moreover, emerging powers cannot become truly legitimate global powers if they keep picking quarrels with all (or almost all) of their neighbours. For China, global legitimacy may not be possible without regional legitimacy. One might point, as John Mearsheimer does, to the US as an exception, and say that as a rising power, it could coerce and threaten its immediate neighbours and pursue expansionism in the form of the Monroe Doctrine, but it did not become a *legitimate* global power until after it abandoned the Monroe Doctrine in the late 1920s.

The 'rise of China' may be an outdated term since China has already 'arrived' as a great power and potentially a superpower. China dominates the speculations about the future security landscape of Southeast Asia. However, any concerns that Southeast Asian states will collectively bandwagon with China, has proven to be unfounded. Some Southeast Asian countries have moved closer to China than others. Those who have moved closer include Cambodia and Laos, both of whom had developed close economic and security ties with China for some time. But the most important shift towards China has been the Philippines under the Duterte government.

The territorial dispute in the South China Sea is a key factor shaping China's relations with ASEAN, even though not all ASEAN members are parties to the conflict. It links extra-regional geopolitics, especially the rise of China and the US–China competition, with the intra-regional dynamics of Southeast Asia. Over the past decade, the conflict has escalated following China's construction of artificial islands and the militarization of several features that it claims to be its own. China rejected the verdict of the July 2016 Permanent Court of Arbitration (on a case brought by the Philippines) that ruled against Chinese claims to sovereignty over the islands.[278] In brief, the Court rejected Chinese claims to have historically exercised exclusive control over the islands, ruled that the disputed islands do not generate extended maritime zones, found China to have violated Philippines's sovereign right in its exclusive economic zones, and criticized China's land reclamation and artificial island construction in seven features for severely damaging the marine environment.[279]

ASEAN's main approach to the conflict has been to seek a Code of Conduct in the South China Sea. Some progress over this was reported in August 2018, when Singapore's Foreign Minister, Vivian Balakrishnan, announced that ASEAN countries and China have reached a Single Draft South China Sea Code of Conduct Negotiating Text (SDNT). According to an early leaked draft, the Code is 'not an instrument to settle territorial disputes or maritime delimitation issues'. [280] Rather, as Greg Poling, Director of the Asia Maritime Transparency Initiative at the Centre for Strategic and International Studies (CSIS) argues, 'What the code of conduct is intended to do is to manage the disputes to prevent them from escalating, and basically to allow the freezing of the thorny territorial questions, while states can manage the resources and manage tensions in the near to medium term.'[281]

The willingness of China—which has been delaying the Code because it felt the timing was not right—to move forward can be explained by the fact that it has already completed a substantial degree of construction and militarization of its occupied islands. There are several issues that need to be resolved before the Code can be formalized, such as China's demand that joint military exercises between any of the parties to the code and any external power/s, should be prohibited without advance notification and consent of the parties to the Code. This is seen as directed against the US and its allies and as such will be unacceptable to them. If such barriers are overcome through further negotiations, the conclusion of such a code of conduct will be an important measure of stabilizing the South China Sea dispute.

As its power grows and the South China Sea dispute worsens, China's attitude towards ASEAN and other Asian regional bodies has shifted. China was angry that ASEAN moved too close to the US during the Obama era.[282] To counter America's influence with ASEAN, China promoted its own regional initiatives, both multilateral and bilateral, like the Asian Infrastructure Investment Bank (AIIB) and the Belt and Road Initiative (BRI), leaving ASEAN out of both fora.

The BRI: Boon or Burden?

The BRI has encountered pushback in Southeast Asia, especially from Malaysia since its 2018 elections.[283] It has also faced growing resistance in Indonesia, while Thailand continues to maintain a cautious approach towards it.[284]

The reasons behind this vary from country to country. In Indonesian domestic politics especially, criticism of the Jokowi government's embrace of BRI by Islamic groups and presidential candidate Prabowo Subianto in the lead up to the 2019 elections was a major factor. Domestic politics also affected Malaysia's attitude, as the newly elected coalition government under Prime Minister Mahathir Mohamad immediately announced its desire to renegotiate BRI projects, which it considered to be unnecessary and expensive.[285] Since then, Malaysia has renegotiated its high-speed rail project under the BRI and cut the costs by a third. Even in Cambodia, perhaps the closest political ally of China in ASEAN, the major port of Sihanoukville is funded by Japan.[286] Japan remains a counter to China in Southeast Asia's infrastructure projects. Myanmar's relations with China have been repaired somewhat despite the stalled Myitsone dam project, and the NLD government of Aung San Suu Kyi has revived some BRI projects, mainly to gain Chinese diplomatic support over the Rohingya issue.[287] Overall, Southeast Asian countries maintain a cautious approach to the BRI. While none oppose it outright in the manner of India and a few seem happy to keep some BRI projects so as not to offend China, they also keep their exposure to the BRI limited. The ambivalent reactions from Southeast Asian countries could be one reason for China's apparent decision to scale back and recalibrate the BRI, including adding more debt-relief measures, as announced by Chinese leader Xi Jinping at the 2nd BRI Forum in April 2019.[288]

The differing perceptions and attitudes among Southeast Asian countries towards China is neither unusual nor unexpected. Southeast Asia and ASEAN have seldom spoken in one voice when it comes to dealing with outside powers. For example, during the Cold War, Malaysia and Indonesia took a softer stance towards Vietnam, then an ally of the Soviet Union, and were openly hostile towards ASEAN, compared to Singapore and Thailand, which were openly pro-US. These divisions have in the past not proven unmanageable. Nor have they precluded ASEAN from developing a substantial measure of cooperation and a shared 'community-building' agenda. There is no reason to believe that ASEAN cannot do likewise now.

Southeast Asia's misgivings about Chinese power were revealed in a recent 'State of Southeast Asia' survey published in January 2019 by a Singapore-based think-tank. When asked, 'How do you view China's re-emergence as a major power with respect to Southeast Asia?' 45.4 per cent of the respondents thought that 'China will become a revisionist power with an intent to turn Southeast Asia into its sphere of influence.' Moreover, less than one in ten respondents (8.9 per cent) saw China as 'a benign and benevolent power'.[289] In the 2022 survey, to the same question, 41.7 per cent of those who responded equated China with being a revisionist power. This response was the top response for eight ASEAN member states, except Cambodia and Thailand. The perception of China being revisionist was most acute in the Philippines (62 per cent) and Myanmar (56 per cent).[290] The 2023 survey showed that nearly 50 per cent of the respondents have either 'little confidence' or 'no confidence' in China doing the 'right thing to contribute to global peace, security, prosperity, and governance'.[291]

COVID-19 did not help China's trust deficit. The PRC's mask diplomacy in Asia has produced mixed results, with complaints about poor quality of masks that do not prevent the spread of the infection.[292] China's strenuous efforts to offer a narrative that presented itself first as a victim that quickly conquered the virus did not suffice to erase misgivings over the origins of the virus from China. Indeed, regional papers like Singapore's *Straits Times* routinely headlined it as the Wuhan virus or the China virus before Trump called it as such.[293] In light of this, China's delays and denials in handling the initial outbreak only serves to deepen her negative image among her Asian neighbours.

Nonetheless, the ultimate outcome depends not on Chinese power or ideology but on Chinese behaviour towards its neighbours. Here, China's flexibility and ability to adapt to new challenges are not to be underestimated. Most of Southeast Asia still does not want confrontation with China and would be receptive to a softer Chinese diplomatic and military approach to the region.

America Wakes Up?

Southeast Asia's relations with the US have changed since the Obama administration's 'pivot to Asia'. The Trump administration's departure from liberal internationalism, or the liberal international order, is not a major worry for Southeast Asian countries because the administration has continued its engagement policy towards the region, although with less emotion and energy than the Obama administration. Trump quickly dumped the Trans-Pacific Partnership (TPP), but this may not be of major consequence to ASEAN 'as a group', since the TPP did not encompass most Southeast Asian countries. More importantly, the Trump administration also dropped Obama's 'rebalancing' strategy and adopted the 'Indo-Pacific' idea, one element of which is the Quadrilateral Security Dialogue (QUAD) involving the US, Japan, Australia, and India.[294] Like Obama's 'rebalancing' strategy, Trump's Indo-Pacific approach relies heavily on US military presence and deployments. But unlike rebalancing, the Indo-Pacific approach is a strategic framework for the US to deal with a wider region encompassing East and Southeast Asia as well as India and the Indian Ocean as a single strategic theatre. The Indo-Pacific approach does contain some novel elements, such as the renaming of the US Pacific Command to the US Indo-Pacific Command (without any significant changes to its mission however) and a much more active and frequent program of Freedom of Navigation Operations (FONOPS) in the disputed waters of the South China Sea. It is the latter which is of greater consequence in reassuring Southeast Asian countries apprehensive about China's role in the region.

In general, the perceptions of the US as a global power and a regional leader have declined, especially when it comes to geopolitics and strategy. According to the aforementioned 'State of Southeast Asia' survey, 'nearly six out of ten respondents (59.1 per cent) think US power and influence at the global stage has deteriorated'.[295] Moreover, when asked, 'How confident are you of the US as a strategic partner and provider of regional security?' 68.1 per cent of the respondents were unsure of or had little confidence in America's reliability as a strategic partner and provider of regional security.[296] In contrast, in the 2022 survey, 45.8 per cent of the respondents perceived that the level of American engagement with Southeast Asia under Biden increased or increased significantly. This optimism ranked high in Brunei, Laos, Myanmar, Singapore, Thailand, and Vietnam. Only Cambodian respondents predominantly felt that American engagement with the region decreased.[297] In 2023, the perception of trust toward the US increased marginally from the previous year, from 52.8 per cent to 54.2 per cent. Unlike their scepticism in 2022, Cambodia's level of trust in the US moved up to 85.1 per cent.[298] Overall, America's perception under the Biden administration has improved remarkably in the region.

Allies, Partners, and Followers

Among other regional powers, Japan has stepped up its engagement with Southeast Asia, as a response to China's increasing power and, especially, owing to concerns about the BRI. Japan has vigorously pursued its own Indo-Pacific strategy, which complements the US approach, but has a much stronger economic dimension, focusing on infrastructure, maritime resources, and support for ASEAN's economic integration. Japan's relations with China have slightly improved in recent months, but this is unlikely to dampen the Sino-Japanese competition that is evident in Southeast Asia.[299]

India too has intensified its engagement with Southeast Asia, in keeping with Prime Minister Narendra Modi's 'Act East' policy. A hallmark of this policy, compared with the 'Look East' policy of Modi's predecessors, is a deeper and more comprehensive strategic approach to Southeast Asia and East Asia, including a more wide-ranging and pro-active military engagement. India has embraced the Indo-Pacific concept, but with some reservations about the QUAD as a strategic concept, due to the legacy of its non-aligned past (now said to have shifted to a policy of 'multi-alignment') as well as a concern not to provoke China.[300] Overall, Southeast Asian countries seem to welcome India's Act East policy, and generally see it as a positive factor in regional stability. While Vietnam and Myanmar are most supportive of India's role in Southeast Asia, Indonesia remains somewhat wary of India's ambitions in the region, which might compete with Jakarta's own. Moreover, Southeast Asian countries are somewhat disappointed with the substance of India's commitment to the region, especially in the economic sphere, where China remains far ahead.

The decline of America's soft power in Asia (leaving the Middle East and Central Asia aside) may be mainly due to the disappointment with the Trump administration's disregard of the region than due to any long-term deep-rooted factors. It had much to do with the heavy-handed way Trump dealt with America's traditional allies, South Korea and Japan, including demanding more rent to station American troops.[301] Trump's inability to show up at the East Asia Summit hosted by Thailand in November 2019, or send a cabinet level delegate, was seen by

ASEAN as a snub. Perceptions of America therefore declined due to the Trump administration's inconsistent and inept handling of the pandemic. However, they went up under the Biden administration, as noted above in the 2022 and 2023 State of Southeast Asia surveys.

US–China Military and Economic Balance

A regional conflict in Asia involving the US and China will undercut America's military advantages, which includes superior weapons, training, and doctrine. As a RAND Corporation study puts it, the US–China military balance is subject to the 'three asymmetries—of distance, time, and stakes,' and these favour China in a US–China confrontation.[302]

Before COVID-19, according to data from the Stockholm International Peace Research Institute (SIPRI), East Asia in 2019 accounted for 19 per cent (China alone was 14 per cent) of total world defence spending, second only to North America's 39 per cent (all but 1 per cent of this by the US), and well above West Europe at 13 per cent. Adding South Asia to East Asia's share, Asia cumulatively accounted for 23.6 per cent.[303] A key trend here was China's relentless military buildup to reduce the gap with the US. Between 2010 and 2019, China increased its defence spending by 85 per cent, while the US cut it by 15 per cent. To be sure, the spending gap remains wide. In 2019, the United States spent $732 billion on defence, compared to China's $261 billion.

China has pursued an aggressive military modernization program to close the gap with the US in certain key areas that matter in regional conflicts in Asia. Its growing inventory of advanced anti-ship and traditional ballistic and cruise missiles allows China a substantial Anti-Access Area Denial (A2AD) capability. This would make it difficult for the US to intervene in conflicts closer to Chinese territory, including the East China Sea, Taiwan, and South China Sea. China's growing fleet of submarines would also act as a deterrent to US naval deployments in Taiwan and the South China Sea conflict situations. While China has built up military installations in artificially constructed islands in the South China Sea, they remain highly vulnerable to a US strike in the event of an armed confrontation. China still remains substantially behind the US when it comes to projecting its forces. In a conflict where the US can use military access in allied territory, China could find itself unable to deploy its forces in the Western Pacific or support those already in the South China Sea, a case of turning Chinese 'A2AD on its head'.

Owing to these factors, the military balance remains in America's favour, especially if the US retains its alliances in the region that provide, if not forces, but access to key military installations in Japan, South Korea, and Southeast Asia. However, in recent years, this balance is tilting in China's favour. According to Elbridge Colby, a former US Deputy Assistant Secretary of Defence, 'The military balance between the US and China in Asia is very delicate and trending in an unfavourable direction in this decade for the US and its allies.'[304] In a 2023 report released by senior researchers at RAND, the PLA's quantitative and qualitative assessments of weapons technology, force structure, and organizational relationships have 'received the attention of Xi Jinping himself', who is personally keen on redressing the military balance relative to China's primary military benchmark, the US.[305] The shift in balance is not only due to China's proactiveness, but also because of creeping doubts about Washington's ability and willingness to fulfil its treaty commitments and protect its allies. In the words of a former senior strategic analyst at Australia's top intelligence agency, China's leaders are banking on America's retreat from Asia, so Beijing 'has a freer hand to militarily coerce smaller neighbours' to become the dominant regional power.[306]

The pre-existing rift between the two states got exacerbated during the Trump administration, when the US imposed tariffs and technology restrictions related to the sale of semiconductors on

China. Biden's policies also curbed American investments in Chinese tech companies. These issues were compounded by COVID-19, when 'politically driven accusations' squandered opportunities for cooperation to tackle a common global threat.[307] Their competition peaked in July 2023, when both the US Secretary of State Anthony Blinken and his Chinese counterpart Wang Yi attended ASEAN meetings, where each tried 'to convince Southeast Asian states to distance themselves from the other'.[308]

In a desire to ease tensions, the two countries' presidents met in November 2023, to establish cooperation on numerous issues ranging from the safe use of artificial intelligence, to providing humanitarian assistance to Gaza, ensuring the smooth passage of goods through the Black Sea and gathering support for postwar reconstruction in Gaza and Ukraine.[309]

When Elephants Fight: Southeast Asia in US–China Rivalry

COVID-19 not only affected states' domestic capabilities to manage its spread, it also affected the regional military balance between China and its Southeast Asian neighbours. While the ten nations that belong to ASEAN singly or collectively are no match for China militarily, some of them are developing capabilities to police and defend their coastal areas and economic zones from Chinese encroachment. China's military spending in 2019 exceeded ASEAN's by more than five times. The pandemic induced cuts and budgetary appropriations and reallocations away from defence, which tilted the regional military balance further in China's favour.

Until now, Southeast Asia's position in the US–China competition has been called 'hedging,' or avoiding taking sides in the rivalry, while watching the competition unfold. Recently, some analysts have argued that such hedging has ended,[310] and the region may be aligning with China. But there is little evidence that Southeast Asia as a region has moved to a 'post-hedging' stage. It has not abandoned its 'co-engagement' (a more realistic description of ASEAN's position than hedging) of US and China, either.[311] Nor is there any decisive sign of the region choosing sides in the US and China rivalry. But the challenge to ASEAN's 'co-engagement' policy now comes not just from the fear of China's rise or the attractions of BRI, but the fact that the US under the Trump administration suffered a great deficit in credibility and trust in Southeast Asia and the fear that this could be repeated in the next election cycle.[312]

When it comes to Chinese and/or Western influence, these should not be seen as zero-sum. The West may have more soft power in Southeast Asia for the time being. But soft power is fickle and its true impact on geopolitics is hard to measure. As the case of China demonstrates, the popularity of US or Western education or culture in Southeast Asia does not necessarily translate into favourable geopolitical alignments with the US/West. In so far as great power rivalry is concerned, Southeast Asia will continue trying to carefully navigate the emerging rivalry for the indefinite future. But the assertion by some that Southeast Asia might have stopped hedging and may be moving towards aligning with China is premature. Southeast Asia will keep its engagement with all powers. Lee Hsien Loong, Singapore's former Prime Minister, has suggested that ASEAN countries may be forced to choose sides in the US–China rivalry.[313] But one wonders what form this might take. Will it mean some countries, such as Singapore, joining the US in an alliance against China? Singapore's relations with the US are already beginning to demonstrate this. Singapore is the closest in the region to being considered by the US as being in a virtual or de facto alliance. On the Chinese side, will some ASEAN countries move to develop a military alliance with China? This is unlikely, as evident from the pushback against the

BRI from Southeast Asian states. The chances are higher that as a region, Southeast Asia will maintain some distance among all the major powers, without allowing any single power to dominate the region. This has been ASEAN's historical security philosophy and is unlikely to change significantly.

The conventional wisdom about Asian security today is that the rise of China is creating an imbalance of power in the continent. This is misleading. There was never really a 'balance' of power in Asia in the conventional sense. Asia has always been a region of US primacy, if not outright hegemony, although the latter term might apply if hegemony is understood in terms of military power projection. Even today, the US outspends China in defence by four and half times. China may be aspiring to anti-access/area denial, but it is nowhere close to upstaging America's military superiority in Asia. The idea of an Asian balance of power—an equilibrium of power—is a myth without much regard for what the term of balance of power actually means.

On the contrary, the relative rise of China may indeed be creating something of a military equilibrium for the first time in Asian history. If realists are right that a balance of power contributes to stability, this cannot be bad for the region as a whole and for its smaller states. After all, a few proponents of balance of power claim that the protection of small states by denying hegemony to any single power is one of its virtues. This is not to say that there is no balancing happening between China and the United States and its allies, but it is defensive, rather than offensive in nature, and it is accompanied by other forces favouring regional stability.

The US rebalancing policy unquestionably responds to China's rise, but there are three important things about it that are often forgotten by analysts. First, it is an outgrowth of 'hedging policy' and retains many elements of an open and flexible measure that does not write off peaceful Chinese behaviour.

Second, rebalancing does not represent a dramatic shift in US military deployment in the region. It mainly reverses the 60–40 per cent ratio of deployment between Europe/Middle East and Asia. Finally, it is not a policy of pre-emptive containment, even though many Chinese analysts claim it is, to score propaganda points. US–China economic ties, not just trade but a virtual mutual assured destruction situation in financial links, demonstrate how different this relationship is from America's containment of the Soviet Union. As such, the rebalancing policy is not a pre-emptive strategy of containment but a countervailing posture that gives China ample room for rising peacefully—which is exactly what it claims to want to do—while preventing it from acquiring a Monroe-Doctrine-like regional hegemony. Chinese analysts and officials would do well to accept this posture. At the same time, China is not pursuing, and is hardly capable of pursuing, a policy of expansionism of the kind a rising Germany did in the late 19th and early 20th centuries or as Japan did before World War II. This is critical for both Western and Asian hyper-realists to acknowledge. Comparing China's ascendancy to Germany or Japan only serves to hyper-sensationalize and make manifest through policy changes and reorientations. Scholars and policymakers would do well to move away from emphasizing the confrontational nature of US–China relations.

One final point to add here about Southeast Asia's future between the US and China is the need for analysts to focus on national trends and outlook from individual Southeast Asian states, and not merely understand the region as a monolith, or 'focus selectively on a few states that tend to align with the US—as though they represent the Southeast Asian view.' In a track 1.5 workshop held in June 2023 at Kuala Lumpur, ASEAN states expressed varying priorities and differing strategies for how to respond to the US and China's increasing rivalry. For example, 'some states like Vietnam and Malaysia feel greater pressure from a Sino-American competition and have intensified their pursuit of "active" and "dynamic" neutrality. Other states, like Cambodia see major power competition as an opportunity to diversify relations and choice.'[314]

The varying stances of Southeast Asian states towards China is particularly evident in the deals that got finalized during the 50th ASEAN-Japan Friendship and Cooperation summit that took place in December 2023. On the sidelines of the summit, Japan stepped up its bilateral security ties with several ASEAN states, like Malaysia, Indonesia, Philippines, and Vietnam, while acknowledging that 'many countries are reluctant to choose sides' between Japan and China and that Japan is 'mindful of the situation and not trying to get them to choose sides.'[315]

ASEAN and 'Europe's Past'

Another reason why ASEAN's external situation is not as stark as that portrayed by the pessimists is the gross misreading of the 'Europe's Past, Asia's Future' argument, which is taken seriously by pundits and the media, like *The Economist* through an abuse of historical parallels and superficial analogical reasoning. There is little reason to accept the view that the rise of China is taking place in an environment that is similar to what existed in Europe after the unification of Germany in the late 19th century. Any comparison between Asia now and Europe before World War I shows more differences than similarities. It is far from clear that China is a revisionist power, a category that assumes that the existing international system denies it opportunities and privileges that it needs to become a global power. In reality, China is on its way to becoming a global player within the existing international system. This does not mean it will not seek changes to that system, but it seems China is challenging those aspects of the system—especially the leadership and direction of global institutions—that are almost universally accepted as unfairly advantageous to the West and are becoming increasingly anachronistic. Moreover, China is far from being alone in challenging them. Others, including democratic India, Brazil, Russia, and South Africa, seek the same changes. In fact, China has more reasons to keep the status quo as a sitting permanent member of the UN Security Council, a position it routinely uses to shape the international system to its advantage, say by denying proposals that seek to terminate, expand or modify the Security Council permanent membership.

Moreover, European multipolarity before the world wars was not accompanied by deep and wide-ranging economic interdependence. Interdependence—including the much-vaunted interdependence between Germany and the UK—was relatively thin and was based primarily on trade. In contrast, the most crucial element of economic interdependence in Asia is not trade, but transnational production networks, which did not exist in pre-war Europe. ASEAN is an integral part of those production networks,[316] initially triggered by Japan in the 1980s, and now sustained by China. Add finance and investment to the picture, and it becomes clear that economic interdependence in Asia and the Asia-Pacific (involving the US) increases the costs of war to a much greater degree than it was in Europe's 'past'.[317] If anything, Asia increasingly resembles Europe's present. Its financial and production networks are no less significant, and about 55 per cent of total trade is intra-Asian, compared to about 65 per cent for EU's internal trade, even though Asia does not have anything close to the extensive bureaucratic apparatus of the EU. This is a form of regionalization that deserves to be recognized on its own terms, rather than on the basis of the increasingly questionable EU-centric criteria.

Although ASEAN is often faulted for its low levels of intra-ASEAN trade, a situation that might not change much despite the realization of the ASEAN Economic Community in the near future, this is offset by the fact that ASEAN is an integral part of East Asian trade, production, and financial interdependence, which has only grown more extensive with the gradual entry of India. This form of interdependence is not only non-ideological, but it is also the most inclusive regional interdependence in the world today, in contrast to Europe's interdependence, which does not really cover Russia.

Another reason for the farcical 'Europe's past' analogy is that European multipolarity was also established and nourished by colonialism. This not only caused conflict among the powers, contributing to Germany's rejection of the status quo as a latecomer to the colonial game, but also undercut the benefits of economic interdependence. Asian powers today are *not* colonial powers. Competition for energy and other resources do not amount to colonial competition. Not only are such resources available in the market, but the costs of going to war to obtain them surely outweigh the benefits in today's increasingly destructive mode of warfare. Although the Chinese economy has diverted some investment away from ASEAN and Chinese manufactured goods pose a threat to ASEAN's industries in some sectors, this is a far cry from a neocolonial situation. ASEAN's openness to the economies of all outside players and to market- and multinational-driven industrialization offsets any such prospect of Chinese colonization or competition among the great powers such as China, Japan, the US, EU, and India for ASEAN resources and markets. This means that no one player has the capacity or advantage to gain political dominance in the region.

Not only economic interdependence, but regional economic and security institutions in Asia are also more inclusive than Europe's. There is no NATO in Asia, a real blessing in geopolitical terms. China is a member of all East Asian and Asia-Pacific regional bodies, in contrast to Russia's exclusion from NATO and the EU. Asian regional institutions are often disparaged as 'talk shops', and some of that criticism is well-deserved. There is no question that ASEAN needs to shift gear from dialogue to action and adopt a more problem-solving approach. It needs to overcome the persisting 'non-intervention' mindset of its members by emulating not the EU (the wrong role model) but the African Union (AU), especially when it comes to collective peacekeeping. ASEAN has more resources but less willpower to do regional peacekeeping than the AU, so it should achieve more success than the AU if it garners the requisite political will.

But Asia's regional institutions are also not merely 'talk shops'. They have produced results. One singular misconception about Asian regional institutions is that they are 'led' by ASEAN. ASEAN only has itself to blame for propagating this unhelpful myth. Its role is better described as a hub and agenda-setter, a convening power with normative and social leadership. Lacking structural power (the ability to compel or coerce) and material resources, ASEAN has used socialization and persuasion to engage not only other Southeast Asian and East Asian countries, but *all* the great powers of the current international order. What might be Asia's security order today had there been no ASEAN? At the very least, there would be a lot less opportunity for dialogue and diplomatic interactions among the major powers with an interest in Asia, and the prospects for a pre-emptive US containment of China would have been greater. ASEAN leaders, the late Lee Kuan Yew in particular, strongly discouraged the US from taking such a course, emphasizing the region's role in settling the region's affairs. Other contributions of ASEAN include keeping intra-Southeast Asian conflicts at a relatively low level,[318] and providing Cambodia, Vietnam, and later, Myanmar, a readymade forum to help them return to the international system after decades of self-destructive isolation. Anyone who says these developments were made possible only because of sanctions by the Western countries has a poor understanding of Southeast Asian history and politics.

In short, the Asian strategic environment is not just about a power shift, but also a paradigm shift.[319] In the aftermath of World War II, Asia's security environment was marked by economic nationalism and autarky (import-substitution), security bilateralism (America's 'hub-and-spoke' alliances), and political authoritarianism. Asia today is marked by an unmistakable economic liberalism and interdependence, a much greater degree of security multilateralism, and democratic politics (the last one constraining China's capacity for regional hegemony through ideology). What is more, the emergence of these trends predates Chinese assertiveness. Instead of being shaped by China and great power politics, as Mearsheimer and other traditionalists argue, Asia's changing regional environment is more likely to shape Chinese and great power behaviour.

Chapter 7

A Region in Crisis

As Southeast Asia neared the end of the second decade of the 21st century, it was facing major challenges to its political, strategic, and economic fabric. Some of these, such as the rise and growing assertiveness of China, had been anticipated over a decade ago. Others, such as the end of the US-centred 'unipolar moment', the rise of populism around the world, including in the West, the backlash against globalization, and the election of a rabidly anti-internationalist presidential regime in the US, were not. While the relative decline of the US as a superpower has been talked about before, the order that the US built, the Liberal World Order, seemed robust and even expansive under the Obama-Hillary Clinton foreign policy leadership that was firmly in place at the onset of the 2010s. Few had foreseen how fast and far that order would unravel until the 2016 US presidential elections.[320]

Entering the 2020s, Southeast Asia as a region, and ASEAN as the main regional organization, faced uncertainties about the future from external and intra-regional dynamics. These include the continuing contest over and militarization of the South China Sea dispute, domestic political uncertainties in member states, non-traditional security challenges like a global pandemic, environmental degradation, economic uncertainty triggered by the US–China trade dispute, and the slowing of economic globalization. Southeast Asia is also deeply affected by the ongoing global power shift and other changes associated with a transition from the unipolar US-dominated international order to a more uncertain period.

A House Divided?

The overall state of intra-ASEAN relations appears generally stable, however, there are fissures in bilateral relations. For example, Singapore–Malaysia relations were strained by the return of Mahathir Mohamad as Prime Minister of Malaysia, whose first term as Malaysian Prime Minister was marked by a hardline approach towards Singapore. Issues straining the bilateral ties include his efforts to scrap the high-speed railway project between the two countries and tensions over air space rights and maritime boundary demarcation in the Johor Straits.[321] But these and other intra-ASEAN disputes can be contained, as can other ongoing bilateral disputes such as the Thai–Cambodia conflict over the Preah Vihear temple.

The intra-ASEAN military dynamics remain fluid. While doubling their total defence spending over the last decade and a half (up to early 2018) in absolute terms, the ASEAN member countries have more or less kept their spending unchanged as a percentage of their total GDP.[322] They continue to buy a range of weapon systems, but this is in many cases, such as for Philippines and Indonesia, due to the need to modernize their hopelessly obsolete systems. Rather than outright intra-ASEAN competition, a range of other factors are influencing the defence acquisitions by ASEAN states, such as a shift from their historic counter-insurgency focus, concern over China's military build-up, and shared threats such as terrorism and piracy. Hence there is little evidence of an intra-ASEAN arms race destabilizing the region.

ASEAN has been, and will likely remain, a 'nascent security community', a group of states which have developed habits of peaceful cooperation and learnt to resolve their disputes without outright war. The key test for a security community is not the absence of conflict, as some mistakenly assume, but the reluctance of members to resolve those conflicts by resorting to deliberate and direct use of military force. In this sense, barring unforeseen circumstances, ASEAN's trajectory is unlikely to change.

Southeast Asia's own internal situation is a cause for concern, however. First, ASEAN is a much bigger entity now than when it was established in 1967. Membership expanded in the 1990s to bring in Vietnam, Laos, Myanmar, and Cambodia, with East Timor likely to become the eleventh member. Second, ASEAN's functions have also expanded significantly. In its early days, ASEAN's role was mainly political and security-oriented (although not in the military sense), expressed in the form of initiatives like the proposal for a Zone of Peace, Freedom, and Neutrality (ZOPFAN) in Southeast Asia. While economic development was a shared goal, trade liberalization, the staple of regional organizations everywhere, did not enter its agenda until the late 1970s, and even then, in a rather limited sense. ASEAN today deals with a whole range of issues. Economic cooperation has expanded from the idea of an ASEAN FTA to a much more comprehensive ASEAN Economic Community, which technically enters into force later this year. While it continues to reject turning itself into a military alliance, ASEAN militaries cooperate, bilaterally and multilaterally, on intelligence-sharing, counterterrorism, and maritime security. Through initiatives like the ASEAN Political-Security Community and ASEAN Socio-Cultural Community, ASEAN also deals with a range of transnational issues, like environmental degradation, air pollution, pandemic preparedness, energy security, food security, migration and people-smuggling, drug-trafficking, human rights, and disaster management.

ASEAN no longer confines itself to only addressing and managing security issues in Southeast Asia. By helping to create and anchor wider Asia-Pacific institutions such as the ARF, and the EAS and involving itself centrally in APEC, ASEAN today is a much larger regional and even a global actor, with varied consequences. But these extensions impose burdens with which even a more resource-rich regional body can barely cope. ASEAN's institutional machinery is hopelessly out of capacity in dealing with its wider responsibilities. An expanded membership means greater disagreements and quarrels, especially involving latecomers to the ASEAN Way. The most serious breakdowns of consensus and unity have involved new members. Cambodia, as ASEAN's chair, disastrously refused to issue a joint ASEAN Communique in 2012 to please China, rejecting the position of fellow members, Philippines and Vietnam, on the South China Sea dispute. Another instance is Myanmar, whose entry in 1995 brought ASEAN a great deal of international embarrassment and whose handling of the Rohingya issue had a similar effect. The entry of Vietnam, Laos, and Myanmar brings ASEAN closer to China physically. Vietnamese membership means that ASEAN is embroiled deeper into the South China Sea conflict with China, implying that national security issues are likely to dominate the regional security agenda.

Yet another challenge to ASEAN in the latter half of the 2010s was the uncertain leadership of Indonesia. The Jokowi government after entering office in 2014 initially downgraded Indonesia's leadership role in ASEAN, at least in comparison to its predecessor, Yudhoyono's involvement. ASEAN was moved from being *the* cornerstone of Indonesian foreign policy to being *a* cornerstone.[323] ASEAN could ill-afford to lose a proactive Indonesian role. Not only is Indonesia the most populous nation and the region's largest economy, it is also ASEAN's only G-20 member and has a record of mediation and good offices in both intra-ASEAN and extra-ASEAN conflicts (the latter including the South China Sea). Indonesia is also a thought leader; the idea of an ASEAN Security Community, which morphed into the ASEAN Political-Security Community today, came from Jakarta. Its ability to combine democracy, development, stability, and peaceful Islam is a singular achievement in the world today, and thus a key element of ASEAN's normative pull before the international community. Thankfully, towards the end of his term, especially in 2023 when Indonesia assumed the role of ASEAN Chair, Jokowi had strengthened its involvement in ASEAN. It remains to be seen if his successor would maintain a high level of commitment to ASEAN which would be a critical factor in sustaining ASEAN centrality.

In dealing with great power rivalry, ASEAN's big advantage was and remains that there is currently no alternative to ASEAN's convening power in the region. The great powers of the Asia-Pacific, namely China, Japan, India, and the US, are not capable of leading Asian regional institutions because of mutual mistrust and a lack of legitimacy, even for countries such as Japan and India.[324] Renewed great power competition does not undermine but supports ASEAN's centrality and indispensability.

But ASEAN cannot take full advantage of this situation if it becomes a house divided against itself, if the domestic politics in key member states detract from their engagement in ASEAN, and if the organization suffers from a lack of leadership. To revitalize itself, ASEAN should perhaps do what a large corporation facing declining competitiveness and profitability does: downsize. Not in terms of its membership, or its staff, which are small anyway, but in terms of issue areas. This does not mean removing itself from the South China Sea issue, as suggested by Cambodia, which forgets that there might not be an independent Cambodia today had ASEAN not engaged in conflicts outside of its membership. (Neither Cambodia nor Vietnam were ASEAN members when the latter occupied the former.) Instead, ASEAN should focus more on issues within Southeast Asia and its immediate environment, and forget about the Korean Peninsula, the Taiwan Strait, and the India–Pakistan conflicts. These are now discussed through the ARF and EAS, but as the convener and agenda-setter, ASEAN should give more focused attention to the South China Sea dispute, no matter what China says. On transnational and global challenges, ASEAN should share more responsibilities with middle powers, such as South Korea, Australia, and Canada.

ASEAN's global membership structure does help it to pursue global and transnational issues and share or delegate leadership to others, audit its commitments, drop less urgent issue-areas and focus selectively on the more important and urgent items. It should make greater use of global and interregional institutions (such as the Asia-Europe Meeting, the various UN bodies, and the G-20 through Indonesia) to build cooperation in areas that cover but go beyond Southeast Asia, rather than taking them on directly. This would include climate change, health issues, terrorism, and disaster management. Moreover, ASEAN should seek rationalization of the purposes and functions of regional bodies in which it participates. There is overlap in the ARF, APEC, ASEAN + 3, EAS, and ASEAN's Post-Ministerial Meetings (ASEAN-PMC). Creating a division of labour and building better synergy among them would reduce ASEAN's burden. The body should cut the number of meetings attended by its secretariat staff by a third from over 1,000 per year now, and better train and deploy expanded core staff, selectively and more purposefully. It should use a professional international agency to handle the recruitment of its core secretariat staff and eliminate political manipulation while enhancing professionalization.

ASEAN's marginalization—even death—from changing great power behaviour has been predicted a few times before, and each time it was proven to be exaggerated. This was the case when the United States withdrew from Vietnam in 1975, allowing China and the Soviet Union to expand their influence.

The conflict between China and Soviet-ally Vietnam over the latter's invasion of Cambodia in December 1979 caused fears of a 'new Cold War' in Southeast Asia. The end of the Cold War led analysts to predict a scramble among China, Japan, and India to fill the resulting 'power vacuum', especially in view of the end to Russia's naval presence in Vietnam and the removal of American military bases from the Philippines. On each occasion, ASEAN emerged stronger, not only because these prophecies proved to be exaggerated, but also because ASEAN stepped up its act to cope with the new strategic developments. The Bali Summit in 1976, the decade of persistent diplomacy to end the Cambodia conflict through the 1980s, and the launch of multilateral dialogues in the early 1990s, are examples of responses to changing great power politics. If ASEAN fails to adjust course now, it might not be so lucky this time.

Economic Challenges

Before COVID-19, Southeast Asia's economic outlook looked positive. This changed as the pandemic swept the region and the world, with many countries suffering a dramatically reduced GDP. But Southeast Asia was not the only place to take the hit. The impact of the COVID-19 pandemic resulted in a fivefold decline in ASEAN's GDP in comparison to its growth at the start of the new millennium.[325] Southeast Asia made a turnaround as the pandemic eased with a growth rate of 5.2 per cent.[326] But a key lesson here is that, as in the past, economic growth in Southeast Asia will remain critically dependent on external factors beyond the capacity of the regional countries.[327] For example, in recent years, the recurrent COVID-related lockdowns in China, Russia's invasion of Ukraine, and a general slowdown in global economic outlook have all negatively affected the region's economic growth. [328]

To be sure, the impact of the external shocks could be mitigated by the region's generally good economic fundamentals, increased intra-ASEAN trade, growing investment under the ASEAN economic community, renewed growth of the tourism sector, and strong domestic demand. An end to the US–China trade conflict would also help.[329] Some Southeast Asian countries, especially Vietnam, have benefitted from the adjustments to global supply chains that got triggered by the US–China trade war. As American and other multinational companies affected by higher US tariffs on Chinese imports into the US consider relocating their manufacturing elsewhere, they look to Southeast Asian countries.[330] On the other hand, the persistence of the US–China trade war and a potentially ramped up geopolitical conflict between the two, along with growing antipathy towards globalization in the West, might dampen Southeast Asia's economic prospects. As Derwin Pereira, a regional consultant, puts it,

> Economically, Southeast Asia is an integral part of global value chains of production in which the economic superpowers— the US, China, the European Union, Japan and India— occupy nodal positions. Without those value chains, the Association of Southeast Asian Nations would lose its catalytic role in the global economy. Deglobalization, brought about by the Sino-American trade war, would hurt the superpowers but it would be more ominous for ASEAN, whose regional rationale is founded on its global relevance. Diminishing interdependence and integration would undermine that rationale.[331]

Southeast Asia is a major hub for global trade, but the trade growth in the region has declined (as it did globally since the 2000s) and trade may no longer be a growth driver for the region. At the same time, intra-regional linkages cannot compensate for it. This also creates new vulnerabilities for the region. Southeast Asia has bought some immunity to adverse external economic forces by developing its own ASEAN Economic Community, which has benefitted the least developed members of ASEAN, even if it is on slow realization (relative to the formal timetable). Also helpful to ASEAN is greater intra-Asian trade integration through the Regional Comprehensive Economic Partnership (RCEP), agreed to in Bangkok in November 2019.[332] But the overall volume of intra-ASEAN trade remains less than a quarter of ASEAN's total trade.

Another major challenge to Southeast Asia's economic future is the Middle-Income Trap (MIT). The MIT refers to a situation in which a country after reaching a per capita income level of between $10,000 and $15,000, stagnates, as it loses its initial advantages that led to high growth, like abundant cheap labour, high investment rates, and low wage competitors. Overcoming the trap requires substantial investment in human capital and innovative technological and managerial resources. The World Bank estimates that in 1960, only 13 out of 101 middle-income economies escaped the trap and made the transition to high-income economies by 2008.[333]

Southeast Asia is not immune to MIT. Malaysia is already in this trap, and three other countries, namely Indonesia, Thailand, and the Philippines, risk falling into it as their income approaches the $10,000 level. A study of these four ASEAN countries found that they failed to undertake successful industrial upgrading after recovering from the Asian financial crisis in 1997/1998, thereby reducing their resource-export dependency like the policies pursued by Japan, South Korea, Singapore, Taiwan, and Hong Kong. Instead, their resource export dependence might have increased due to the strong recovery of primary commodity prices after the 1997 financial crisis, which tempted them to divert more investment from the manufacturing sector to primary industries. Another factor behind their failure to move up the industrial chain to avoid the MIT could be their lack of domestic multinational companies in the manufacturing sector, which are essential for manufacturing and exporting parts and components to international multinational corporations (MNCs).[334] Unless this situation is mitigated, the MIT could become a real and substantial threat to the future economic progress of Southeast Asia, especially the ASEAN-4. The ASEAN-4 seem to be aware of the MIT and are ostensibly willing to undertake measures to avoid it.[335] Mahendra Siregar, the current Indonesian ambassador to the US and the former chair of the Indonesian Investment Coordinating Board (BKPM), insisted to me in an interview that the middle-income trap is not an option for Indonesia. But the task is not easy. The less developed of the ASEAN-4, Indonesia and Philippines, need to balance growth with equity (through subsidies and social protection) given their large populations of poor people. Other factors that undercut policy measures taken to avoid the MIT include political instability (as has engulfed Thailand from 2014 to now), and economic corruption and mismanagement (as in Malaysia under the Najib government till 2018).

COVID's Impact

The experience of COVID-19 not only showed Southeast Asia's vulnerability to transnational threats, but also the varying conditions and capabilities among the regional nations in responding to them. The effects of the pandemic on Southeast Asian countries depended on individual states' economic resilience and health infrastructure capacities. For example, Indonesia and Philippines were the hardest hit countries in terms of reported fatalities while Singapore was the least. National responses to COVID-19 in Southeast Asia varied in terms of effectiveness. Regional cooperation through ASEAN was not very substantial, despite the region's prior experiences with pandemics like Avian flu and SARS, and it mostly concerned information-sharing and monitoring. ASEAN countries, like most others, closed their borders to each other as well as to the outside world. Overall, ASEAN's response to COVID-19, as a regional organization, was not particularly noteworthy. Ralph Cossa, an American expert on ASEAN, contended, perhaps with a dose of overstatement that, 'ASEAN has been a useful "club" with some notable economic achievements over the years, but it has offered nothing in this particular crisis. There has been no "ASEAN response" to the pandemic; each country has acted on its own.'[336]

COVID-19 did not significantly reduce support in Southeast Asia for globalization. But this also means the region's economic prospects are too closely tied to the global economy and economic trends in the wider Asian region. Southeast Asia is a subset of Asia, and Asia's integral place in globalization makes it especially vulnerable to economic disruptions such as that caused by COVID-19. And the impact of crisis-induced economic decline on Southeast Asia and Asia in general can hardly be overestimated. Decades of robust economic growth allowed Asian governments to reduce poverty, promote domestic stability, and improve regional security by creating a web of interdependence. While initially based on trade, economic growth and interdependence in Asia became broader with accelerating investment, financial flows, regional production networks, and variegated supply chains, whereby a single product, be it a car, a computer, or a smartphone, is manufactured across several national jurisdictions. Japan was the key early driver of these networks, but slowly and inexorably, China became the centre of Asia's regional economy.

One aspect of this vulnerability to the vagaries of globalization has to do with regional security. Decades of economic growth and globalization has led to growing interdependence among regional countries. This has contributed to greater regional security. Nobody argued that economic interdependence alone would prevent war, but there is little question that it makes war so costly that countries are discouraged from going to war except as a very last resort. That logic still holds, but it is becoming increasingly fragile. The US–China trade war has already dealt a blow to US–China interdependence. But here COVID-19 might have a major impact, as countries learn the vulnerability created by supply chain disruptions triggered by the pandemic. To add to this, the US under Trump blasted the idea of production networks, calling it a 'crazy idea' and vowed to make the US more self-reliant in vital products.[337]

It will take more time and much more effort to break China's position in regional supply chains and to find alternatives. Not only did China have a head start, but its combination of infrastructure, skilled labour, and established networks in the region through the Chinese diaspora, are not easily replicated by other Asian nations, such as Vietnam or India. Also, to avoid US tariffs, China is already moving some of its production capacity to Southeast Asia.

An Ecological Crisis

Among non-traditional security challenges in Southeast Asia, ecological security deserves serious consideration. Southeast Asia could be one of the worst affected regions in terms of environmental disasters brought on by deforestation and climate change. The region 'has the highest rates of deforestation of any major tropical region, followed by Latin America and Africa.'[338] A recent calculation by a multinational research team estimated that 'Southeast Asia lost 82,000 square kilometres (31,700 square miles) of forest to croplands between 2000 and 2014.'[339] The ADB estimates that unmitigated climate change could cause an 11 per cent drop in Southeast Asia's GDP by the end of the 21st century.[340] Key sectors affected would be agriculture, tourism, and fishing. Southeast Asia has also experienced an average increase in temperature every year since 1960. The Global Climate Risk Index compiled by Germanwatch lists Vietnam, Myanmar, Philippines, and Thailand among the ten countries in the world most affected by climate change.[341] Vietnam, which has been recognized for its high growth potential, has been ranked by the World Bank 'as one of five countries most likely to be affected by climate change'.[342]

Environmental degradation caused by deforestation and commercial plantation farming has been a major factor behind the recurring air pollution (haze) affecting Indonesia, Malaysia, and Singapore, most recently in 2019.[343] The World Bank estimated the economic costs to Indonesia of the 2015 haze at more than $16 billion, which equals to about 1.8 per cent of Indonesia's GDP.[344] Apart from heavy economic costs, the haze has also caused political tensions among the neighbours.

Another non-traditional challenge to Southeast Asian regional stability concerns demographics and technology. Sixty per cent of ASEAN's 630 million population is under thirty-five years old.[345] Some estimates predict a declining population in ASEAN by 2050 due to declining birth rates, hinting that a 'demographic dividend that helped drive ASEAN's strong economic growth from at least the 1990s' may be coming to an end.[346] The total fertility rate (the number of children that women give birth to in their lifetime) of Singapore, Thailand, Malaysia, and Vietnam is already below 2.1, the level necessary to keep a population stable.[347] Many Southeast Asian countries are experiencing decline in working age population growth, with Singapore and Malaysia being the worst affected. This hints at labour supply problems that have the potential to hamper economic growth.[348] Yet the presence of migrant workers and the reliance on imported labour is becoming an increasingly sensitive and controversial issue, even for Singapore, which has traditionally been open to immigration. This portends problems for the region's economic growth and political stability.

One potential solution to ASEAN's demographic challenge is popularization of digital technologies. It has been said that 'ASEAN may be able to use digitalization to reduce the burden of the aging society that it is facing. ASEAN countries are particularly sensitive to digitalization and are keen to develop startups that are competitive in terms of digital technology.'[349] But the rapid development of technology may create new challenges for ASEAN, especially from what has been called the Fourth Industrial Revolution, which 'refers to a set of highly disruptive technologies, such as artificial intelligence (AI), robotics, blockchain, and 3D printing, that are transforming social, economic, and political systems and putting huge pressure on leaders and policy-makers to respond.'[350] Southeast Asia has one of the world's fastest growing population of internet users with Brunei having the highest internet penetration rate at over 119 per cent, attributable to consumers having multiple internet subscriptions simultaneously.[351] But disparities are high among ASEAN members when it comes to technology adoption. The poorer Southeast Asian countries, especially Vietnam, Cambodia, and Laos, acutely face the need to upgrade their manufacturing technology to move up the supply chain or face the reversal of the economic growth they enjoyed in recent years.

With a relatively young population, Southeast Asia is in a good position to take advantage of the Fourth Industrial Revolution. The digital economy in ASEAN is projected to grow to $200 billion by 2025.[352] But, given intra-regional disparities, taking advantage of the fourth industrial revolution will depend critically on regional cooperation.

Chapter 8

Demons and Angels: The Future of Southeast Asia

The Demons Are Rising

Southeast Asia is not new to intensified great-power rivalry. But the previous major episode of military confrontation—the Cold War from 1950s to 1990s—actually contributed in no small way to the rise of Asia, including Southeast Asia. In its fight against Soviet- and Chinese-inspired communism, the US extended a security umbrella over the pro-Western nations and the sea lanes in the region. The Cold War also stimulated common purpose and unity among nations—Indonesia, Malaysia, Singapore, Thailand, and Philippines—due to their fear of being entangled into great-power intervention. This led to the creation and consolidation of ASEAN. Moreover, investments from Japan, a US ally and Asia's fastest rising economy in the 80s, helped the industrialization of several Southeast Asian countries. The resulting rapid economic growth created greater domestic and regional stability.

But the tide is turning now. The past few years have been especially challenging for Asia. China has started flexing its growing military and economic muscles in the region. The US has broken its engagement with China. America and China have moved from being reluctant partners to outright rivals. This has drawn in other powers, like Japan, India, Russia, and Australia, and has raised the prospects of a new Cold War in Asia. Southeast Asian states are under pressure to choose sides in this contest. At the same time, the COVID-19 pandemic, and the 'de-globalization' process set in motion by the 2008 global financial crisis, cloud the region's economic and security prospects.

From Trade to Tribute?

China's spectacular rise casts a profound shadow over Southeast Asia's future. Will China revive a former tributary relationship over the region and establish a regional hegemony? Answering this requires a careful look at China's territorial claims in the South China Sea, its military build-up, its economic policy, especially the Belt and Road Initiative, and its soft power in Southeast Asia. Chinese foreign policy especially under Xi Jinping has been far more assertive than that espoused by any of his predecessors. Deng Xiaoping's cautious approach has been abandoned. But does it mean China is now willing and able to impose a sphere of influence over the region, to the exclusion of other major powers? In answering this question, this chapter will look at some of the limitations of Chinese power, including its own economic and military strength, its own policy of 'peaceful rise', and its calculations about how far it should go to turn the region into a Chinese dependency. An escalation of the South China Sea dispute due to a dramatic increase in China's militarization of the islands, and other actions such as active challenge to the US Freedom of Navigation Operations and its declaration of an Air Defence Identification Zone over South China Sea could pose a severe threat to Southeast Asia's security outlook.

To worsen matters, China's changing attitude towards ASEAN and other multilateral institutions in Asia challenge

Southeast Asia's resilience. While ostensibly committed to this principle, some of China's policies affect ASEAN's unity. China's cultivation of relations on a primarily bilateral basis, such as through its Belt and Road Initiative is one such example. Also, there is no common ASEAN position on the BRI, much to China's delight, as it prefers bilateral interactions over multilateral relations. China's South China Sea approach has also divided ASEAN, with Cambodia and Philippines under Rodrigo Duterte aligning their countries with China and making it harder for ASEAN to develop a common stand towards China. This in turn has undermined intra-ASEAN cohesion, without which ASEAN can hardly maintain its 'driver's seat' role in the regional architecture.

Alone without America?

When the Sino-centric model was at its peak, the US did not exist as a global power or even as a nation (except during the late Qing period). Its emergence as a dominant power since the end of World War II (or a little earlier) is one of the most important challenges to any revival of Chinese centrality. But when it comes to the US, a major question about Asia's future is whether the US has 'staying power' in the region. Does it have the political will and military wherewithal to counter Chinese advances and protect its own interests? Some Asian and Western experts argue that without US military presence, Asia would not have achieved the degree of stability and development it has enjoyed since the end of Vietnam War. This claim needs to be seriously questioned. Was Asia's stability and growth really due to America's presence or was it due to other factors, such as policies undertaken by regional governments? Another perennial question is whether the US has staying power in the region. This depends on its own domestic politics and consideration of its strategic interests, which keep changing with different US administrations, especially under the most recent three Presidents—Obama, Trump, and Biden.

Flashpoints and Fears

The US–China rivalry is not the only or even the most far-reaching source of insecurity in Southeast Asia. There are other sources, like domestic strife, ethnic rivalries, separatist movements, and to some extent, radicalism. Moreover, not all flashpoints of interstate conflicts in Asia are the product of the US–China rivalry or likely to be shaped by it. Their sources of outbreak and potential for escalation vary widely. For example, the India–Pakistan rivalry is very different from the conflicts in the South China Sea, Taiwan Straits, or the Korean Peninsula, when it comes to the impact of the Sino-US conflict in shaping their outcomes.

The South China Sea conflict is widely seen as one of Asia's most likely flashpoints of war, with some speculating that it might trigger World War III. But is this hype or justified fear? To be sure, the prospects for China and ASEAN coming to an accommodation and compromise might seem to have receded with China's creation of artificial territory in the seas, despite efforts by ASEAN and China to find a diplomatic solution, and with the growing involvement of US and other powers in the area. But that does not make the South China Sea conflict the scene of a major conflagration. While the South China Sea may represent one of the biggest tests of Chinese dominance in the region, it is not the region's worst nightmare. Ironically, in other regional conflicts, where outright armed conflict is likely to be far more disruptive and destructive, prospects for war remain less likely, due to balance of power projection capabilities between the US and China (including China's growing A2AD ability) and nuclear deterrence.

Democrats and Dictators

Anti-military and pro-democracy protests in Myanmar after the 2021 coup

In the 1980s and 1990s, Southeast Asian countries like Indonesia, Malaysia, Thailand, and Singapore avoided political liberalization owing to their economic 'performance'. They also claimed that economic growth under authoritarian rule improved domestic stability. But three of the four, Indonesia, Thailand, and Malaysia, have since experienced instability. Another regional laggard, Myanmar, routinely experiences instability and witnessed its democratic experiment collapse with the 2021 coup. Hence, the argument that economic development alone can ensure stability is questionable. At the same time, Indonesia after Suharto has proven that there may be a virtuous cycle between democracy, economic development, and stability/security; that the three can indeed go hand in hand. Yet, questions about Southeast Asia's political future remain. Can Southeast Asian countries manage their political stability without democratization? Can they adopt the Chinese and Vietnamese models of ensuring economic growth while staying authoritarian? Or does the region's long-term stability and development depend on political liberalization and more democracy? In conjunction with this, failure to ensure regime legitimacy through democratic politics may also contribute to growing radicalization resulting in major terrorist attacks such as the Bali Bombings of 2002. This could aggravate the regional and global terrorist threat posed by radical extremism.

An Uncertain Future

Southeast Asia's economic outlook is clouded by the US–China trade war and the effects of the COVID-19 pandemic. Despite the region's generally good economic fundamentals, and the possibility that Southeast Asia may benefit from the adjustments to global supply chains triggered by the trade war, the persistence of the Sino-American economic and geopolitical conflict, along with growing antipathy towards globalization in the West, casts a shadow over the region's economic future.

There is also the possibility of a major financial crisis like the 1997 Asian financial crisis that originated in Southeast Asia, which could cause widespread social and political upheaval (like the fall of Suharto in Indonesia in 1998). While no one can make definitive predictions, policymakers should be prudent to take them into serious consideration when assessing and preparing for the future.

When Elephants Fight

Back in the 1950s and 60s, Southeast Asia was viewed by Western geopolitical experts as the 'Balkans of the Orient' and a 'region of revolt'. Its newly independent states were seen as 'dominos' that were about to fall in the tide of Soviet- and Chinese-backed communist movements. By the 1980s, however, perceptions had changed. Southeast Asia had become part of East Asia's 'economic miracle' and the 'Asian century'.

ASEAN's past achievements have been impressive, but it now faces critical challenges. These challenges include intra-ASEAN disputes, differences over how to deal with the Sino-US competition and competing approaches to regional cooperation that are promoted by the US and China. Also, the ASEAN Way of consensus and non-interference, and the idea of ASEAN's centrality may be becoming inadequate in dealing with new threats and challenges, which may lead to ASEAN's obsolescence.

These developments have the potential to make Southeast Asia a pawn in the hands of the great powers, while simultaneously destroying the region as a distinct idea. Amidst these developments, as the fate of the region looks increasingly uncertain, the question arises: has Southeast Asia passed its 'use-by-date'?

ASEAN's commitment to developing its three communities, namely the ASEAN Economic Community, the ASEAN Political-Security Community, and the ASEAN Socio-Cultural Community, is critical to its future. Over the past few years, ASEAN has made a good deal of progress in developing capacity for cooperation against terrorism, piracy and disaster relief, but has lagged in the areas of human rights (which is developed through institutions such as the ASEAN Inter-Governmental Commission on Human Rights- a rather weak and ineffectual body) and refugee protection. ASEAN's response to the Rohingya crisis did show divisions over human rights, but in reality, it reflected the potency of domestic forces. Malaysia's (under the Najib government) strident criticism of Myanmar was partly intended to burnish his Islamic credentials and divert attention from his domestic troubles. But ASEAN needs to make more progress in regional cooperation to gain the support of the region's people. In this context, the *State of Southeast Asia Survey* found that:

The main concern about ASEAN is the perception that ASEAN has not 'delivered' for its 650 million population. Nearly three quarters of the respondents (72.6 per cent) express their disappointment that 'the tangible benefits of ASEAN are not felt.' . . . Rounding off the top three concerns is the fear that 'ASEAN is becoming the arena for major power competition' (62 per cent) and ASEAN's inability to 'cope with fluid political and economic developments' (61.9 per cent).[353]

A Broken Mirror?

A shared identity is an important factor in ensuring Southeast Asia's stability and cooperation. If the international order of a region is generated purely by a balance of power system, such stability is likely to be fragile and unstainable in the long-term. Moreover, regional identity is key to building the ASEAN community, including its economic, socio-cultural, or political-security communities. At the same time, regional identity is subject to challenge and change due to changing political, strategic, and economic currents in the region and beyond.[354]

The sense of an ASEAN identity has grown in keeping with ASEAN's progress in developing the three aforementioned regional communities. A survey published in 2017 by the Jakarta-based Economic Research Institute for ASEAN and East Asia (ERIA) found that 'awareness of ASEAN increased significantly after 2014.' More importantly, the survey revealed that 'more than three-fourths of all respondents felt 'moderately' to 'very much' as ASEAN citizens. Combined with those who indicated feeling 'somewhat' as ASEAN citizens, a sense of ASEAN belongingness was shared by virtually all the respondents. To be sure, much of this identity is due to the publicity surrounding the ASEAN Economic Community (which came into force in 2015), as well as the natural effect of geographic proximity. But it is significant that for a regional organization, which unlike the European Union has no program for a common citizenship, only 3 per cent of the survey respondents said they did not feel like they were ASEAN citizens.'[355]

Apart from its need to strengthen regional cooperation, ASEAN is also facing challenges to its 'centrality' in the regional cooperation agenda. China's pursuit of bilateralism has divided ASEAN, with Cambodia and Philippines (under Duterte at least) showing greater deference to Beijing in return for aid and diplomatic cover. As such, for ASEAN to remain relevant and survive, it must prioritize the identity-making and identity-preserving regional agendas.

From Far East to the Indo-Pacific

Another challenge to Southeast Asia comes from the Indo-Pacific concept. This is a recent construct. It emerged as a way of linking the Indian and Pacific Oceans and giving greater recognition to the role of India and Indonesia in any regional strategic formulation. But the Indo-Pacific idea has taken on more life and meaning with, as noted earlier, the Trump administration's adoption of the concept and the renaming of the Pacific Command to the Indo-Pacific Command.

Regions are like fashion—they change their names and colour with passing time and taste. For example, the larger geographic space within which Southeast Asia is located has been variously called 'Far East', 'Asia' (1940s–50s), 'Asia-Pacific' (1960s–80s), and 'East Asia' (1990s–2000s).

The Indo-Pacific name is distinct from previous names for the broader region of which Southeast Asia is a part. While the term 'Far East' came from imperialists (Britain in particular), 'Asia' from nationalists, 'Asia-Pacific' from economists, and 'East Asia' from culturalists, the Indo-Pacific comes from military-strategists. The Indo-Pacific concept has become a major signpost of

Sino-US rivalry. The US promotes it as a military-strategic approach, which China rejects as 'containment'. While India, Japan, and Australia are on the side of the US, Southeast Asian countries are trying to stay neutral.

The Indo-Pacific idea is anchored in the QUAD, comprised of the US, Australia, Japan, and India. Though not a formal alliance, given China's ascendancy, the QUAD has intensified its security and economic ties. As of 2021, leaders in all four countries became more aligned in their shared concerns about China's increasingly assertive behaviour in the region and invested in defining a constructive agenda of cooperation. All four navies participated in their first joint exercise, Malabar, in November 2020. The member states also convened working groups on COVID-19 vaccines, climate change, and technological innovation and supply-chain resilience.[356]

Despite the QUAD's convening and enacting tangible measures reflective of its raison d'etre, the idea of Indo-Pacific is contested, even among its proponents. This is revealed in the terminology used by the US and Indonesia to articulate their respective visions for the Indo-Pacific. Briefly stated, the US wants a 'free' and 'open' (FOIP) Indo-Pacific,[357] while Indonesia seeks an 'open' and 'inclusive' Indo-Pacific.[358] Thus, the US does not use 'inclusive' while Indonesia does not use 'free'. The US idea of a 'free' Indo-Pacific identifies domestic political openness and good governance as key ingredients, putting itself at odds with China, while Jakarta's stress on 'inclusive' implies that its policy is not meant to isolate China. It is of interest that Japan adopted the US language of 'free and open' Indo-Pacific,[359] while India is taking a middle path, calling for a 'free, open, and inclusive Indo-Pacific Region'.[360]

As a leader of ASEAN, Indonesia is uncomfortable with the US approach, seeing it as exclusionary and aimed at isolating China. Moreover, Jakarta sees the QUAD as a strategic coalition of outside powers, without ASEAN involvement. Jakarta is also developing an ASEAN-centred Indo-Pacific strategy which is more consistent with ASEAN's principle of inclusiveness, consensus-building, and stressing a non-military orientation. Indonesia is keen on seeing the Indo-Pacific idea develop as a political and diplomatic approach.

In June 2019, ASEAN adopted a largely Indonesian-conceived plan for the Indo-Pacific ('ASEAN Outlook on Indo-Pacific' or AOIP), after some objections from Singapore and Cambodia. While some Western observers have dismissed the importance of AOIP because it does not target China specifically or carry compliance measures, these ASEAN 'experts' miss the point: this is how ASEAN has been doing its business since its founding. The document is written in typical ASEAN speak, but it is an act of diplomatic and political assertion by ASEAN. By adopting it, ASEAN is telling the world that the Indo-Pacific idea, hitherto pushed by outside powers like Japan, Australia, India, and the Trump administration, is also ASEAN's business, and that ASEAN has its own way of developing this concept, while not letting outside powers dominate the 'discourse' on the Indo-Pacific. The ASEAN document is 'inclusive' and avoids the adjective 'free' which is seen as anti-China. This is meant to make the document palatable to China. At the same time, it contains references to 'freedom of navigation', which should satisfy Washington. In this manner, ASEAN is playing its classic role as regional consensus-builder, which is all the more essential at a time of rising bilateral tensions between the US and China.

Last but not the least, it legitimizes role of Indonesia as the only country that can stand up to both China and the US or indeed to all other major powers. This is critical for ASEAN centrality. One expects that both the US and Indonesian conceptions of the Indo-Pacific will continue. While the US will pursue its own vision in cooperation with close allies like Japan, the Indonesian formulation is more likely to hold in ASEAN diplomacy and might draw in China, which remains suspicious of the Indo-Pacific idea.

Centre or Periphery?

To boost its resilience, Southeast Asia needs to step up regional cooperation. Key to this is to maintain what is known as 'ASEAN centrality'. This implies that ASEAN should remain at the centre of the regional architecture, especially in multilateral institutions and dialogues, such as the ASEAN Regional Forum (ARF), East Asian Summit (EAS), ASEAN Defence Ministers Meeting (ADMM) in the Asia-Pacific or Indo-Pacific region and that all major powers should respect ASEAN's role on the 'driver's seat' of regional cooperation. Relatedly, 'ASEAN centrality' implies that no 'outside' power, be it the US, China, India, Japan, or Russia, should develop a regional institution or dialogue on its own initiative that would undermine or compete with ASEAN's role.

But in recent years, the idea of 'ASEAN centrality' has come under challenge. One major reason for this is the performance of regional institutions like the ARF and EAS and the criticism that they have never grown out of their 'talk shop' mode. While the claim is somewhat exaggerated, as these institutions remain important as fora for consultations and norm-setting, there is little question that they need to reform and even reinvent themselves to stay relevant. This would require the ARF to move beyond a confidence-building role to one that performs preventive diplomacy, if not conflict-resolution. There have been plenty of suggestions to this effect; it is time to implement them. As I have argued elsewhere, existing crisis management mechanisms which have bene undertaken primarily on a bilateral basis, such as those between China and the US or between China and Japan, should be multilateralized, as has happened in the financial domain, where the initial bilateral currency swap arrangements were accompanied by a multilateral component called the Chiang Mai Initiative Multilateralization (CMIM). The EAS needs to create a convening mechanism for quick consultations on unfolding regional crises, like natural disasters and financial meltdowns. The strengthening of the ADMM+, which has shown promise because of its smaller size than the unwieldy ARF, is also imperative.[361] Moreover, 'ASEAN centrality should not preclude giving non-ASEAN members more voice (hence stake) in setting the agenda and the direction of the ARF and the EAS.'[362]

To maintain its centrality and even relevance, ASEAN should strengthen itself institutionally, while preserving the core elements of its security matrix. First, while ASEAN centrality has traditionally meant being the anchor or driver of Asia-Pacific security architecture, in the altered context of great power rivalry, centrality would also involve not veering in the direction of any power or group or ideology. Not taking sides in great-power rivalry is a key element of Southeast Asia's security matrix, which must be safeguarded. The true ASEAN Way means choosing the Middle Way.

Second, centrality does not mean neutrality, which is neither practical nor necessary, and goes against another grain of Southeast Asia's strategic matrix—its inclusive approach to security. Hence, ASEAN must not abandon its 'co-engagement' of both US and China and all the major powers. Working to preserve these two elements of its strategic matrix is the best way ASEAN could remain key to the regional stability of Southeast Asia and the Indo-Pacific.

Angels Awaiting?

Southeast Asia's return to geopolitics can thus be framed around the competing forces of conflict (demons) and stability (angels). The demons include the US–China rivalry, and territorial conflicts in the South China Sea, and an offensive form of Chinese hegemony, while the angels include economic openness and linkages, ideological tolerance, and regional cooperation. It is these angels that Asia needs to invoke to exorcise its demons and escape a geopolitical nightmare. To fight the demons, Asia, including Southeast Asia, can benefit from some angels, or major changes that have taken place in the region since World War II. Three are especially noteworthy.

First, Asia started its journey after World War II with inward-looking economies tied more to their former colonial masters than to each other. They were dependent more on natural resources and import-substitution than on manufacturing and export promotion. But through the decades, economic nationalism and self-reliance gave way to regional interdependence and integration into the global economy.

Second, Asia's security architecture, in the immediate aftermath of World War II, was defined by a hub-and-spoke bilateralism centred around America's alliances. There was not only no Asian NATO, but also no Asian mechanism for security cooperation or common security. ASEAN only emerged in the late 1960s and did not take off until the 1990s. Since then, Asia has developed a much more elaborate system of security cooperation: bilateral, subregional, and multilateral. While regional institutions have not done a great job, without them the region would be significantly more unstable.

Third, during much of the first decades after World War II, Asian countries were ideologically divided, owing to the effects of the Cold War. But these ideological divisions became less important as more and more countries embraced capitalism, if not democracy. Many countries also underwent political liberalization, including democratic transitions in South Korea and Taiwan, and in Indonesia, Philippines, and Cambodia in Southeast Asia, that were staunchly authoritarian for much of the Cold War. To be sure,

Burma's transition has been reversed, and Thailand's democracy has stunted. But Malaysia offers more hope for a multi-coalition polity resulting in more democratic politics.

The visible, if incomplete, shift from economic nationalism to interdependence, from security bilateralism to multilateralism and from ideological competition and authoritarianism to political liberalization, if not outright democratization, does provide reasons for optimism for Southeast Asia in the post-Cold War period. The region's future stability depends on whether these shifts continue or get reversed. Growing US–China rivalry, Trumpism, and the COVID-19 pandemic might have disrupted the transformation. While economic integration within Asia and between Southeast Asia and East Asia is deepening with the Regional Comprehensive Economic Partnership (RCEP), this does not include India or the US, two of the key players in the region. Security multilateralism seems less promising now than a decade ago, while ideological divides seem to be resurfacing in China–US relations.

Despite concerns over the growing US–China competition, Southeast Asia has not abandoned its 'co-engagement' with both countries. Nor is there any decisive sign of the region choosing sides in the US and China rivalry. This might change if China becomes more assertive (which would lead more regional countries to turn to the US) or the US suffers a major decline in its credibility and trustworthiness as a strategic partner in the region (which will draw the region into the Chinese orbit).

Towards the Future

What direction might Southeast Asia take then? No one has the geopolitical crystal ball. Conventional thinking suggests three possible directions.

The first is for Southeast Asia to muddle through and continue business as usual. Under this scenario, most Southeast Asian countries refrain from taking sides between the US and China or hedge their bets on their geopolitical competition. This used to be the position of most small nations in Southeast and South Asia. But it has become increasingly hard to sustain. In reality, countries like Singapore have already tilted towards the US, while others like Cambodia and Laos have moved towards China. As the US–China rivalry intensifies, more and more ASEAN members will find it difficult to hedge, or sit on the fence. Ultimately, despite the economic linkages with China (which also serve China's interests), smaller Asian countries such as ASEAN members may move closer to the US, especially under a democratic administration that might give them a comparable degree of presidential attention and respect as Barack Obama did.

A second scenario is a Sino-centric order. An extreme version of this would be a Chinese Monroe Doctrine in the region. In this scenario, many, if not all Asian countries, would bandwagon with China either due to economic and security benefits or Chinese coercion. This was, to me, never a very likely scenario, as I had argued in a 2004 essay in *International Security*. COVID-19 makes it even less likely. This time though, China's own actions, more than anything else, prevents any prospect for the emergence of a Sino-centric region.

A third scenario is a region less dependent on China or admiring of its ideology and tilting more towards the US and the West. Strange as it may seem to some, this is more likely, especially if the US changes course in dealing with its own allies and ASEAN. This is much easier than most people think.

But Southeast Asia's geopolitical future can also be framed around an alternate history where there is no centre. This is an alternative to the strategic notion of the Indo-Pacific. It comes from the pre-colonial Indian Ocean network, the world's largest maritime trading network before the rise of Europe, and transatlantic trade. It brought together East Asia and the Indian

Ocean, including China and India, but without being dominated by either. It was a non-hegemonic way of managing commerce and security. Using this as a model, Asia could further its economic linkages, multilateral institutions and ideological tolerance, all of which are the key drivers of peace and stability. As China expands its economic and military reach, it is becoming less of an East Asian actor and more of an Indo-Pacific actor. As a large frog in a larger pond, this may turn out to be a constraining factor in China's ability to dominate Asia. If properly pursued, the Indian Ocean's past, based on a free, non-imperial and vibrant trade and cultural network, can help Asia exorcise the demons of history and embrace its angels.

If Southeast Asia must think in terms of a return of history, that history cannot be the Sino-centric order of East Asia. Any attempt to recreate that order would trigger opposition, from the US as well as regional powers. It is time to think of another history, which offers the vision of an open, non-imperial system. Instead of looking to China's Tributary system as a model, Southeast Asian leaders and the public need to invoke the traditions and principles of the pre-colonial Indian Ocean. Asia's demons are inspired by Europe's, America's, and China's own imperial pasts, while the angels come from its growing economic linkages, multilateral institutions and ideological tolerance and the historical example of a free, non-imperial and vibrant Indian Ocean trade and cultural network. Reorienting Asia back to that future deserves serious consideration in our historical imagination and geopolitical designs.

PART IV

STUDYING SOUTHEAST ASIA

Chapter 9

The Emergence and Evolution of Southeast Asian Studies[363]

The emergence of 'Southeast Asian studies' was the result of two related and closely interacting forces in the post-war period.[364] The first was the slow but steady recognition of an emerging idea of Southeast Asia as a region on its own right. This, in itself, was a late, contrived and contested process. It involved rejecting Southeast Asia as a cultural appendage of either China or India.[365] Partly responsible for this rejection is what Reid has called the 'turning away' tendency in states existing in the closest proximity to larger powers, that is, Burma and Vietnam (as well as the Philippines in relation to the US).[366] A related development is the quest for an 'autonomous history' of the region.[367] Political and strategic developments, including the Southeast Asia Command (SEAC) established by the Allied Forces fighting Japan during World War II, made Southeast Asia a more familiar geopolitical concept. But as late as 1955, the sponsors of the Asia-Africa Conference in Bandung—a group comprising India, Pakistan, Ceylon (later Sri Lanka), Burma (later Myanmar) and Indonesia—were still calling themselves officially as the 'Conference of the South-East Asian Prime Ministers'. The existence of this group, also known as the Colombo Powers, suggests that the concept of Southeast Asia excluding Pakistan, India, and Sri Lanka (which would be later classified as belonging to 'South Asia') had not yet fully arrived, at least in the political and diplomatic arena.

The second important factor was the institutional development of Southeast Asian studies. Initially, European scholars were key to the debate over Southeast Asia's cultural matrix and autonomy.[368] Subsequently, 'the centre of this new field [Southeast Asia] was undoubtedly the United States',[369] a 'coincidence between Southeast Asia's birth as a concept and the triumph of world power.'[370] In the US, the First and the Second Indochinese Wars had a major influence in advancing the concept of Southeast Asia and Southeast Asian studies as a field of study.[371] The increasing prominence of the United States for the field of Southeast Asian studies was reflected in the establishment of 14 Southeast Asian Studies departments between 1947 and 1972 and a tenfold increase in specialists on the region from 1940 to 1984.[372]

Despite this growth, Southeast Asian Studies in the US would remain plagued by self-doubt (about the field, not the individuals working in it). Benedict Anderson, a leading scholar in the field, not only found the number of active scholars publishing regularly in the field to be too small, but also labelled the quality of the 'academic study of the politics of Southeast Asia in North America', now the centre of gravity in the field, as 'feeble and fragile'.[373] Among the reasons which he identified for this state of affairs was fluctuation 'in Washington's concern with that region'. 'Most of us recognize the bitter irony that the heyday of Southeast Asian studies in the widest sense was the era of the Vietnam War.'[374] The consequence of 'political marginality', combined with 'disciplinary marginality', encouraged 'journalistic moonlighting' and 'a deep seated lack of sense of purpose' among the scholars of Southeast Asia.[375]

Doubts about Southeast Asian studies have persisted. Anderson maintained his earlier critique of Southeast Asian studies by arguing in 1992 that 'no very convincing intellectual case has been made for the field, which continues to rest on visibly shaky foundation'.[376] Around the same time, Charles Keyes contended that 'Southeast Asia does not exist as a place', and 'Southeast Asian studies does not exist as a distinctive field of studies'.[377] In 1995, Ruth McVey, mindful of the origins of the field during the World War II-era South East Asia Command, feared that the 'shallow [a] genealogy of the field only emphasized the field's insecurity, threatening it with absorption into more established academic empires.'.[378] In her words, 'The study of Southeast Asia was conceived in a powerful but narrow ideological framework that was of foreign origin but has been strongly internalized by the region's postcolonial ruling elites ... Nonetheless, global and regional forces, and the corrosive power of time, are looking to loosen its grip.'[379] Speaking of these forces, some scholars have noted the 'decline' of Southeast Asia as a region, partly due to its growing interdependence with Northeast Asia, as well as the resurgence of its two big civilizational neighbours, China and India.[380] The fate of Southeast Asian studies could be the same as that of Southeast Asia as a region, about which there is renewed uncertainty. 'Whether Southeast Asia will acquire greater coherence in the future, or become increasingly irrelevant, is a question that cannot be answered.'[381]

If doubt was the chief enemy of the Southeast Asia specialist, desire is their best ally. By desire, I mean the interest and determined efforts of Southeast Asian specialists to self-identify with the field despite the uncertainties over the future of their area studies. This desire had been sustained and fuelled by three factors: diversification, regional dynamism, and, above all, indigenization. In 1982, Kernial Singh Sandhu, the then director of the newly established Institute of Southeast Asian Studies, challenged the pessimism about the state of Southeast Asian studies by pointing to 'the dynamism of the region and ... the obvious academic attention to research on Southeast Asia.

Institutions dedicated to Southeast Asia are springing up around the world . . . People who have ignored the region for hundreds of years are now trying to catch up.'[382] Emmerson found the reasons for the field's continued existence in the willingness of its own specialist community to identify themselves with it. In his view, Southeast Asian studies 'do exist' because, among other things, 'at least for the time being, enough people speak, teach, learn and write as though "Southeast Asia" did exist for us to give them the benefit of the doubt.'[383] Furthermore, 'most of them are *willing to identify themselves as "specialists" of that area*, to allow deans and donors to do so, and to speak, write, meet, and raise money as if there were something called Southeast Asia out there after all.'[384] If this view is accepted, one might take that the field is socially constructed from within, rather than held together by any exogenous factors such as war and crisis, especially since the end of the Vietnam War.

A 'Feeble and Fragile' Region

But mere desire is not a sufficient basis for sustaining Southeast Asian studies. Given the uncertainty over the name of the region, its 'feeble and fragile' support base, and its 'shallow genealogy' in the Cold War milieu, one way to ensure the survival of the field is to broaden its support base or to place it on a wider footing. But how is this done? Part of the answer would seem to be locating the field within the rearticulated and broader relevance of the area studies tradition. This means going beyond the traditional inward-looking nature of area studies and accentuating its transnational and comparative aspects. But this is no easy task, as the area studies tradition has itself been under question, especially from discipline-based approaches and from the pressures of globalization. Indeed, this challenge was a primary external source of doubt about Southeast Asian studies, compounding the aforementioned misgivings about the field's geopolitical lineage and quality deficit that came from inside the field.

The area studies tradition is distinguished by an emphasis on field research, a certain amount of multi-disciplinarity, and, above all, a life-long devotion to studying a nation or region. A disciplinary approach, by contrast, seeks to identify 'lawful regularities, which, by definition, must not be context bound'. Discipline-based scholars aspire to be social scientists, who 'do not seek to master the literature on a region, but rather to master the literature of a discipline'.[385] Area studies scholars were attacked in the 1990s by discipline-based scholars for being little more than '"real estate agents" with a stake in a plot of land rather than an intellectual theory'. Their work was described variously as 'a-theoretical', 'journalistic', and 'mushy'. They were faulted for not knowing statistics, for 'offering resistance to rigorous methods for evaluating arguments', for not generating 'scientific knowledge', and for being 'cameras', rather than 'thinkers'.[386] In contrast, disciplinary social science was seen as being more theoretical, and hence their contributions and insights more 'universally applicable and globally useful'.[387]

The proponents of area studies have struck back. James Scott warned that purely disciplinary approaches, centred on formal theory, would fail to illuminate 'real societies and the conduct of historically situated human agents'.[388] Moreover, discipline-based scholars have come to the defence of area studies. While acknowledging that 'exclusive specialization in a particular area . . . misses the connections between developments in different parts of the world', Peter Katzenstein, a disciplinary scholar of international relations, argues that area studies is crucial for three reasons: (1) analysing transnational relations, (2) as the basis for 'contingent generalizations that go beyond specific locales', and

(3) to compensate for the 'superficial and speculative' connections that strictly disciplinary perspectives make 'to the variegated experiences of various parts of the world'.[389]

But even some of the key proponents of the area studies approach concede that in its traditional version, it can be a 'double-edged sword'. As Arjun Appadurai notes, on the one hand, area studies was 'a tiny refuge for the serious study of foreign languages, alternative worldviews, and large-scale perspectives on socio-cultural change outside Europe and the United States', and was 'one of the few serious counterweights to the tireless tendency to marginalize huge parts of the world in the American academy and American society more generally'. At the same time, he conceded that area studies also suffered from 'a certain over-identification with the regions of its specialization', and had 'grown too comfortable with its own maps of the world, too secure in its own expert practices, and too insensitive to transnational processes both today and in the past.'.[390]

In the field of Southeast Asian studies, a certain amount of disconnect between the area studies tradition and disciplinary approaches persisted. This is especially evident in the study of issues related to the international relations (as opposed to foreign policy), regionalism, and security of Southeast Asia. These areas have struggled to gain recognition from scholars from the area studies community, which has been, and continues to be, dominated by those who study history, geography, sociology, languages, and so on. The baggage of war and national security (e.g., Southeast Asia Command, Vietnam War, etc.) has been part of the reason for the discomfort of some area studies specialists in accepting contemporary international relations and security scholars. Moreover, regionalism and regional identity-building issues sit somewhat uncomfortably with the usual inclination of Southeast Asian specialists to train and contribute in a country-specific approach, rather than deal with the region in its wholeness (the trees to the exclusion of the forest).

A further external source (with powerful echoes from some scholars within the field) of doubt about 'Southeast Asian studies' is the general sense of uncertainty about the future of area studies in an era of globalization.[391] 'The whole globalization discourse has benefited the social sciences, not area studies,' claims David Ludden.[392] One argument here is that globalization has produced shared experiences across regions and created transnational communities of affected people (victims) across issue areas which cannot be examined strictly in terms of geography or national origins. Willa Tanabe writes that the 'area study scholars perhaps failed to recognize the importance of global forces . . . the most critical issues today are those that cross borders . . . Area studies must cross borders to remain relevant.'[393]

Globalization challenges the importance of some of the more salient claims of traditional area studies, such as its emphasis on language studies. English has unquestionably emerged as the language of globalization. Another challenge posed by globalization concerns the relevance of 'region' as a unit of analysis. Some perspectives on globalization hold that it is not only undermining the nation-state, but also rendering the concept of 'region' less distinctive and hence analytically, less useful.

Like the challenge of discipline-based approaches to Southeast Asia, that posed by globalization can also be overstated. It is arguable that the post-Cold War international system is increasingly regionalized, and that regional level of analysis and regional actors/institutions have an increasing autonomy which cannot be understood simply by focusing on developments and forces at the global level.[394] Just as globalization has not rendered the nation-state irrelevant, it has not dampened regional identities and might even have strengthened it. Emmerson contends that globalization has helped to reduce orientalism in Southeast Asian studies which is a positive development.[395] James Scott credits globalization for promoting greater indigenous scholarship in Southeast Asia.[396]

While the challenges to Southeast Asian studies, from self-doubt, disciplinary scholarship, and globalization, have proven to be somewhat exaggerated, they have nonetheless led to a growing recognition for the need for adjustments and changes in the area studies tradition, especially with calls for broadening its foundations and locating it in the wider processes of social, economic and political change. Such efforts move it beyond the traditional conception of regions or areas as relatively self-contained units. An important example of this change can be found in the 'regional worlds' approach developed by a University of Chicago project. The project offered new 'conceptual, strategic, and practical . . . approach to area studies'. It sought to move area studies from an approach 'driven by conceptions of geographical, civilizational and cultural coherence', or 'trait geographies', towards 'process geographies' that take a more dynamic and interactive view. Regions or areas are not 'objective clusters of cartographic, material or cultural facts'. The 'process geography' perspective sets forth 'new ways to approach both space and time in relation to "areas"' with space becoming more flexible and porous and time becoming less sequential and cumulative'.[397]

In this sense, 'regional worlds' are neither wholly self-contained entities, nor purely extensions of global dynamics. 'Multiple regions overlap and contradict one another to form complex webs of power, interaction, and imagination that are constantly in motion.'[398] As one of the key people behind the project, Arjun Appadurai, notes: 'All world areas now produce their own pictures of the world and not just of themselves.' The challenge for area studies should thus be to 'recognize that areas are not just places but are also locations for the production of other world-pictures, which also need to be part of our sense of these other worlds'.[399] In responding to the challenge of globalization, area studies scholars could offer regional perspectives on wider world issues, and not just concentrate on explaining Southeast Asian dynamics.

In short, the call for redefining Southeast Asian studies involves accepting the regional space as more porous and flexible, and adopting a more dynamic and interactive view of the regional space. It involves locating area studies in the wider context of global processes, (instead of rejecting, embracing globalization), and taking a comparative view of regional dynamics. Such broadening calls for new approaches to Southeast Asian studies. Below, I outline two, which I call transnational area studies and discipline-based regional studies.

The Spectre of Comparisons?

Will Southeast Asian studies benefit from a comparative approach? One breed of Southeast-Asian-studies scholars, though primarily trained in regional affairs, or in the area studies tradition, are also interested and involved in comparative research into other regions or are into more transnational or global phenomena.

Benedict Anderson's work is an important example of the transnational area studies approach. Although known as a Southeast Asianist, his most famous work, *Imagined Communities*, is not a work on Southeast Asia alone. Rather, it traced what is undoubtedly one of the most powerful transnational forces of the modern era: nationalism, and it does so by placing it in the wider context of technological, social, economic, and political changes in Europe and around the world. In his book, *The Specter of Comparisons: Nationalism, Southeast Asia and the World*, he goes a step further, drawing attention to the fact that nationalists are apt to resort to comparisons to imagine their own identity. An extract from the blurb of the book is especially suggestive here. Citing the Indonesian President Sukarno's attempt to inspire and justify nationalism in Indonesia by invoking Hitler's 'clever' depiction of the ideals of German nationalism, Anderson marvels at this example of:

> an anti-colonial leader . . . viewing Europe and its history through an inverted telescope, as Europeans often regard other parts of the globe. Strange shifts in perspective can take place when Berlin is viewed from Jakarta, or when complex histories of colonial domination straddle what counts as the founding work of a national culture in a language its people no longer read. The 'specter of comparisons' arises as nations stir into self-awareness, matching themselves against others, and becoming whole through the exercise of the imagination.[400]

The substance and approach of *Specter of Comparisons*, as well as *Imagined Communities*, make one thing quite clear. It is not exactly what one might call the 'structured, focused' comparison method, which is favoured by international relations scholars. In this method, comparisons have to follow strict conventions, including 'a well-defined research objective and an appropriate research strategy', clear specification of independent and dependent variables, including variables that offer 'policy leverage', and 'doability' (cases should not be chosen simply because they are 'interesting').[401] The *Imagined Communities* fails this social scientific test. But how lucky are we all for it?

At the same time, Anderson's study of nationalism is not so much a work of comparison, but of diffusion. Here one finds one of the best examples of the area specialist's contribution to the study of diffusion. Anderson locates Indonesian nationalism in the wider context of time (past) and space (other locations) in the spread of nationalism. His observation that his interest in 'wider and more pretentiously theoretical-universal, considerations and framings' (the hallmark of a disciplinary scholar), came about 'at a time in [his] life when the possibilities of serious and immersed fieldwork in Southeast Asia [the traditional hallmark of an area specialist] were, for all kinds of reasons, diminishing,' is especially revealing. It not only suggests that comparisons can produce a useful alliance between area studies knowledge and disciplinary knowledge, and that comparisons can take off from an area studies vantage-point, but also that comparative studies can be *enhanced* by the study of diffusion.[402] Such enhancement occur when one goes beyond discussing similarities and differences to identifying how these come about. While he acknowledges that comparisons are inevitable, he does not appear to be convinced that they are benign (as the term 'spectre' conveys that sense of foreboding). But comparisons can be fruitful and pleasurable in the quest for knowledge. The term 'spectre' implies there is something self-serving, or even darkly political, absurd, and fanciful, about comparisons. But there are also other types of comparisons that can illuminate the context of that politics and place Southeast Asian dynamics in a sharper and wider global context, as the 'regional world' project has called for. Comparative studies help make the field of Southeast Asian studies more inclusive, drawing in others, including those whose primary field is not Southeast Asia.

Anderson's work and the new notion of area studies in the 'regional worlds' project points in the direction of transnational area studies. But these are not alone. The area studies approach to Southeast Asia contains within itself elements that can be generalized and made as the basis of comparisons. Let me offer some examples. Hans Dietrich Evers points to many concepts developed by Southeast Asian Studies scholars which aided not just the comparative study of Southeast Asian countries, but also came to be used for social research elsewhere and became 'standard concepts of textbook social science'. Among the examples he cites are J.S. Furnivall's 'plural societies' and J.H. Boeke's 'dual organization'.[403] Furnivall's 'plural societies', outlined in a work published in 1939, described a distinct Southeast Asian form of social organization, which had developed in Burma, Malaya, and the Dutch East Indies toward the end of colonial rule. This organization consisted of three social orders: the natives, the Chinese, and the Europeans, who co-existed and interacted in the material and economic spheres while maintaining their respective cultural distinctiveness.[404] Another concept was Boeke's 'dualistic economies' or 'dual organization'. Originally published in 1940, it presented a model describing how capitalist economic development under colonial rule, including the influx of mass products from the metropolitan countries, produced an economic duality in which the lower stratum of society sank into greater poverty while the upper stratum became richer, urbanized, and Westernized.[405]

Other concepts identified by Evers include Geertz's 'agricultural involution' (comparing Javanese social development with that of Japan) and John Embree's 'loosely structured social systems' (contrasting Japanese and Thai rural society). While some of these concepts cannot be directly applied to regions beyond Southeast Asia, they do provide the basis of comparison with similar phenomena in other regions. Recent works on norm dynamics, including the idea of 'constitutive localization' of norms, took off from the historian O.W. Wolters' concept of localization in Southeast Asian culture and art, the 'idea of the local initiative' derived from Dutch economic historian Jacob van Leur's work on Indonesia, and British art historian and archaeologist Quaritch Wales's concept of 'local genius' demonstrate the enduring transportability and applicability of ideas beyond their regional 'confines'.[406]

Regionalism and Southeast Asian Studies

Of late, Southeast Asian studies have been deeply impacted by Southeast Asian regionalism. Initially in the Southeast Asian studies tradition, the study of regionalism and transnational patterns had not been popular. As one study published in 1984 found, the area studies tradition has traditionally favoured country-specific perspectives over study of regional or transnational patterns, such as regional organizations, geopolitics and international organizations, international trade, international alliances, diplomacy, imperialism, and colonialism.[407] Moreover, scholarship studying the politics or society of more than one country within Southeast Asia had remained scarce. The diversity of Southeast Asia imposed a 'major constraint on scholars who attempt[ed] to analyse the region as a whole' and wished 'to deal holistically with the area'.[408] As a result, 'rather than attempting to deal with Southeast Asia as a whole, Western social scientists have instead become country specialists.'[409]

While diversity and disunity renders problematic an approach that looks beyond the domestic politics and foreign policies of individual countries and covers regional patterns and interactions at both state and non-state levels, it is still warranted.[410] This is not only because the region has developed a history of regionalism since ASA in 1961 and ASEAN in 1967, but also because a good deal of the region's problems (and solutions to them) are regional or transnational in scope (ranging from human rights, financial volatility, environmental degradation, pandemics, piracy and terrorism, drugs, human trafficking, and other forms of transnational crime).

There have been important exceptions to the area specialists' lack of interest in Southeast Asian regional interactions and regionalism. Investigations into regional patterns of international relations were pioneered within the area studies tradition by distinguished scholars like Evelyn Colbert, Russell Fifield, George Kahin, Michael Leifer, Don Emmerson, Sheldon Simon, and Donald Weatherbee, among others. But some Southeast Asian specialists remain sceptical about regionalism.[411] Anderson, who devotes fewer than two pages to Southeast Asian regionalism in his *Specter of Comparisons* book, dismisses ASEAN as inconsequential and 'impotent'. Yet this assertion ignores ASEAN's role in keeping intra-mural tensions (e.g. the Sabah dispute, Singapore–Indonesia and Singapore–Malaysia security tensions) to a manageable level. What about the grouping's role in helping the political resolution of the Cambodia conflict? Could it be the reason why the organization, as Anderson concedes, 'has managed to have itself taken seriously in international diplomacy'?[412]

Above all, it is ironic that for someone who coined the term 'imagined community', Anderson judges ASEAN from a functional or 'efficiency' criterion: its impotence. Anderson does unwittingly suggest a principal contribution of ASEAN when he observes: 'It is a striking fact that when ASEAN was formed, in 1967, invitations to join it were issued to all the existing states in Southeast Asia (and to none outside it).'[413] He is slightly wrong here—Ceylon (Sri Lanka) did receive an invitation to join ASEAN in August 1967, but refused for political reasons (and when it applied to be a member of the organization a decade later, it received a firm rejection). But what the above suggests is that ASEAN was a turning point in the *imagination* of Southeast Asia by its elites through a contrived sense of regionness involving 'all the existing states in Southeast Asia (and to none outside it)', i.e. excluding the big powers such as India (member of the conference of South East Asian Prime Ministers in 1955) and China. This role in regional identity-building, which was to develop further in the following decades is ASEAN regionalism's principal contribution, despite its functional limitations.

In recent years, the growth of disciplinary approaches to Southeast Asia has made the study of regionalism and ASEAN much more visible.[414] These scholars draw upon new theories of international relations, especially constructivism and the 'new regionalism' approaches.[415] Despite the limitations imposed by the region's diversity and disunity, such work has contributed not only to greater knowledge of regional processes at work within

Southeast Asia, but also to theory development at the global level, especially to constructivism (with it view of regions as dynamic, socially-constructed units) and comparative regionalism.[416] This contribution is consistent with the 'regional worlds' approach, which calls for greater attention to the two-way flow of ideas and learning between the regional and the global levels. Some of the literature also places ASEAN within the context of inter-regionalism,[417] reminiscent of Subrahmanyam's 'connected history' approach. In either case, they have enriched Southeast Asian studies and enhanced the contribution of Southeast Asian studies to general international relations theory and literature.

Moreover, the new scholarship on Southeast Asian and Asian regionalism increasingly acknowledges the limitations of applying Western theories that are of doubtful value in the local context, thereby helping to render the field of comparative regionalism less Eurocentric. This Eurocentrism has been increasingly acknowledged and challenged. The EU's supranational bureaucratization and legalism, with the ultimate goal of creating a post-sovereign system, is seen as a poor fit, both normatively and functionally, for ASEAN and others. Different regionalisms are more likely to be judged in terms of their set goals and within their own historical and political contexts than by simply applying the criteria supplied by the EU experience.[418]

This is where the area studies tradition and disciplinary perspectives can really come together. As noted at the outset, comparative studies is not just about finding the similarities and differences between two areas, but also about how ideas and institutions travel from one to another and produce mutual learning. As we know from recent works in international relations theory, diffusion is not replication but localization, whereby, as noted earlier, local actors selectively borrow and redefine outside ideas and institutions to suit their context and need based on preexisting beliefs and practices. In this process, the agency belongs not just to the transnational idea entrepreneurs at the point of origin but also to their intended target audience at the receiving end.[419] To get a proper understanding of diffusion, we need the depth and richness of context that the area studies approach is known to provide. But to understand the causal mechanisms and processes by which ideas and institutions travel is where disciplinary perspectives can make their contribution. In other words, the area studies approach makes comparisons and diffusion more sensitive to local context, allowing the comparativist scholar to fulfil the recognition of 'significant values of each culture within its own context'. The disciplinary approach provides theoretical and methodological toolkits that explain the causal processes of diffusion and make comparisons more systematic and of greater universal value. It is this synergy that makes comparisons productive and alluring to the Southeast Asian specialist, which ultimately is a pleasure, and not a spectre.

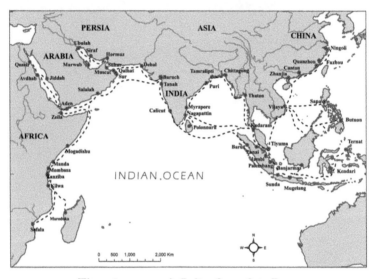

*The main ports on the Indian Ocean Spice Route
(Early 16th Century A.D.)*

Chapter 10

The Indo-Pacific Idea: Myth and Reality

Addressing a seminar on regional cooperation in Bangkok in 2021, I said: 'Asia' was built by nationalists, 'Asia-Pacific' by economists, 'East Asia' by culturalists, 'Indo-Pacific' by strategists.[420] A perceptive reader suggested that Far East was coined by imperialists, and I agreed and added it.

The history of the naming of regions bears this out. Far East, as well as Near East and Middle East, were essentially hangovers from the imperial era. Originally mentioned by the Portuguese to designate the location of India, it became a familiar term in global geopolitics under the British empire. In 1947, the UN established the United Nations Economic Commission for Asia and the Far East (ECAFE) in Bangkok. But it was renamed as the United Nations Economic Commission for Asia and the Pacific (ESCAP) in 1974, because some Asian leaders objected, asking: 'Far from where? East of what?'

Asia was a province of the Roman Empire and originally centred on the Anatolian region of modern Turkey. The idea of 'Asia' in the modern era was anchored on pan-Asianism. One version of pan-Asianism became a tool of Japanese imperialists to exclude and expel Western powers from the region. But as Japan's s effort failed, an anti-colonial version of pan-Asianism became a common platform for Asian countries, championed by India's Jawaharlal Nehru, China's Sun Yat-sen, and Japan's Okakura Kazuo. The two Asian Relations Conferences of 1947 and 1949 held in New Delhi were the highpoint of this effort.

But India's efforts to lead pan-Asianism by convening two Asian Relations Conferences and establish a permanent political organization—the Asian Relations Organization—petered out with its defeat in the Sino-Indian War of 1962.

With this, the idea of pan-Asianism also died. India, the early leader of Asian regionalism, left the movement, partly due to its own domestic preoccupations, its greater interest in leading global non-alignment, and its loss to China in the 1962 war. China too was sidelined; while preaching non-intervention, Mao was actively promoting communist subversion throughout Southeast Asia. Moreover, the economic realities of Asia were also changing.

From then on, the Asia-Pacific idea (with and without the hyphen) took off. This occurred with the creation of a number of economic forums, such as the Pacific Basin Economic Council (PBEC, 1967), Pacific Trade and Development Conference (PAFTAD, 1968), and PECC (Pacific Economic Cooperation Council, 1980). The key role in these were played by economists, businesspeople, and policy experts. In 1989, governments stepped in by creating the Asia Pacific Economic Cooperation (APEC). In 1994, the ASEAN Regional Forum—the first Asia-Pacific multilateral security group—was established in Bangkok. But these bodies, based on considerations of interdependence and benefit, lacked any sense of shared culture and identity.

This changed after the 1997 Asian financial crisis. Suddenly Asia-Pacific fell out of fashion, due to the resentment over America's unwillingness to come to the rescue of crisis-hit Southeast Asia and the Bush administration's summary rejection of Japan's Asian Monetary Fund initiative. The idea of East Asia took over. Malaysian leader Mahathir Mohamad led this anger by proposing an East Asian Economic Grouping (EAEG), renamed EAEC to stress its informal nature. The EAEC took on a culturalist, even mildly racist flavour when some analysts called it East Asia minus the Caucasians (or for that matter the Indians). But the East Asia Vision Group (EAVG), promoted by Korean leader Kim Dae Jung, advanced a more positive 'vision' in a 2001 report, not only describing East Asia as 'a distinctive and crucial region in the world', but also calling for 'fostering the identity of an East Asian community'. Such an identity, the report stressed, would be based on 'shared challenges, common aspirations, and a parallel destiny'. Interestingly enough, these were some of the exact words in Chinese leader Xi Jinping's idea of a 'Community of Shared [or common] Destiny'.

But when the East Asia Summit (EAS) held its first meeting in Kuala Lumpur in 2005, it had discarded Mahathir's membership vision. India, Australia, and New Zealand were allowed to join, on the grounds that East Asia was a functional, rather than a geographic concept. The real reason was that some countries, including Indonesia and Singapore, sought to balance China with the participation of other powers. US and Russia joined the group in 2011. Here, security trumped identity.

In the meantime, Japan, China, South Korea, and ASEAN had set up ASEAN Plus Three (APT) in 1997, with its main brief being financial cooperation, which, in 2000, would lead to the Chiang Mai Initiative (CMI)—a bilateral and multilateral currency swapping system that members could draw on in the event of attacks by currency speculators or as a buffer against financial volatility. While the idea of East Asia persists, the EAS and ASEAN Plus three have not lived up to their early expectations.

The EAS has been stymied by the US–China rivalry. It is at this juncture when the Indo-Pacific idea came into vogue. Although the term was not new, it was a 2007 paper on India–Japan security cooperation by a retired Indian naval officer, Gurpreet Khurana, which gave it contemporary policy prominence. Another version, which initially seemed to gain some traction, was proposed by Indonesia's Foreign Minister Marty Natalegawa. His vision of the Indo-Pacific came into focus in 2013 with his proposal for an Indo-Pacific Treaty of Friendship and Cooperation, modelled after ASEAN's existing Treaty of Amity and Cooperation (ASEAN TAC).

The term was initially sidelined in US policy, which under the Obama administration was promoting 'rebalancing' or 'pivot'. The head of the US Pacific Command was more sympathetic, using 'Indo-Asia-Pacific' in 2013 in a speech in Jakarta.[421] The Trump administration dumped the 'pivot' and embraced the Indo-Pacific, and the Biden administration continued this embrace.

The lesson here is that regions are not named purely or mainly by geography, but are often shaped by strategic, economic and cultural drivers. Because of this, regions are not permanent entities and their names and boundaries change.

Going a step back in history to illustrate this, the emergence of 'Southeast Asia' as a region had much to do with the Allied Southeast Asian Command (SEAC) of World War II. But strategic factors are never enough to sustain a regional organization. Regional identity and participation are important. Contrary to what people might think, Great Powers are not always the best agents of creating or naming regions, especially when they try to design regional bodies after their own interest and leadership. This can be seen from the fate of Japan's Greater East Asia Co-Prosperity Sphere, created to advance Japanese imperialism in the period leading upto World War II. The Southeast Asia Treaty Organization (SEATO), set up by the US in 1954 as part of its anti-communist strategy, attracted only two Southeast Asian members—Thailand and Philippines—and died unceremoniously in 1975. By contrast, the Association of Southeast Asian Nations, established in 1967 with five nations of the region and none from outside, not only survived but took an ever more important role in regional order-management.

But 'Southeast Asia' itself also shows how fluid regional definitions can be. The five official sponsors of the 1955 Asia-Africa Conference—the Bandung conference—Indonesia,

Burma, India, Pakistan, and Ceylon, called themselves the Conference of South East Asian Prime Ministers. Today, no one considers the last three of these as part of Southeast Asia, but of 'South Asia'.

Regions also die. The US used 'Southwest Asia' to fight the Soviet occupation of Afghanistan through the 1980s and then coined 'AfPak' (Afghanistan–Pakistan) as part of its war on terror in the area, in which both nations were viewed as a single theatre of strategic policy and military operations. Both names have died out, although Southwest Asia existed and still remains as a general but little used term for designating the western part of Asia.

Is Indo-Pacific doomed to disappear? To answer this, consider three major differences between Indo-Pacific and previous names, such as East Asia and Asia-Pacific.

For one thing, this is an ever more culturally and politically diverse area than East Asia. Economic links within Indo-Pacific are weaker than those in Asia-Pacific or East Asia. India is not well integrated into East Asia or the transpacific production networks that were crucial to the Asia-Pacific idea. New Delhi is not an APEC member and has pulled out of the RCEP negotiations out of concern of Chinese competition. India's interest in the Indo-Pacific idea owes to security considerations, especially to counter China, as well as to achieve a geopolitical prominence that it does not and cannot enjoy in the Asia-Pacific or East Asia constructs.

This reminds us once again that Asia-Pacific had emerged after economic interdependence had set in. It was a way of rationalizing economic links, inviting production networks led by Japan. Indo-Pacific is based on a strategic vision that is aiming to create a strategic convergence or interdependence, which is much more narrow, and it is mainly based on an imagined strategic convergence of a few leading nations. Analysts, and certainly China itself, view the Indo-Pacific as a not-so-thinly veiled front against China, promoted by its major adversaries, without a single Southeast Asian nation being at its core.

This leads to a second point. While 'Asia-Pacific' and East Asia are anchored on multilaterals—such as APEC, ARF, EAS, the Indo-Pacific so far rests on minilaterals, such as the Quadrilateral Security Dialogue (QUAD) comprising the US, Japan, India, and Australia. The Indo-Pacific Economic Framework (IPEF) promoted by the US is another minilateral. Minilaterals do matter. But they are usually preferred by big powers rather than small ones. The IPEF as an effort to create economic structure has been half-hearted and is probably destined to fail. The Indo-Pacific idea also lacks the support of a vibrant track II community, like PECC and the Council on Security Cooperation in the Asia-Pacific (CSCAP).

Third, Asia-Pacific was founded on ASEAN centrality, which the Indo-Pacific framing undercuts, or has the potential to undercut. Asia-Pacific also had outside powers, but ASEAN came to be on the drivers' seat. In the Indo-Pacific, ASEAN has been relegated to a passenger's seat, despite its own version of the Indo-Pacific as presented in the 2019 ASEAN Outlook on Indo-Pacific (AIOP).

The AIOP is a limited response out of fear of being sidelined by the QUAD approach to the Indo-Pacific. The AIOP also shows how the Indo-Pacific idea suffers from an aspirational gap: between the US idea of 'free' and 'open', terms meant to isolate China, and the China 'inclusive' vision of Indonesia and the AOIP. This leads to competing visions of the Indo-Pacific idea.

These considerations should be cause for caution for analysts and policymakers that are overly enthusiastic about the Indo-Pacific idea. To endure, the Indo-Pacific architecture must become more inclusive and multilateral and non-hegemonic. The historical Indian Ocean region, before the arrival of European imperial powers, was a thriving commercial and cultural region that no one—whether India or China—dominated but everyone benefitted from.

Through history, the Indian Ocean has belonged to no single power, neither China nor India or A combination of powers. It was not India's Ocean, but one in which India was one of several actors, among the most consequential, but not hegemonic. The actors (for India as well as other countries in the Indian Ocean interactions) were not just India's rulers, but more importantly, its monks, priests, merchants, adventurers, and labourers. Neither was the Indian Ocean a Chinese sphere of influence. Although many Southeast Asian states including Srivijaya, Malacca, and Siam had tributary relations with China, the trade was neither dominated nor managed by China.

Chinese admiral Zheng He's ship in woodblock print

From time to time, big powers did make coercive forays into the Indian Ocean, such as the southern Indian Chola kingdom's attacks on Southeast Asian port cities in the eleventh century and the Chinese admiral Zheng He's imperial voyages in the fifteenth. But for the most part of its history, before the era of European colonization, trade and cultural interactions in the Indian Ocean were managed by smaller port-cities or coastal states: Malindi, Mogadishu, Kilwa, Zanzibar, Aden, Hormuz, Calicut, Kalinga, Nagapattinam, Samudra Pasai, Srivijaya, and Malacca. It was a pluralistic world, and a remarkably open trading environment. It is the pre-colonial Indian Ocean trading system, rather than the Mediterranean or any other body of water, that was the genuine precursor for 'free trade', which is falsely credited to Britain and the US. Unlike British or American promotion of 'free trade' in modern times, or that of the Roman Empire in the ancient Mediterranean, free trade in the Indian Ocean was achieved without the hegemony of any single civilization or power. It was this vibrant cultural and political universe whose impact is substantial in shaping Asian civilization. The future Indo-Pacific can learn from that experience.

Notes

1 Fisher, Charles A. 1962. Southeast Asia: The Balkans of the Orient? A Study in Continuity and Change. *Geography* 47, 4: 347–67.
2 Osborne, Milton. 1970. *Region of Revolt: Focus on Southeast Asia.* Oxford: Pergamon Publishers.
3 Kim, Young. 1995. *The Southeast Asian Economic Miracle.* Oxfordshire: Routledge.
4 Emmerson, Donald K. 1984. Southeast Asia: What's in a name? *Journal of Southeast Asian Studies* 15, 1: 1–21.
5 Holt, Sean M. 2022. Five countries, other than China, most dependent on the South China Sea. *CNBC*, November 17.
6 Steinberg, David Joel. 1988. *In Search of Southeast Asia: A Modern History.* Honolulu: University of Hawaii Press.
7 van Leur, Jacob. 1955. *Indonesia Trade and Society: Essays in Asian Social and Economic History.* The Hague: W. Van Hoeve Press.
8 Wales, H.G. Quaritch. 1951. *The Making of Greater India: A Study in Southeast Asian Culture Change.* London.
9 Wolters, Oliver W. 1999. *History, Culture, and Region in Southeast Asian Perspectives.* Singapore and Ithaca: ISEAS and Cornell University Southeast Asia Program.
10 Emmerson. Southeast Asia: What's in a name? *Journal of Southeast Asian Studies.*
11 Wolters. *History, Culture, and Region in Southeast Asian Perspectives.*
12 Ibid.

13 Ibid.
14 Tambiah, Stanley J. 1977. The galactic polity: The structure of traditional kingdoms in Southeast Asia. *Annals of the New York Academy of Sciences* 293, 1: 69–97.
15 Reid, Anthony. 1988. *Southeast Asia in the Age of Commerce, Vol. 1: The Lands Below the Winds*. New Haven: Yale University Press.
16 Ibid.
17 Ibid.
18 Ibid.
19 Acharya, Amitav. 2021. Journey to the east: The Hindu-Buddhist making of Southeast Asia. *The Diplomat*, 15 February.
20 Majumdar, R.C. 1955. *Ancient Indian Colonisation in South-East Asia*. Baroda: University of Baroda Press.
21 Adas, Michael. 1974. *The Burma Delta: Economic Development and Social Change on an Asian Rice Frontier*. Madison: University of Wisconsin Press.
22 Arasaratnam, S. 1969. Some notes on the Dutch in Malacca and the Indo-Malayan trade, 1641–1670. *Journal of Southeast Asian History* 10, 3: 480–90.
23 Osborne, Milton. 1979. *Southeast Asia: An Introductory History*. Crows Nest, Australia: Allen & Unwin.
24 SarDesai, D.R. 2012. *Southeast Asia: Past and Present*. New York: Routledge.
25 Acharya, Amitav. 2012. *Civilizations in Embrace: The Spread of Ideas and the Transformation of Power*. Singapore: Institute of Southeast Asian Studies.
26 Wolters. *History, Culture, and Region in Southeast Asian Perspectives*.
27 Tai, Michael. 2019. *China and her Neighbours: Asian Diplomacy from Ancient History to the Present*. London: Zed Books
28 Wake, Christopher H. 1964. Malacca's early kings and the reception of Islam. *Journal of Southeast Asian History* 5, 2: 104–28.

29 Sutherland, Heather. 2003. Southeast Asian history and the Mediterranean analogy. *Journal of Southeast Asian Studies* 34, 1: 1–20.
30 Coedes, Georges. 1968. *The Indianised States of Southeast Asia*. Ed. Walter Vella. Honolulu: East-West Center Press.
31 Ptak, Roderich. 1998. In Memoriam: Denys Lombard (1938–1998). *International Institute for Asian Studies Newsletter* 16.
32 Braudel, Fernand. 1995. *The Mediterranean and the Mediterranean World in the Age of Philip II*. Berkeley: University of California Press.
33 Sutherland, Heather. Southeast Asian History and the Mediterranean Analogy.
34 Ptak, Roderich. In Memoriam.
35 Braudel, Fernand. *The Mediterranean and the Mediterranean World*.
36 Sutherland. Southeast Asian History and the Mediterranean Analogy.
37 One approach that is especially suitable for this purpose is 'Parallel-Oriented Comparative History'. See Skocpol, Theda and Margaret Somers. 1980. The uses of comparative history in macrosocial inquiry. *Comparative Studies in Society and History* 22, 2: 174–97.
38 Reid, Anthony. 1993. The last stand of autonomous states in Southeast Asia and Korea, 1750–1870: Problems, possibilities, and a project. *Asian Studies Review* 17, 2: 103–20.
39 Lieberman, Victor. 2003. *Strange Parallels: Southeast Asia in Global Context, 800–1830*. Cambridge: Cambridge University Press.
40 Subrahmanyam, Sanjay. 1997. Connected histories: Notes towards a reconfiguration of early modern Eurasia. *Modern Asian Studies* 31, 3: 735–62.
41 Smail, John R.W. 1961. On the possibility of an autonomous history of modern Southeast Asia. *Journal of Southeast Asian History* 2, 2: 72–102.

42 Lieberman. *Strange Parallels: Southeast Asia in Global Context.*
43 Ibid.
44 Ibid; Lieberman, Victor. 1993. Local integration and Eurasian analogies: Structuring Southeast Asian history, 1350–1830. *Modern Asian Studies* 27, 3: 475–572.
45 Subrahmanyam. Connected Histories.
46 Subrahmanyam, Sanjay. 1998. Notes on circulation and asymmetry in two Mediterraneans. Ed. Claude Guilott et al. Wisebaden: Harrassowitz.
47 Subrahmanyam. Connected Histories.
48 Fifield, Russell. 1983. Southeast Asia as a regional concept. *Southeast Asian Journal of Social Science* 11, 2: 1–14.
49 Gordon, Bernard K. 1966. *The Dimensions of Conflict in Southeast Asia.* New Jersey: Prentice Hall.
50 Ibid.
51 Ibid.
52 _____ 2022. Trade integration deepens in Asia and the Pacific amid pandemic. *ADB News Release*, 9 February.
53 My approach to the study of regions and regionalism shares many elements of Benedict Anderson's approach to the study of nationalism and the nation-state. There are many parallels between 'imagining the nation' and 'imagining the region'. Particularly, Anderson's focus on the collective 'imagining' of the nation by a nationalist elite is mirrored in my explanation of Southeast Asian region-building as a process of elite socialization. But drawing upon the work of Wolters, Reid, and others, I place more emphasis on the role of traditional political-cultural frameworks and pre-capitalist commerce (while Anderson focusses on print capitalism) in building modern social identities. I also believe that the term 'proximities' more accurately reflects the degree of socialisation and bonding evident in the case of Southeast Asia than the term 'communities' used by Anderson to

describe nations. Although a certain sense of community can develop within the region, as has been the case in Southeast Asia, the continued salience of state sovereignty (despite claims about its alleged obsolescence and erosion) makes regional communities fundamentally different from nation-states. Southeast Asia is still a region inhabited by highly sovereignty-conscious actors.

54 Acharya, Amitav. 2012. *The Making of Southeast Asia: International Relations of a Region*. Ithaca: Cornell University Press.
55 This chapter has been adapted from a previously authored article, cited as: Acharya, Amitav. 2016. Studying the Bandung Conference from a global IR perspective. *Australian Journal of International Affairs* 70, 4: 342–57.
56 Indonesian Ministry of Foreign Affairs. 1955. Opening Address given by Sukarno.
57 Ibid.
58 Phillips, Andrew and Tim Dunne. 2015. The 'Bandung Divide': Australia's lost opportunity in Asia? *The Conversation*, 23 April.
59 UK High Commissioner of Ceylon to Commonwealth Relations Office, 18 January 1955, D2231/60, FO 371/116976, TNA, PRO.
60 UK High Commission Telegram 33, 5 January 1955, D2231/22, FO 371/116975.
61 Acharya, Amitav. 2009. *Whose Ideas Matter? Agency and Power in Asian Regionalism*. Ithaca: Cornell University Press; Acharya, Amitav. 2013. *Rethinking Power, Institutions, and Ideas in World Politics: Whose IR?* Abingdon: Routledge. Acharya, Amitav. 2014. Who are the norm makers? The Asian-African conference in Bandung and the evolution of norms. *Global Governance* 20, 3: 405–17.
62 Marnham, J.E. 'Communication from Colonial Office, London to A.A.W. Landymore, Foreign Office, London on 12

April 1955. London: The National Archives. D2231/195/B, FO 371/116979.
63 Cable, J.E. 'Afro Asian Conference.' UK Foreign Office, Far Eastern Department, 1955. London: The National Archives. DP 35/6096, FE 106/287/1.10.
64 Ibid.
65 Tarling, Nicholas. 1992. 'Ah-Ah': Britain and the Bandung Conference of 1955. *Journal of Southeast Asian Studies* 23, 1: 74–111.
66 'Draft Guidance Telegram to All Missions, 'How it Evolved."' In Cable, J. E. UK Foreign Office, Far EasternDepartment. 1955. 'Afro Asian Conference.' London: The National Archives. D2231/123, FO 371/116978.
67 Ampiah, Kweku. 2007. *The Political and Moral Imperatives of the Bandung Conference of 1955: The Reactions of the US, UK, and Japan*. Leiden: Brill.
68 British Embassy, Tokyo. 'Extract from the United States intelligence report No. 4488 of 6/1/55.' 17 January 1955. London: The National Archives. D/2231/85, FO 371/116977.
69 Makins, Roger. 'Addressed to Foreign Office telegram No. 132.' *Telegram from British Embassy, Washington, to Foreign Office, London*. 26 February 1955. London: The National Archives. D/2231/119, FO 371/116966, Set 10.
70 US Department of State. 'Memorandum of a Conversation, Department of State, Washington, April 8, 1955 2:35 p.m.' In *Foreign Relations of the United States, 1955–1957 Volume II, China*. Washington: US Department of State, Office of the Historian, 1955a.
71 Crombie, G. E. 'Communist Aims at Afro-Eurasian Conference.' *Communication from Commonwealth Relations Office to F. S. Tomlinson, Foreign Office, London*. 25 April 1955. London: The National Archives. D2231/297, FO 371/116982.

72 Nehru, Jawaharlal. 1955. Jawaharlal Nehru's speech to the political committee of the Asia-Africa conference, 23 April.
73 Khudori, Darwis. 2018. *Bandung Legacy and Global Future: New Insights and Emerging Forces*. New Delhi: Aakar Books.
74 UK Foreign Office, Research Department, London. 'A Review of the Afro-Asian Conference.' 5 May 1955. London: The National Archives. D2231/368, FO 371/116986.
75 Sid-Ahmed. Mohamed. 2005. The Bandung Way. *Al-Ahram Weekly*.
76 Ibid.
77 Jack, Homer A. 1955. *Bandung: An On-the-Spot Description of the Asian-African Conference, Bandung, Indonesia* Chicago: Toward Freedom.
78 Ministry of Foreign Affairs, Indonesia. 1955. Final communiqué of the Asian-African conference of Bandung. 24 April.
79 Acharya. *Whose Ideas Matter?*
80 Ministry of Foreign Affairs, Indonesia. Final communiqué.
81 Nehru. Speech to the political committee.
82 Ministry of Foreign Affairs, Indonesia. Final communiqué.
83 Reus-Smit, Christian. 2013. *Individual Rights and the Making of the International System*. Cambridge: Cambridge University Press.
84 Kahin, George McTrunan. 1956. *The Asian-African Conference: Bandung, Indonesia, April 1955*. Ithaca: Cornell University Press.
85 Crocker, W. R. 'Personal Impressions by the Australian Ambassador to Indonesia – Far Eastern Department.' 1955. London: The National Archives. DO35-6099.
86 National Archives. CO 936-350.
87 US Department of State. 'US Department of State Intelligence Report No. 6903, 27 April 1955, 'Results of the Bandung Conference: A Preliminary Analysis."' In *Dispatch from British Embassy, Washington, to Foreign Office, London*. 1955. London: The National Archives. D2231/373, FO 371/116986.

88 UK Foreign Office. Review of the Asian-African Conference.
89 Morland. Some Impressions of the Bandung Conference by R.W. Parkes.
90 Kahin. *The Asian-African Conference.*
91 Sukarno. 1955. Opening speech at the Bandung conference.' *Asia-Africa Speaks from Bandung.* Jakarta: Ministry of Foreign Affairs.
92 Abdulghani, Roselan. 1964. *The Bandung Spirit.* Jakarta: Prapantja Press.
93 Bull, Hedley, and Adam Watson. 1984. *The Expansion of International Society.* New York: Oxford University Press.
94 Acharya. *Whose Ideas Matter?*
95 Abdulghani. *The Bandung Spirit.*
96 UK High Commission. "Afro-Asian Conference' - Telegram to Commonwealth Relations Office,' 2 May 1955. London: The National Archives. FC1041/828, FO 371/115049.
97 Ibid.
98 Crocker, W. R. 'Personal Impressions by the Australian Ambassador to Indonesia – Far Eastern Department.' 1955. London: The National Archives. DO35-6099.
99 This chapter is adapted from the author's book: Acharya, Amitav. 2012. *The Making of Southeast Asia: International Relations of a Region.* Ithaca: Cornell University Press. It also draws on a paper drafted for the 'Singapore Biennale 2013: If the World Changed,' Singapore Art Museum, 2013.
100 Melchor, Alejandro. 1975. Security issues in Southeast Asia. Jakarta: Centre for Strategic and International Studies.
101 Ibid.
102 Hall, D.G.E. 1968. *A History of South-East Asia.* London: Palgrave Macmillan.
103 Gordon, Bernard K. 1966. *The Dimensions of Conflict in Southeast Asia.* New Jersey: Prentice Hall.

104 Ibid.
105 Association of Southeast Asia. 1962. *Report of the Special Session of Foreign Ministers of ASA*. Kuala Lumpur / Cameron Highlands: Federation of Malaya.
106 Ibid.
107 Ibid.
108 Ibid.
109 Ibid.
110 Ibid.
111 Ibid.
112 Acharya. *The Making of Southeast Asia: International Relations of the Region*.
113 Ghazali bin Shafie, Muhammad. 1982. Confrontation leads to ASEAN. *Asian Defence Journal*.
114 Malik, Adam. 1975. Regional cooperation in international politics. Jakarta: Centre for Strategic and International Studies.
115 Rajaratnam, S. 1968. Statement at the Second ASEAN Ministerial Meeting in Jakarta, August 6, 1968.' Ed. Boni Ray Siagian. Jakarta: Department of Information and ASEAN National Secretariat.
116 Onn, Hussein. 2021. Opening speech at second meeting of ASEAN Economic Ministers, Kuala Lumpur, March 8–9, 1976. Ed. Thakur Phanit. Bangkok: International Studies Centre.
117 Acharya, Amitav. 2001. *Constructing a Security Community in Southeast Asia: ASEAN and the Problem of Regional Order*. London: Routledge.
118 Ibid.
119 Ghazali bin Shafie, Muhammad. 2000. *Malaysia, ASEAN and the New World Order*. Bangi: Universiti Kebangsaan Malaysia Press.
120 Ibid.

121 Solidum, Estrella. 2003. *The Politics of ASEAN: An Introduction to Southeast Asian Regionalism*. Singapore: Marshall Cavendish.
122 Romulo, Carlos, P. 1978. A perspective on ASEAN. *Asia-Pacific Community*, 2: 1–6.
123 Onn. Opening Speech at second meeting of ASEAN Economic Ministers.
124 Lacanlale, Agerico. 1982. Community formation in ASEAN's external relations. Ed. R.P. Anand and Purificacion Quisumbing. Quezon City and Honolulu: University of the Philippines Law Center and East-West Center Culture Learning Institute.
125 Capie, David, and Paul Evans. 2007. *The Asia-Pacific Security Lexicon*. Singapore: ISEAS-Yusof Ishak Institute.
126 Harris, Stuart. 1996. The regional role of 'Track Two' diplomacy. In *The Role of Security and Economic Cooperation Structures in the Asia Pacific Region: Indonesian and Australian Views*, ed. Hadi Soesastro and Anthony Bergin. Jakarta and Canberra: Centre for Strategic and International Studies and Australian Defence Studies Centre.
127 Ibid.
128 Paribatra, Sukhumbhnad. 1997. ASEAN Ten and its role in the Asia Pacific. Paper presented at the 'Asia in the XXI Century' conference, April 28–29.
129 Hernandez, Carolina. 1995. One Southeast Asia in the 21st century: Opportunities and challenges. Paper presented at the 1995 Convention of the Canadian Council for Southeast Asian Studies, October 27–29, Quebec City, Canada.
130 Acharya. *The Making of Southeast Asia*.
131 Emmerson. Southeast Asia: What's in a name?
132 Reid, Anthony. 1999. A Saucer Model of Southeast Asian identity. *Southeast Asian Journal of Social Science* 27, 1: 7–23.

133 Smail, John R.W. 1961. On the possibility of an autonomous history of modern Southeast Asia. *Journal of Southeast Asian History* 2, 2: 72–102.

134 Emmerson, Donald K. 1984. Beyond Western surprise: Thoughts on the evolution of Southeast Asian Studies. In *Southeast Asian Studies: Options for the Future,* ed. Ronald A. Morse, Lanham, MD: University Press of America.

135 McVey, Ruth. 1995. Change and continuity in Southeast Asian Studies. *Journal of Southeast Asian Studies* 26, 1: 1–9.

136 Ibid.

137 Fifield, Russell H. 1976. Southeast Asian Studies: Origins, development, future. *Journal of Southeast Asian Studies* 7, 2: 151–61.

138 Ness, Garry and Martha Morrow. 1984. Assessing U.S. scholarly resources on Southeast Asia. In *Southeast Asian Studies: Options for the Future,* ed. Ronald A. Morse, Lanham, NY: University Press of America.

139 ASEAN, 'Declaration of ASEAN Concord II (Bali Concord II).' 11 May 2012. https://asean.org/speechandstatement/declaration-of-asean-concord-ii-bali-concord-ii/.

140 ASEAN. *ASEAN 2525: Forging Ahead Together* (Jakarta: ASEAN Secretariat, 2015) http://www.asean.org/storage/2015/12/ASEAN-2025-Forging-Ahead-Together-final.pdf.

141 Intal, Jr., Ponciano S. et.al. 2017. Voices of ASEAN: What does ASEAN mean to ASEAN peoples? Jakarta: Economic Research Institute for ASEAN and East Asia.

142 This chapter is based on Acharya, Amitav. 1995. Human Rights in Southeast Asia: Dilemmas of foreign policy. *Eastern Asia Policy Papers* 11. The paper was commissioned by the Canadian International Development Agency (CIDA).

143 Awanohara, Susumu, Michael Vatikiotis and Shada Islam. 1993. Vienna Showdown. *Far Eastern Economic Review* 156, 24: 16–17.

144 Hernandez, Carolina. ASEAN Perspectives on human rights and democracy in international relations: Problems and Prospects. Working Paper of the Centre for International Studies, University of Toronto, no. 1995-1.

145 Davies, Mathew. 2014. An agreement to disagree: The ASEAN human rights declaration and the absence of regional identity in Southeast Asia. *Journal of Current Southeast Asian Affairs* 33, 3: 107–129.

146 Fairclough, Gordon. 1993. Standing Firm. *Far Eastern Economic Review.* 22–3.

147 Awanohara, Vatikiotis and Islam. Vienna Showdown.

148 _____1993. Take pragmatic line on human rights: Kan Seng. *The Straits Times*, 17 June.

149 Talib, Ahmad. 1991. Don't preach, West told. *New Straits Times*, 20 July.

150 _____1993. Alatas: No nation can judge others on human rights. *The Straits Times*, 16 June.

151 Mahbubani, Kishore. 1992. New areas of ASEAN Reaction: Environment, Human Rights and Democracy. *Asean-ISIS Monitor*, 5. Such an emphasis on communitarianism has not escaped criticism. According to one critic: 'The pre-industrial societies of Asia, as elsewhere, did place community and the obligation to it ahead of individuals and their rights. But this observation does not license a leap to the claim that modern East Asian societies are consequently not suited to the observance of human rights or liberal democracy because of residual Confucianism. This ignores the historical discrediting of Confucianism, the emergence of revolutionary left-wing politics and the development in South Korea, Taiwan, Hong Kong and Singapore of

the most un-Confucian practices associated with rapid industrial growth such as corporate conglomerates with twelve-hour working days for the executives, the breaking up of community through massive urbanization, the necessity of parliamentarism for legitimacy, government by military elites and the militarization of politics.' Tremewan, Christopher. 1993. Human Rights in Asia. *The Pacific Review* 6, 1: 17–30.

152 ASEAN. Joint communique of the Twenty-Sixth ASEAN Ministerial Meeting. Singapore, July 23–4, 1993.
153 Talib. Don't preach, West told.
154 _____ 1993. KL will continue to speak up: Foreign Minister. *The Straits Times*. 22 June.
155 ASEAN. Joint communique of the Twenty-Sixth ASEAN Ministerial Meeting.
156 ASEAN-ISIS. 1993. *The Environment and Human Rights in International Relations: An Agenda for ASEAN's Policy Approaches and Response*. Jakarta: ASEAN-ISIS.
157 Take pragmatic line on human rights: Kan Seng. *The Straits Times*.
158 Mahbubani. New Areas of ASEAN Reaction.
159 Jones, Sidney. 1993. Human Rights: Basic elements of effective protection. Paper presented at ASEAN-ISIS Asia Pacific Roundtable, June 6–9, Kuala Lumpur, Malaysia.
160 Ghai, Yash. 1994. *Human Rights and Governance: The Asia Debate*. San Francisco: The Asia Foundation, Center for Asian Pacific Affairs.
161 Donnelly, Jack. 1984. Cultural relativism and universal human rights. *Human Rights Quarterly* 6, 4: 400–19; Tremewan. Human rights in Asia.
162 On the role of human rights NGOs in Asia, see: Jones, Sidney. 1993. The Organic growth: Asian NGOs have come into their own. *Far Eastern Economic Review* 156, 24: 23.

163 Jones, Sidney. 1995. The impact of Asian economic growth on human rights. *Asia Project Working Paper*, New York: Council on Foreign Relations.
164 _____1994. Thailand: Rights activists get cold reception. *Bangkok Post*, 26 July.
165 Vatikiotis, Michael. 1994. Going Regional. *Far Eastern Economic Review* 157, 42: 16.
166 Richardson, Michael. 1993. For the planners, a time to decide. *International Herald Tribune*, 18 November.
167 _____Take pragmatic line on human rights: Kan Seng. *The Straits Times*.
168 Mahbubani. News Areas of ASEAN Reaction.
169 This point was made by a senior Singapore Foreign Ministry official. See Mahbubani, Kishore. 1992. The west and the rest. *The National Interest* 28: 3–12.
170 _____Alatas: No nation can judge others on human rights. *The Straits Times*.
171 Ramcharan, Robin. 2000. ASEAN and Non-Interference: A principle maintained. *Contemporary Southeast* Asia 22, 1: 60–88.
172 _____Alatas: No nation can judge others on human rights. *The Straits Times*.
173 RSIS Centre for Non-Traditional Security Studies. Interview with Mr. Rafendi Djamin, Commissioner of Indonesia to AICHR. RSIS Centre for NTS Studies and ICRC Regional Workshop on the Protection of Civilians, Singapore, 15–16 July 2010.
174 Ibid.
175 Ehy Hara, Abubaker. 2019. The struggle to uphold a regional human rights regime: The winding role of ASEAN Intergovernmental Commission on Human Rights (AICHR). *Revista Brasileira de Politica Internacional* 62, 1.
176 The High-Level Dialogue on Human Rights in ASEAN. 'Joint Statement: ASEAN needs a stronger Human Rights

Mechanism.' Organized by the Asian Forum for Human Rights and Development (FORUM-ASIA), ASEAN Parliamentarians for Human Rights (APHR) and the Centre for Strategic and International Studies (CSIS), 9 May 2019.

177 Wu, Chien-Huei. 2016. Human rights in ASEAN context: Between universalism and relativism. In *Legal Thoughts between the East and the West in the Multilevel Legal Order: A Liber Amicorum in Honour of Professor Herbert Han-Pao Ma*, ed. Chang-fa Lo, Nigel N.T. Li, and Tsai-yu Lin, Berlin, Germany: Springer.

178 EEAS Press Team. 2023. ASEAN: 5th policy dialogue on human rights with the European Union takes place in Brussels. *EEAS*, 3 October.

179 UN Office of the High Commissioner for Human Rights. 2017. Report of OHCHR Mission to Bangladesh interviews with Rohingyas fleeing from Myanmar since 9 October 2016.

180 UNICEF. 2019. Bangladesh Humanitarian Situation Report No. 52 (Rohingya Influx). *UNICEF*, 22 July.

181 Ibid.

182 Ha, Hoang Thi, and Ye Htut. 2016. Rakhine crisis challenges ASEAN's Non-Interference Principle. *ISEAS Perspective* 70: 1–8; Lego, Jera. 2017. Why ASEAN can't ignore the Rohingya crisis. *The Diplomat*, 17 May.

183 Ong-Webb, Graham. 2020. Southeast Asia in 2019: Adjustment and adaptation to China's regional impact. *Southeast Asian Affairs* 1: 11–14.

184 ASEAN. 2019. Chairman's Statement of the 34th ASEAN Summit.

185 Human Rights Watch. 2020. ASEAN: Overhaul regional response to Rohingya crisis.

186 Spandler, Kilian. 2020. Lessons from ASEAN's Rakhine response. *East Asia Forum*.

187 Acharya, Amitav. 2022. *Tragic Nation Burma: Why and How Democracy Failed*. Singapore: Penguin Random House SEA.

188 Khoo Ying Hooi. 2020. Southeast Asia's pandemic politics and human rights: Trends and lessons. *LSE Blog*.

189 Maude, Richard. 2022. Human rights in Southeast Asia during the pandemic. *Asia Society Policy Institute and Asia Society Australia Project Report*, 22 November.

190 Huntington, Samuel P. 1991. *The Third Wave: Democratization in the Late Twentieth Century*. Norman, OK: University of Oklahoma Press.

191 Rustow, Dankwart A. 1990. Democracy: A global revolution? *Foreign Affairs* 69, 4: 75–91.

192 Karl, Terry Lynn and Philippe C. Schmitter. 1994. Democratization around the globe: Opportunities and Risks. In *World Security: Challenges for a New Century*, ed. Michael T. Klare and Daniel C. Thomas, New York: St. Martin's Press.

193 Frank, Thomas M. 1992. The emerging right to democratic governance. *The American Journal of International Law* 86, 1: 46–91.

194 Diamond, Larry. 1993. The globalization of democracy. In *Global Transformation and the Third World*, ed. Robert Slater, Barry Schutz and Steven Dorr, Boulder, CO: Lynne Rienner; Diamond, Larry. 1992. Promoting Democracy. *Foreign Policy* 87: 25–46.

195 Fukuyama, Francis. 1992. *The End of History and the Last Man*. New York: Avon Books.

196 Chee, Chan Heng. 1982. Political stability in Southeast Asia. Paper presented to the Seminar on Trends and Perspectives in ASEAN, Institute of Southeast Asian Studies, February 1–3, Singapore.

197 Huntington, Samuel P. 1993. Cart before the horse. *Financial Mail* 129, 5: 39, cited in *The South at the End of the Twentieth Century*, ed. by Larry Swatuk and Timothy Shaw, London: Macmillan.

198 A good deal of this literature was developed at the Asia Research Centre at Murdoch University, Perth in the 1980s and 1990s, and featured scholars such as Garry Rodan, Richard Robinson, Richard Higgott and Kevin Hewison. See for example, *Southeast Asia in the 1990s: Authoritarianism, Democracy and Capitalism,* ed. Kevin Hewison, Richard Robison, and Garry Rodan, St. Leonards, New South Wales: Allen and Unwin. This literature rejected modernization theory and the Third Wave scholarship led by Huntington or the O'Donnell, Schmitter and Whitehead team where a common focus was on the impact of economic growth in fostering democratization. The Murdoch School laid even more emphasis on domestic economic factors, in contrast to the wider perspective of the Third Wave literature, which also took note of bargaining, elite pacts, and to a limited degree, external political factors.

199 This quote is from 1992. *The Wit and Wisdom of Lee Kuan Yew,* ed. Douglas Armine and Lindsay Davis, Singapore: Editions Didier Millet

200 Richardson, Michael. 1993. For the planners, a time to decide. *International Herald Tribune,* 18 November: 5.

201 Talib. Don't preach, West Told.

202 Samad, Nuraina. 1998. PM: "New capitalists" may dominate Asian economies. *New Straits Times,* 5 June.

203 Pitsuwan, Surin. 2017. Democracy in Southeast Asia: Achievements, Challenges and Prospects. *Kofi Annan Foundation Conference Report.*

204 Ibrahim, Anwar. 1994. Asia's new civility. *Far Eastern Economic Review.* 34.

205 See Acharya, Amitav. 1995. Human rights and regional order: ASEAN and human rights management in post-Cold War Southeast Asia. In *Human Rights and International Relations in the Asia-Pacific,* ed. James T.H. Tang, London:

Pinter; Acharya, Amitav. 1995. *Human Rights in Southeast Asia: Dilemmas of Foreign Policy.* Toronto: JCAPS.

206 Mackie, Jamie. 1998. Development and democratisation in East and Southeast Asia. *Agenda: A Journal of Policy Analysis and Reform* 5, 3: 335–46.

207 Albright, Madeleine K. 1998. Opening remarks before the Senate Appropriations Committee Subcommittee on Foreign Operations. Washington D.C.

208 _____1998. An open government saved us: Ramos. *The Straits Times*, 16 June.

209 _____1998. Riots not a call for democracy: Interview with Lee Kuan Yew. *The Straits Times*, 16 June.

210 Singapore Government Press Release. 1998. Asia in crisis: Risks and Chances. Speech by Senior Minister Lee Kuan Yew to the Dusseldorf Industry Club, October 8, Dusseldorf, Germany.

211 _____Riots not a call for democracy. *The Straits Times.*

212 _____*The Wit and Wisdom of Lee Kuan Yew.*

213 _____1970. White House Memorandum of Conversation. The National Security Archive, 26 May.

214 Dori, John and Jams Przystup. 1998. Indonesia after Suharto: How the US can foster political and economic reform. *The Heritage Foundation Report.*

215 _____2000. IMF delays release of loan to Indonesia. *The Wall Street Journal*, 28 March.

216 Larimer, Tim. 1998. Surin: Because of the crisis, we are prone to conflict. *Time*, 2 November.

217 Mitton, Roger. 1998. Divided we stand. *CNN AsiaWeek*, 31 July.

218 Richardson, Michael. 1998. Singapore and Malaysia watch with alarm: Indonesia's neighbours fear wave of refugees.

International Herald Tribune/New York Times, 11 February; Sadli, Mohammad. 1998. The Indonesian crisis. *ASEAN Economic Bulletin* 15, 3: 272–80.

219 Mitton. Divided we stand.
220 Jasin, A. Kadir. 1997. ASEAN stand on Cambodia commendable. *New Straits Times*, 13 July.
221 Acharya, Amitav. 2014. *Constructing a Security Community in Southeast Asia: ASEAN and the Problem of Regional Order*. Oxfordshire: Routledge.
222 Ibid.
223 Mansfield, Edward and Jack Snyder. 1995. Democratization and the danger of war. *International Security* 20, 1: 5–38.
224 Mishra, Pankaj. 2013. After Suharto. *London Review of Books* 35, 19.
225 Mohammed, Arshad and Ed Davies. 2009. Indonesia sows Islam, modernity coexist: Clinton. *Reuters*, 17 February.
226 Acharya, Amitav. 2014. *Indonesia Matters: Asia's Emerging Democratic Power*. Singapore: World Scientific.
227 The World Bank. 2000. GDP Growth (Annual %) – Indonesia.
228 Nugroho, Yanuar and Sujarwoto. 2021. Institutions, outputs and outcomes: Two decades of decentralization and state capacity in Indonesia. *Journal of Southeast Asian Economies* 38, 3: 296–319.
229 Suhartono, Muktita and Daniel Victor. 2019. Violence erupts in Indonesia's capital in wake of presidential election results. *New York Times*, 22 May.
230 Yu, Truston. 2019. Ethnicity is futile: It's time for Indonesia to move towards civic nationalism. *The Jakarta Post*, 22 September.
231 Westminster Foundation for Democracy. Indonesia.
232 Hunt, Luke. 2017. A more taxing time for Cambodia's civil society? *The Diplomat*, 9 August; UN Office of the High

Commissioner for Human Rights. 2021. Cambodia: Stop backsliding and expand freedom – UN expert.

233 Human Rights Watch. 2022. 'Locked inside our homes': Movement restrictions on rights activists in Vietnam.

234 _____2020. Singapore ruling PAP wins elections, but support falls. *BBC*, 10 July; Ooi Kok Hin. 2020. Singapore's election: Why aren't the winners smiling? *The Interpreter*, 21 July.

235 Marston, Hunter. 2021. Civil society and Southeast Asia's authoritarian turn. *New Mandala*, 4 June.

236 Cook, Tim. 2011. Thailand's July election: Understanding the outcome, Interview with Catharin Dalpino. *The National Bureau of Asian Research*, 21 July.

237 Overholt, William H. 2017. Duterte, democracy, and defense. *Brookings Institution Report*, 21 January.

238 Curato, Nicole. 2021. Democratic expressions amidst fragile institutions: Possibilities for reform in Duterte's Philippines. *Brookings Institution Article*, 22 January.

239 Assistance Association for Political Prisoners (Burma). https://aappb.org/.

240 Tomsa, Dirk. 2010. Indonesian politics in 2010: The perils of stagnation. *Bulletin of Indonesian Economic Studies* 46, 3: 309–28.

241 Tehusijarana, Karina, Marguerite Afra Sapiie, Ghina Ghaliya and Nurul Fitri Ramadhani. 2019. It's over: Jokowi wins. *The Jakarata Post*, 22 May.

242 Yeo, George. 2017. 'Civilisational states' like China are less prone to populism. *The Straits Times*, 29 May.

243 Jennings, Ralph. 2020. Why Vietnam is asking other Asian countries to help squelch fake news. *Voice of America*, 1 October.

244 _____2020. Cambodia uses Coronavirus crisis to arrest 17 critics, rights group says. *Reuters*, 24 March.

245 Ganjanakhundee, Supalak. 2020. COVID-19 in Thailand: The securitization of a non-traditional threat. *ISEAS–Yusof Ishak Institute Perspective* 51.

246 Enos, Olivia. 2020. Responding to COVID-19 in Southeast Asia. *Asian Studies Centre Issue Brief* 5058, The Heritage Foundation.

247 Dalpino, Catharine. 2020. Diplomatic doldrums: ASEAN loses momentum in the pandemic as security tensions rise. *Comparative Connections* 22, 2.

248 Gorbiano, Marchio Irfan. 2020. Jokowi uses reshuffle threat to spur cabinet into action. *The Jakarta Post*, 30 June.

249 Sriring, Orathai and Panu Wongcha-um. 2020. Thailand's new finance minister resigns amid economic crisis. *Reuters*, 1 September.

250 Beech, Hannah. 2020. Protests take on Thai monarchy, despite laws banning such criticism. *The New York Times*, 13 August.

251 Lewis, Simon. 2022. Southeast Asian leaders face rights questions, flying shoe on Washington debut. *Reuters*, 12 May.

252 Pitsuwan, Surin. *Kofi Annan Foundation Conference Report*.

253 Ibid.

254 _____ 2023. Cambodia leader Hun Sen to step down, hand over power to son. *Al Jazeera*, 26 July.

255 Kurlantzick, Joshua. 2023. The state of democracy in Southeast Asia is bad and getting worse. *World Politics Review*, 9 August.

256 Nayt Thit. 2023. Myanmar junta goes on the defensive in August, resistance gains ground. *The Irrawaddy*, 31 August.

257 Tin Aung Khaing and Kyaw Lwin Oo. 2023. Ethnic armies' 'Operation 1027' put Myanmar junta on defensive in 2023. *Radio Free Asia*, 30 December.

258 Wong, Andrea Chloe. 2021. SE Asian democratic reversals favour China. *Philippine Daily Inquirer*, 26 March.

259 _____ 2022. An adjustment to global poverty lines. *The World Bank Factsheet*, 14 September.

260 United Nations Development Program. 2022. 2022 Global Multidimensional Poverty Index. *Human Development Reports*, 17 October.

261 Kochhar, Rakesh. 2015. Despite poverty's plunge, middle-class status remains out of reach for many. *Pew Research Centre Report*, 8 July.

262 Alkire, Sabina, Christian Oldiges and Usha Kanagaratnam. 2021. Examining multidimensional poverty reduction in India 2005/6-2015/16: Insights and oversights of the Headcount Ratio. *World Development* 142; _____ 2021. New OPHI article analyses poverty in India using Multidimensional poverty Index v/s Headcount Ratio. *Oxford Department of International Development*, 22 March.

263 Safi, Michael. 2019. Churchill's policies contributed to 1943 Bengal Famine – Study. *The Guardian*, 29 March.

264 Waal, Alex de. 2000. Democratic political process and the fight against fame. *Institute of Development Studies Working Paper* 107.

265 Mya Maung. 1989. The Burma road to poverty: A socio-political analysis. *The Fletcher Forum of World Affairs* 13, 2: 271–94.

266 Nugraha, Purna Cita and Amitav Acharya. 2021. Will Indonesia's trifecta survive COVID-19? *The Jakarta Post*, 20 January.

267 Diamond, Larry. 2004. Moving on up out of poverty: What does democracy have to do with it? *Centre on Democracy, Development and Rule of Law Working Paper* 4.

268 Mahler, Daniel Gerszon, Nichant Yonzan, Christoph Lakner, R. Andres Castaneda Aguilar and Haoyu Wu. 2021. Updated estimates of the impact of COVID-19 on global poverty: Turning the corner on the pandemic in 2021? *World Bank Blogs*, 24.

269 Kurlantzick, Joshua. 2021. COVID-19 and its effect on inequality and democracy: A study of five large democracies. *Council on Foreign Relations Working Paper*.

270 Maude, Richard. 2020. COVID-19, government and security in Southeast Asia. *Asia Society Policy Institute Essay*.

271 Mearsheimer, John. 2001. *The Tragedy of Great Power Politics*. New York, NY: W.W. Norton & Company; Mearsheimer, John. 2006. China's unpeaceful rise. *Current History* 105, 690: 160–62.

272 Kang, David C. 2003. Getting Asia wrong: The need for new analytical frameworks. *International Security* 27, 4: 57–85. For a contrarian view, see Acharya, Amitav. 2003/2004. Will Asia's past be its future? *International Security* 28, 3: 149–64.

273 Friedberg, Aaron L. 1993/1994. Ripe for rivalry: Prospects for peace in a multipolar Asia. *International Security* 18, 3: 5–33; Friedberg, Aaron L. 2000. Will Europe's past be Asia's future? *Survival* 42, 3: 147–60.

274 Bull, Hedley. 1977. *The Anarchical Society: A Study of Order in World Politics*. New York City, NY: Columbia University Press.

275 Deutsche, Karl, and David Singer. 1964. Multipolar power systems and international stability. *World Politics* 16, 3: 390–406.

276 Acharya, Amitav. 2014. *The End of American World Order*. Cambridge: Polity; Acharya, Amitav. 2014. From the unipolar moment to a multiplex world. *YaleGlobal*, 3 July.

277 Bremmer, Ian and Nouriel Roubini. 2011. A G-Zero world: The new economic club will produce conflict, not cooperation. *Foreign Affairs* 90, 2.

278 Heijmans, Philip. 2017. China's plan to buy influence and undermine democracy. *The Atlantic*, 18 October.

279 Phillips, Tom, Oliver Holmes and Owen Bowcott. 2016. Beijing rejects tribunal's ruling in South China Sea case. *The Guardian*, 12 July.

280 The full text of the verdict at: Permanent Court of Arbitration. 2016. *The South China Sea Arbitration* (The Republic of the Philippines V. The People's Republic of China). *The Hague Press Release*, 12 July.

281 Ching, Nike. 2018. South China Sea Code of Conduct gains momentum as China moves to complete militarization. *VOA News*, 22 October.

282 Ibid.

283 Richburg, Keith. 2011. US pivot to Asia makes China nervous. *The Washington Post*, 16 November.

284 Ma, Alexandra. 2018. Malaysia has axed $22 Billion of Chinese-backed projects, in a blow to China's grand plan to dominate world trade. *Business Insider*, 21 August.

285 Lam, Angus. 2020. Domestic politics in Southeast Asia and local backlash against the Belt and Road Initiative. *Foreign Policy Research Institute*, 15 October; _____ 2019. Beware of BRI debt trap. *The Bangkok Post*, 27 April.

286 _____ 2019. RPT-Malaysia says it is keen for more 'fair' deals with China. *Reuters*, 23 April.

287 _____ 2022. Signing of Japanese ODA loan agreement with Cambodia: Expanding Sihanoukville Port through the construction of new container terminals to contribute to the improvement of the logistics environment in Cambodia. *Japanese International Cooperation Agency Press Release*, 8 August.

288 Myers, Lucas. 2020. The China-Myanmar Economic Corridor and China's determination to see it through. *Wilson Centre Asia Dispatches*, 26 May.

289 Yao, Kevin. 2019. China seeks to allay fears over Belt and Road debt risks. *Reuters*, 24 April.

290 _____ 2019. *The State of Southeast Asia, 2019*. Singapore: Institute of Southeast Asian Studies-Yushof-Ishak Institute. The survey was conducted by the

ISEAS-Yushof-Ishak Institute of Singapore with 1,008 respondents drawn from all ten ASEAN member states to ensure that the survey accurately reflects the regional view. The highest responses for the survey came from Myanmar (16.9 per cent), followed by Malaysia (14.5 per cent), Singapore (12.7 per cent), Vietnam (12.3 per cent), Indonesia (11.4 per cent), Thailand (11.4 per cent), the Philippines (11 per cent), Brunei Darussalam (4.5 per cent), Laos (2.9 per cent) and Cambodia (2.4 per cent).
291 Ibid, 2022.
292 Ibid, 2023.
293 Law, Elizabeth. 2020. The bugs in China's mask diplomacy. *The Straits Times*, 2 April.
294 Baharudin, Hariz. 2020. Wuhan Virus: MOH says online chatter that someone in Singapore has died from virus is fake news. *The Straits Times*, 25 January.
295 US Department of State. 2019. A free and open Indo-Pacific: Advancing a shared vision.
296 *The State of Southeast Asia Survey*, 2019.
297 Ibid.
298 Ibid, 2022.
299 Ibid, 2023.
300 Kamata, Jio. 2022. The paradox of China-Japan relations. *The Diplomat*, 22 September.
301 Ladwig III, Walter C. and Anit Mukherjee. 2019. The United States, India, and the future of the Indo-Pacific strategy. *The National Bureau of Asian Research Commentary*.
302 Gallo, William. 2019. Trump says South Korea to pay 'substantially more' for US troops. *VOA News*, 7 August.
303 Kelly, Terrence K, James Dobbins, David A. Shlapak, David C. Gompert, Eric Heginbotham, Peter Chalk and Llyod Thrall. 2014. Developing a U.S. strategy for dealing with China: Now and into the future. *RAND Research Brief*.

304 Tian, Nan, Alexandra Kuimova, Diego Lopes da Silva, Pieter D. Wezeman and Siemon T. Wezeman. 2020. Trends in world military expenditure, 2019. *SIPRI Fact Sheet*.

305 Schuman, Michael. 2023. China could soon be the dominant military power in Asia. *The Atlantic*, 4 May.

306 Cozad, Mark, Jeffrey Engstrom, Scott Harold, Timothy Heath, Sale Lilly, Edmund Burke, Julia Brackup and Derek Grossman. 2023. Gaining victory in systems warfare: China's perspective on the US-China military balance. *RAND Research Report*.

307 Roggeveen, Sam. 2022. China's third aircraft carrier is aimed at a post-US Asia. *Foreign Policy*, 21 June.

308 Christensen, Thomas J. 2020. A modern tragedy? COVID-19 and US-China relations. *Brookings Policy Brief*.

309 Ba, Alice. 2023. In Southeast Asia, US-China competition is more than a two-player game. *USIP Analysis and Commentary*.

310 Cheng, Evelyn. 2023. US-China relations are now more about crisis prevention. *CNBC*, 14 November.

311 Shambaugh, David. 2018. U.S.-China rivalry in Southeast Asia: Power shift or competitive coexistence? *International Security* 42, 4: 85–127.

312 Cheng-Chwee, Kuik. 2020. Hedging in post-pandemic Asia: What, how, and why? *The Asan Forum*, 6 June.

313 Cheng-Chwee, Kwik. 2018. Opening a strategic Pandora's jar? US-China uncertainties and the three wandering genies in Southeast Asia. *The Asan Forum*, 2 July.

314 Wong, Catherine. 2018. Singapore leader Lee Hsien Loong warns region may have to choose between China and US. *South China Morning Post*, 15 November.

315 Ba. In Southeast Asia, US-China competition is more than a two-player game.

316 Yamaguchi, Mari. 2023. Japan and ASEAN bolster ties at summit focused on security amid China tensions. *CTV News*, 16 December.

317 Acharya, Amitav. 1995. Transnational production and security: Southeast Asia's growth triangles. *Contemporary Southeast Asia* 17, 2: 173–85.

318 Economic interdependence discourages war by increasing its costs; it does not preclude war.

319 Acharya, Amitav. 1995. A regional security community in Southeast Asia? *Journal of Strategic Studies* 18, 3: 175–200; Acharya, Amitav. 2014. *Constructing a Security Community in Southeast Asia: ASEAN and the Problem of Regional Order.* New York: Routledge.

320 Acharya, Amitav. 2014. Power shift or paradigm shift: China's rise and Asia's security order. *International Studies Quarterly* 58, 1: 158–73.

321 Zakaria, Fareed. 2008. *The Post-American World.* New York: W.W. Norton. Although Zakaria recognized the rise of new powers like China and India challenging US hegemony, he did not foresee the end of the liberal order but continued to believe in its continuation. See also, Kupchan, Charles. 2013. *No One's World: The West, the Rise of the Rest and the Coming Global Turn.* New York: Oxford University Press. Like other writings on the subject, this book was more about the relative decline of the West, rather than about the decline of the US-led liberal order. The latter was clearly the focus of Acharya, Amitav. 2014. *The End of American World Order.* Cambridge: Polity. This book, published two years before Trump's elections, argued that the US-led liberal world order is ending, regardless of the US itself declining or not.

322 Liu, Sebastian. 2018. Deep waters, close quarters: Malaysia and Singapore's cross-strait disputes. *The Diplomat*, 20 December.

323 Heiduk, Felix. 2018. Is Southeast Asia really in an arms race? *East Asia Forum*, 21 February.

324 Fajrilla Sidiq, Mabda Haerunnisa. 2022. Cornerstone no more? The changing role of ASEAN in Indonesian foreign policy. *The Diplomat*, 5 October.

325 Acharya, Amitav. 2011. Can Asia lead? Power ambitions and global governance in the twenty-first century. *International Affairs* 87, 4: 851–69.

326 _____ 2023. For ASEAN countries, IMF sees slower growth outweighing China reopening. *Reuters*, 31 January.

327 Ibid.

328 Park, Albert. 2022. Asian Development Outlook (ADO) supplement: Key messages. *Asian Development Bank*.

329 McDermid, Charles. 2019. US-China trade war divides Southeast Asia, Belt and Road fears unite it: Survey. *South China Morning Post*, 9 January.

330 Choudhury, Saheli Roy. 2019. US-China trade war could create winners in Southeast Asia: Bain & Co. *CNBC*, 23 November.

331 Pereira, Derwin. 2018. How the US-China trade war will make or break ASEAN. *South China Morning Post*, 16 November.

332 _____ 2019. RCEP deal goes down to wire. *The Bangkok Post*, 4 November.

333 _____ 2014. Escaping the Middle-Income Trap. *Global Economic Symposium*; _____ 2012. The Middle-Income Trap. *The Economist*, 27 March.

334 Kumagai, Satoru. 2018. The Middle-Income Trap in the ASEAN-4 countries from the trade structure viewpoint. In *Emerging States at Crossroads: Emerging Economy, State and International Policy Studies*, ed. K. Tsunekawa and Todo Y, Singapore: Springer.

335 Tho, Tran Van. 2013. The Middle-Income Trap: Issues for members of the Association of Southeast Asian Nations. *ADBI Working Papers* no 421.

336 Cossa, Ralph. 2020. Post COVID-19, the US-China rivalry will only get worse. *PacNet* 29.

337 _____ 2020. Trump again raises idea of decoupling economy from China. *Reuters*, 15 September.

338 Victor, Pamela. 2017. Deforestation – A modern-day plague in Southeast Asia. *The ASEAN Post*, 23 September.

339 Palminteri, Sue. 2018. Southeast Asian deforestation more extensive than thought, study finds. *Mongabay*, 18 July.

340 Raitzer, David A. 2015. *Southeast Asia and the Economics of Global Climate Stabilization*. Manila: Asian Development Bank.

341 Prakash, Amit. 2018. Boiling point. *Finance and Development* (The World Bank) 55, 3.

342 _____ 'Vietnam.' *Global Facility for Disaster Reduction and Recovery (GFDRR)*.

343 Yeung, Jessie. 2019. Indonesian forests are burning, and Malaysia and Singapore are choking on the fumes. *CNN*, 11 September.

344 _____ 2015. Indonesia's fire and haze crisis. *The World Bank* 25 November.

345 _____ 2018. ASEAN in 'good position' to take advantage of tech revolution: PM Lee. *Channel News Asia*, 12 September.

346 _____ 2018. ASEAN economies ill-prepared for old age. *Nikkei Asian Review*, 9 January.

347 Keiichiro, Oizumi. 2018. ASEAN's problem of declining birthrates and population aging: How to cope with widening domestic gaps. *Discuss Japan*, no. 43.

348 Kujis, Louis. 2017. ASEAN's impending demographic troubles. *Brink News*, 4 October.

349 Keiichiro. ASEAN's problem of declining birthrates and population aging.

350 The World Economic Forum and the Asian Development Bank. 2017. *ASEAN 4.0: What Does the Fourth Industrial Revolution Mean for Regional Economic Integration? We Forum.*

351 _____ 2023. Internet penetration in Southeast Asia as of July 2022, by country. *Statista*, 1 March.

352 ASEAN in 'good position' to take advantage of tech revolution: PM Lee. *Channel News Asia*

353 *The State of Southeast Asia Survey 2023.*

354 Acharya, Amitav. 2017. The evolution and limitations of ASEAN identity. In *Building ASEAN Community: Political-Security and Socio-Cultural Reflections.* Jakarta: Economic Research Institute for ASEAN and East Asia.

355 Intal Jr., Ponciano et al. 2017. Voices of ASEAN: What does ASEAN mean to ASEAN peoples? Jakarta: Economic Research Institute for ASEAN and East Asia.

356 Smith, Sheila A. 2021. The Quad in the Indo-Pacific: What to know. *CFR*, 27 May.

357 Pompeo, Michael R. 2018. Remarks on America's Indo-Pacific economic vision. U.S. Chamber of Commerce.

358 Marsudi, Retno. 2018. Kerja diplomasi Indonesia' (Indonesia's diplomatic activity). Paper presented to the Conference on Indonesian Foreign Policy Community, 20 October, Jakarta, Indonesia.

359 Japanese Ministry of Foreign Affairs. 2017. A new foreign policy strategy: Free and open Indo-Pacific strategy.

360 Government of India's Ministry of External Affairs. Address by Foreign Secretary at the Regional Connectivity conference: South Asia in the Indo-Pacific context.

361 For a thoughtful discussion, see: See Seng, Tan. 2019. Is ASEAN finally getting multilateralism right? From ARF to ADMM+. *Asian Studies Review.*

362 Acharya, Amitav. 2016. Security pluralism in the Asia-Pacific. *Global Asia* 11, 1: 12-17.

363 This chapter has been adapted from a previously authored article, cited as: Acharya, Amitav, 2014. Remaking Southeast Asian Studies: Doubt, Desire and the Promise of Comparisons. *Pacific Affairs* 87, 4: 463–483.
364 Acharya. *The Making of Southeast Asia: International Relations of a Region*.
365 Emmerson. Southeast Asia: What's in a name?
366 Reid. A saucer model of Southeast Asian identity.
367 Smail. On the possibility of an autonomous history of modern Southeast Asia.
368 Emmerson, Donald K. 1984. Beyond Western surprise: Thoughts on the evolution of Southeast Asian Studies. In *Southeast Asian Studies: Options for the Futures*, ed. Ronald A. Morse. Lanham, MD: University Press of America.
369 McVey. Change and continuity in Southeast Asian studies.
370 Ibid.
371 Fifield. Southeast Asian studies: Origins, development, future.
372 Ness, Garry and Martha Morrow. Assessing U.S. scholarly resources on Southeast Asia.
373 Ibid.
374 Ibid.
375 Anderson. Politics and their study in Southeast Asia.
376 Reid, Anthony. 2003. Southeast Asian studies: Decline or rebirth? In *Southeast Asian Studies: Pacific Perspectives*, ed. Anthony Reid, Tempe: Arizona State University, Program for Southeast Asian Studies.
377 Keyes, Charles F. 1992. A conference at wingspread and rethinking Southeast Asian studies. In *Southeast Asian Studies in the Balance: Reflections from America*, ed. Charles Hirschman, Charles F. Keyes, and Karl Hutterer, Ann Arbor, Association for Asian Studies.
378 McVey. Change and continuity in Southeast Asian studies.

379 Ibid.
380 Huxley, Tim. 1996. Southeast Asia in the study of International Relations: The rise and decline of a region. *Pacific Review* 9, 2: 199–228.
381 Kratoska, Paul, Remeo Raben and Henk Schulte Nordholt. 2005. Locating Southeast Asia. In *Locating Southeast Asia: Geographies of Knowledge and Politics of Space*, ed. Paul Kratoska, Remeo Raben and Henk Schulte Nordholt, Singapore: Singapore University Press and Athens: Ohio University Press.
382 Sandhu, Kernial Singh, Pushpa Thambipillai, and Triena Ong. 1984. *Southeast Asian Affairs*. Singapore: Institute of Southeast Asian Studies.
383 Emmerson. Situating Southeast Asian studies: Realm, guild, and home. In *Southeast Asian Studies: Pacific Perspectives*, ed. Anthony Reid, Tempe: Arizona State University, Program for Southeast Asian Studies.
384 Ibid.
385 Bates, Robert H. 1997. Area studies and the discipline: A useful controversy? *PS: Political Science and Politics* 30, 2: 166–9.
386 Shea, Christopher. 1997. Political scientists clash over value of area studies. *Chronicle of Higher Education*, 10 January.
387 Ludden, David. 1998. Area studies in the age of globalization. University of Pennsylvania.
388 D'Amato, Silvio, Matteo Dian and Alessandra Russo. 2022. Reaching for allies? The dialectics and overlaps between International Relations and area studies in the study of politics, security and conflicts. *Italian Political Science Review* 52, 2: 153–71.
389 Katzenstein, Peter J. 2005. *A World of Regions: Asia and Europe in the American Imperium* Ithaca: Cornell University Press.
390 Appadurai, Arjun. 1996. *Modernity at Large: Cultural Dimensions of Globalization*. Minneapolis: University of Minnesota Press.
391 McVey, Ruth T. 1998. Globalization, marginalization and the study of Southeast Asia. In *Southeast Asian Studies:*

Reorientations, ed. C. J. Reynolds and R. McVey, Ithaca, NY: Cornell University Press.

392 Ludden. Area studies in the age of globalization.

393 Tanabe, Willa. 'Crisis in Area Studies: An Overview Presented at the SHAPS Forum.' http://www.hawaii.edu/movingcultures/tanabe-crisis.html.

394 Acharya, Amitav. 2007. The emerging regional architecture of world politics. *World Politics* 59, 4: 629–52.

395 Emmerson. Situating Southeast Asian studies: Realm, guild, and home.

396 Reid, Anthony. 2003. Globalization, Asian diasporas and the study of Southeast Asia in the West: A changing perspective from California. In *Asian Migrants and Education: The Tensions of Education in Immigrant Services and Among Migrant Groups*, ed. Michael Charney, Brenda Yeoh and Tong Chee Kiong, Amsterdam: Klawer Academic Publishers.

397 University of Chicago. Regional worlds at the University of Chicago: About the program.

398 Ranchod-Nilsson, Sita. Regional worlds: Transforming pedagogy in area studies and International Studies. *University of Chicago*.

399 Staal, Frits. 2003. The future of Asian studies. *International Institute for Asian Studies Newsletter* 32: 6–7.

400 Anderson. *The Spectre of Comparisons*.

401 George, Alexander L. and Andrew Bennett. 2005. The method of structured, focused comparison. In *Case Studies and Theory Development in the Social Sciences*, ed. Alexander L. George and Andrew Bennett, Cambridge, MA: MIT Press.

402 Anderson. *The Specter of Comparisons*.

403 Evers, Hans-Dieter. 1980. The challenge of diversity: Southeast Asian studies and the development of Social Science. In *A Colloquium on Southeast Asian Studies*, ed. A.B. Shamsul, Chandran Jeshurun and A. Terry Rambo, Singapore: ISEAS Publishing.

404 Furnivall, J. S. 1956. *Colonial Policy and Practice: A Comparative Study of Burma and Netherlands India*. New York: New York University Press.
405 Boeke, Herman. 1953. *Economics and Economic Policy of Dual Societies as Exemplified by Indonesia*. New York: Institute of Pacific Relations.
406 Acharya, Amitav. 2013. *Civilizations in Embrace: The Spread of Ideas and the Transformation of Power*. Singapore: Institute of Southeast Asian Studies; Acharya, Amitav. 2004. How ideas spread, whose norms matter. *International Organization* 58, 2: 239–75; Acharya. *Whose Ideas Matter*.
407 Ness and Morrow. Assessing U.S. scholarly resources on Southeast Asia.
408 Neher. The Social Sciences.
409 Ibid.
410 Acharya. *The Making of Southeast Asia*.
411 Dismissing ASEAN's contribution to regional stability, Anderson argues that it was domestic change from Sukarno to Suharto, and not ASEAN, that led to the resolution of the *Konfrontasi*. Yet this can hardly be evidence of ASEAN's failure, since the idea of ASEAN evolved in tandem with the negotiations to end the *Konfrontasi*, and ASEAN itself was founded after the end of *Konfrontasi*.
412 Anderson, *The Specter of Comparisons*.
413 Ibid, 16.
414 Here one might include the contributions of Peter Katzenstein, Amitav Acharya, Alice Ba, Hiro Katsumata, Jürgen Haacke, Shaun Narine, among others.
415 The difference between 'old' and 'new' regionalism lies in three areas: the multipolar context of the latter (as opposed to the bipolar context of old regionalism); the dominant role of hegemonic actors (or 'hegemonic regionalism' created from 'outside' and 'above') in the creation of old regionalism

as opposed to the 'autonomous' nature of new regionalism(from 'within' and 'below'), and the comprehensiveness and multidimensional nature of new regionalism as opposed to the narrow and specific focus of the old. Hettne, Bjorn and Andras Inotai. 1994. *The New Regionalism: Implications for Global Development and International Security*. Helsinki: UNU World Institute for Development Economics Research.

416 See for one example, Acharya and Johnston. *Crafting Cooperation: Regional International Institutions in Comparative Perspective* (Cambridge: Cambridge University Press, 2007). A key purpose of this book was to compare the institutional-design of ASEAN and the 'ASEAN Way,' with that of the ASEAN Regional Forum, with other regional institutions in Europe, Africa, Middle East and the Americas. Because the starting point was ASEAN, it can be regarded as a contribution to the theoretical and comparative literature on comparative regionalism albeit with a distinctively Southeast Asian starting point. Acharya's other works, namely *Constructing a Security Community in Southeast Asia* and *Whose Ideas Matter*, have also contributed to the wider disciplinary IR literature on norm dynamics and comparative regionalism. See also: Acharya and Stubbs. Theorising Southeast Asian relations: An introduction.

417 Ruland, Heiner and Roloff. *Interregionalism and International Relations*.

418 Acharya and Johnston. *Crafting Cooperation*.

419 Acharya. *Whose Ideas Matter*.

420 https://x.com/AmitavAcharya/status/1413139276561145861?s=20

421 Miles, Donna. 2013. Locklear calls for Indo-Asia-Pacific cooperation. *American Forces Press Service*.